私の少年

MY BOY

1

Hitomi Takano

contents

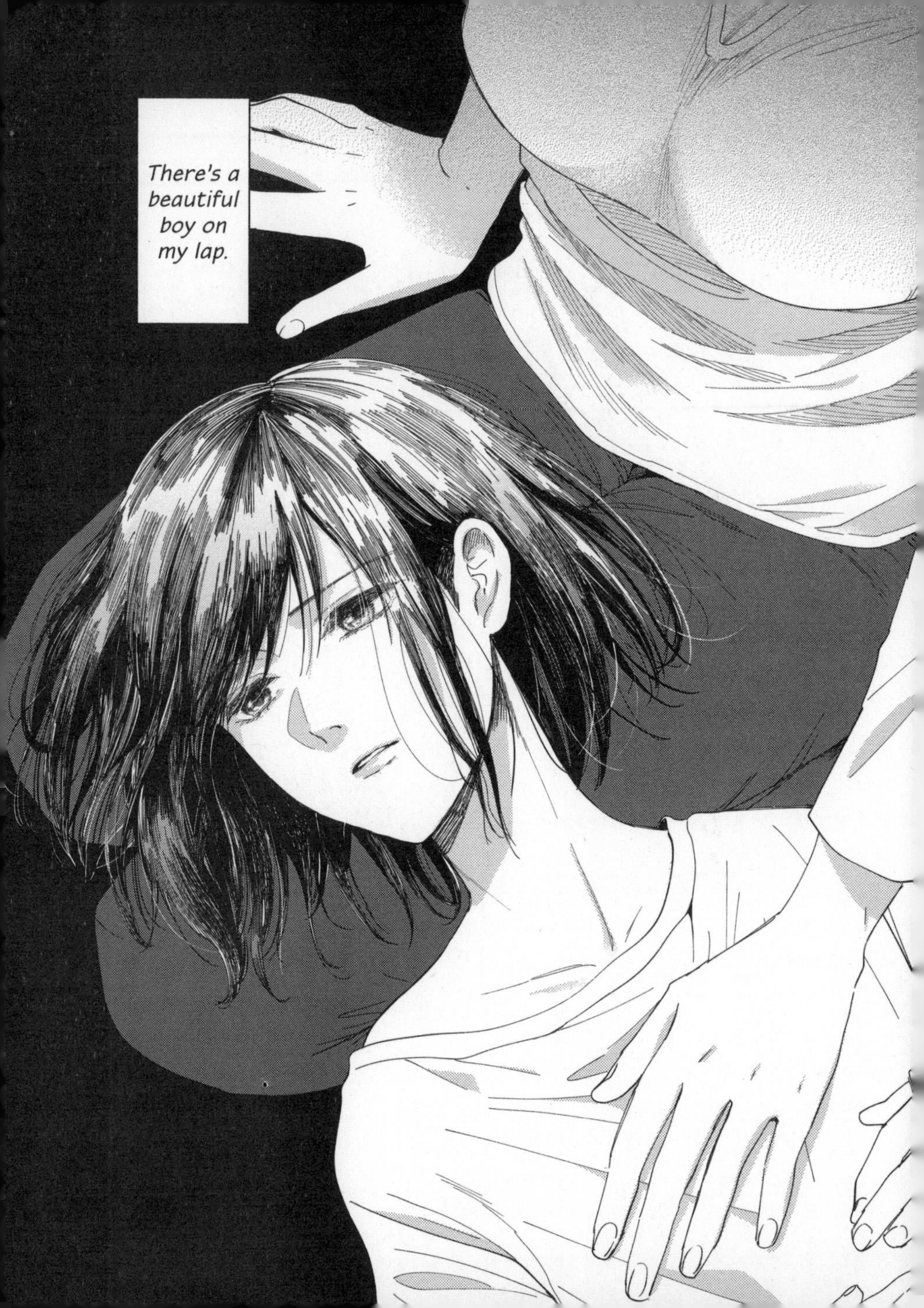
There's a beautiful boy on my lap.

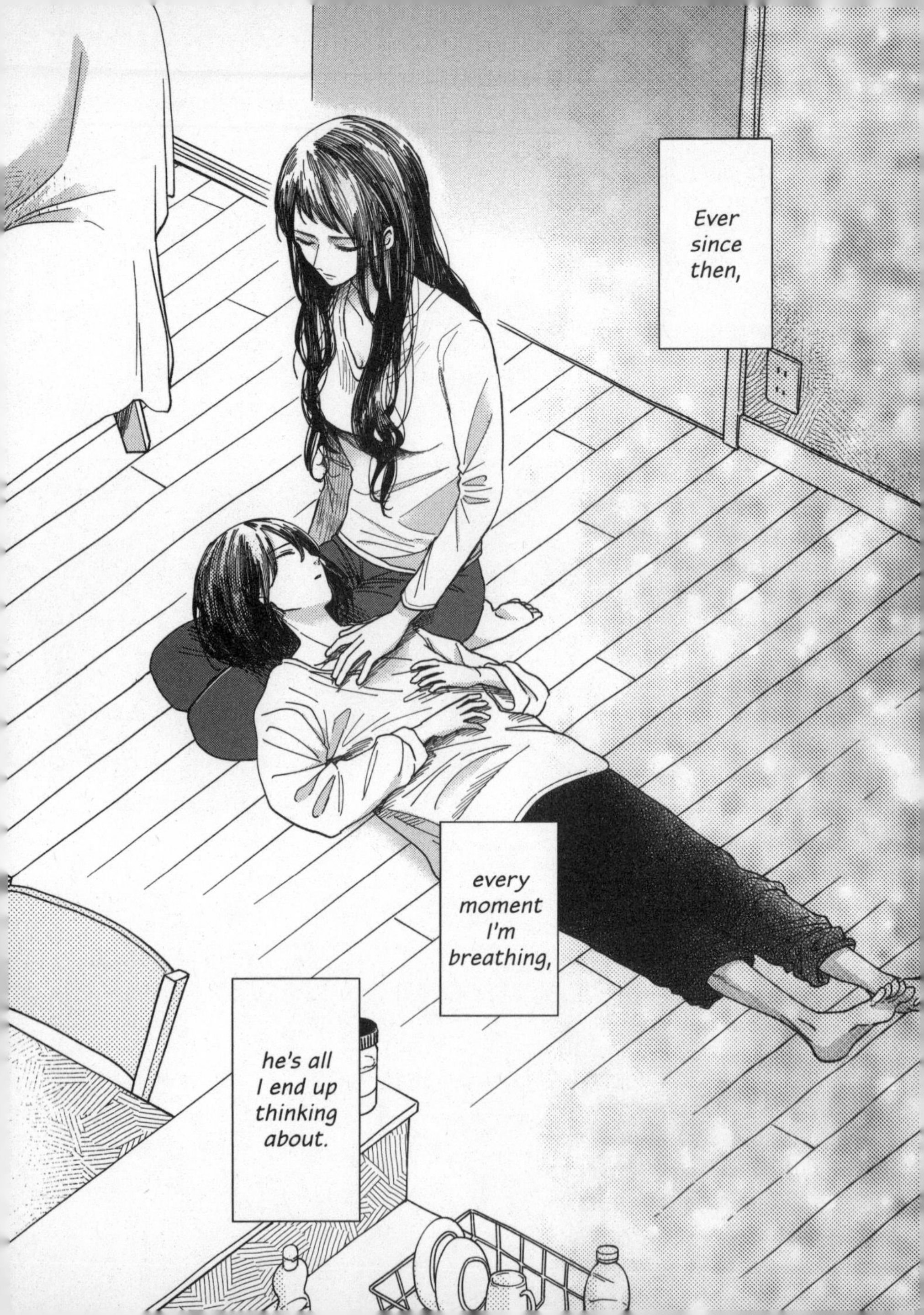
Ever since then,
every moment I'm breathing,
he's all I end up thinking about.

Chapter 1 THERMOMETER

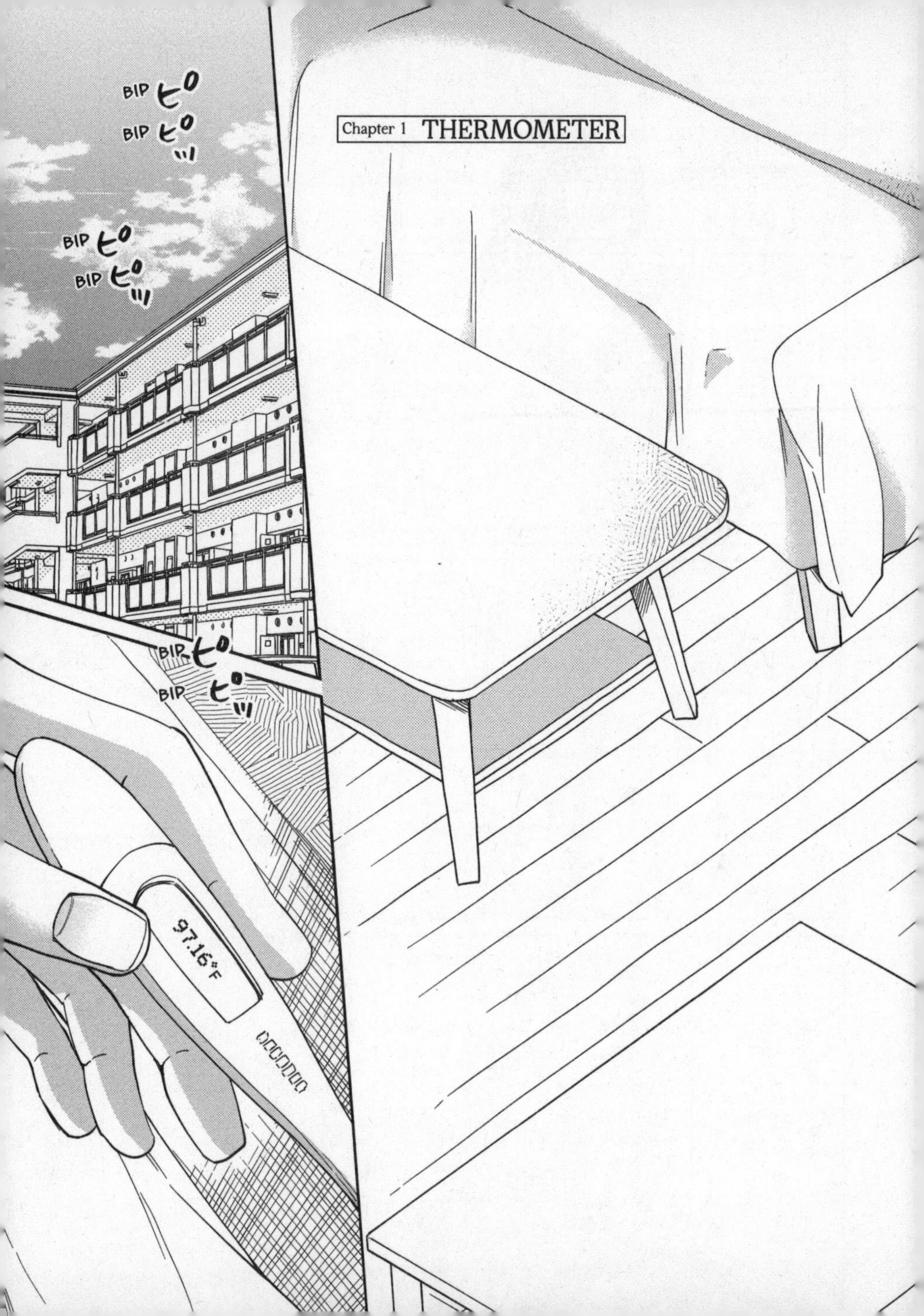
BIP ピ
BIP ピッ
BIP ピ
BIP ピッ
BIP ピ
BIP ピッ
97.16°F

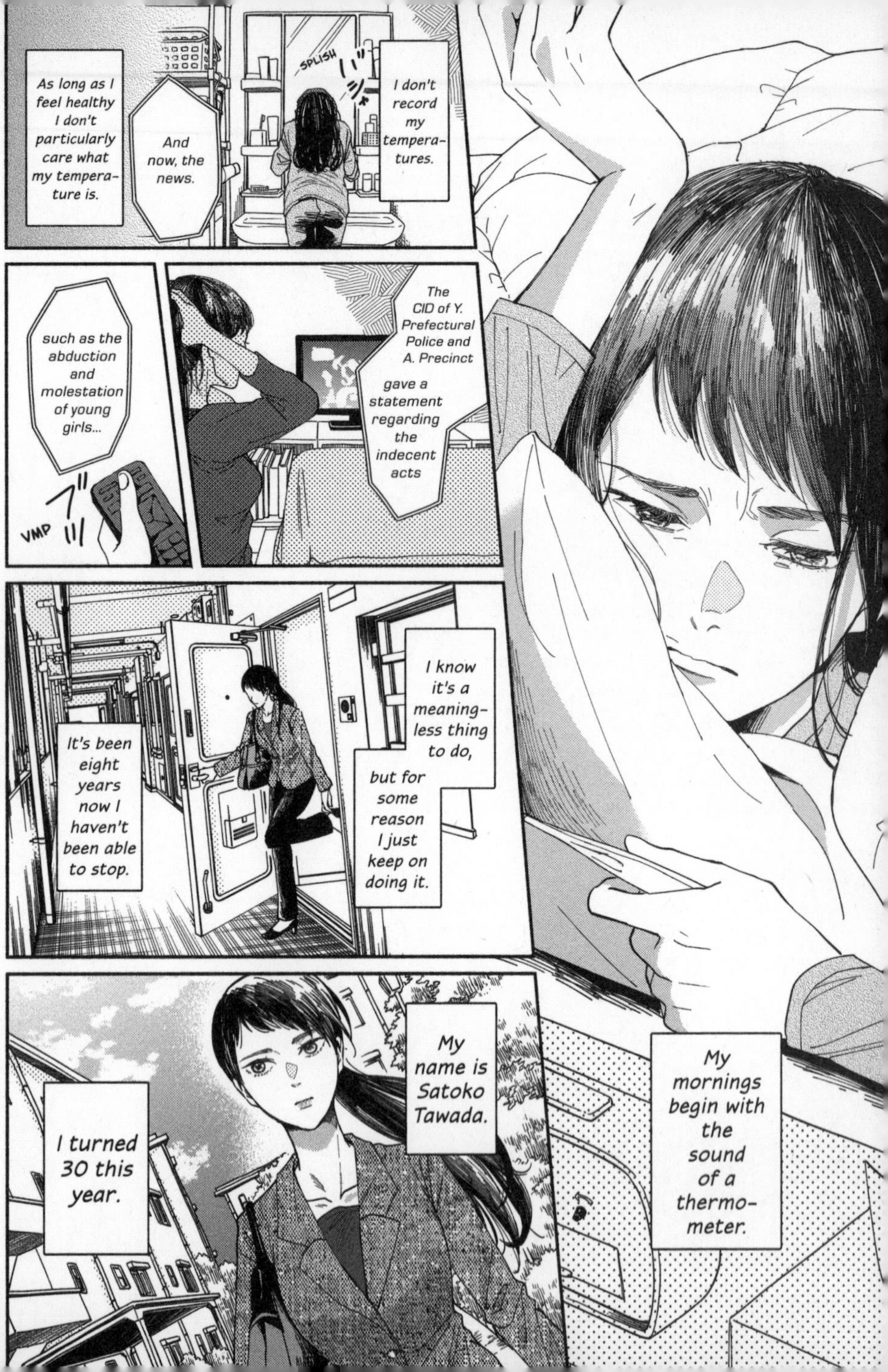

My mornings begin with the sound of a thermometer.
SPLISH
I don't record my temperatures.
And now, the news.
As long as I feel healthy I don't particularly care what my temperature is.
The CID of Y. Prefectural Police and A. Precinct
gave a statement regarding the indecent acts
such as the abduction and molestation of young girls...
VMP
I know it's a meaningless thing to do,
but for some reason I just keep on doing it.
It's been eight years now I haven't been able to stop.
My name is Satoko Tawada.
I turned 30 this year.

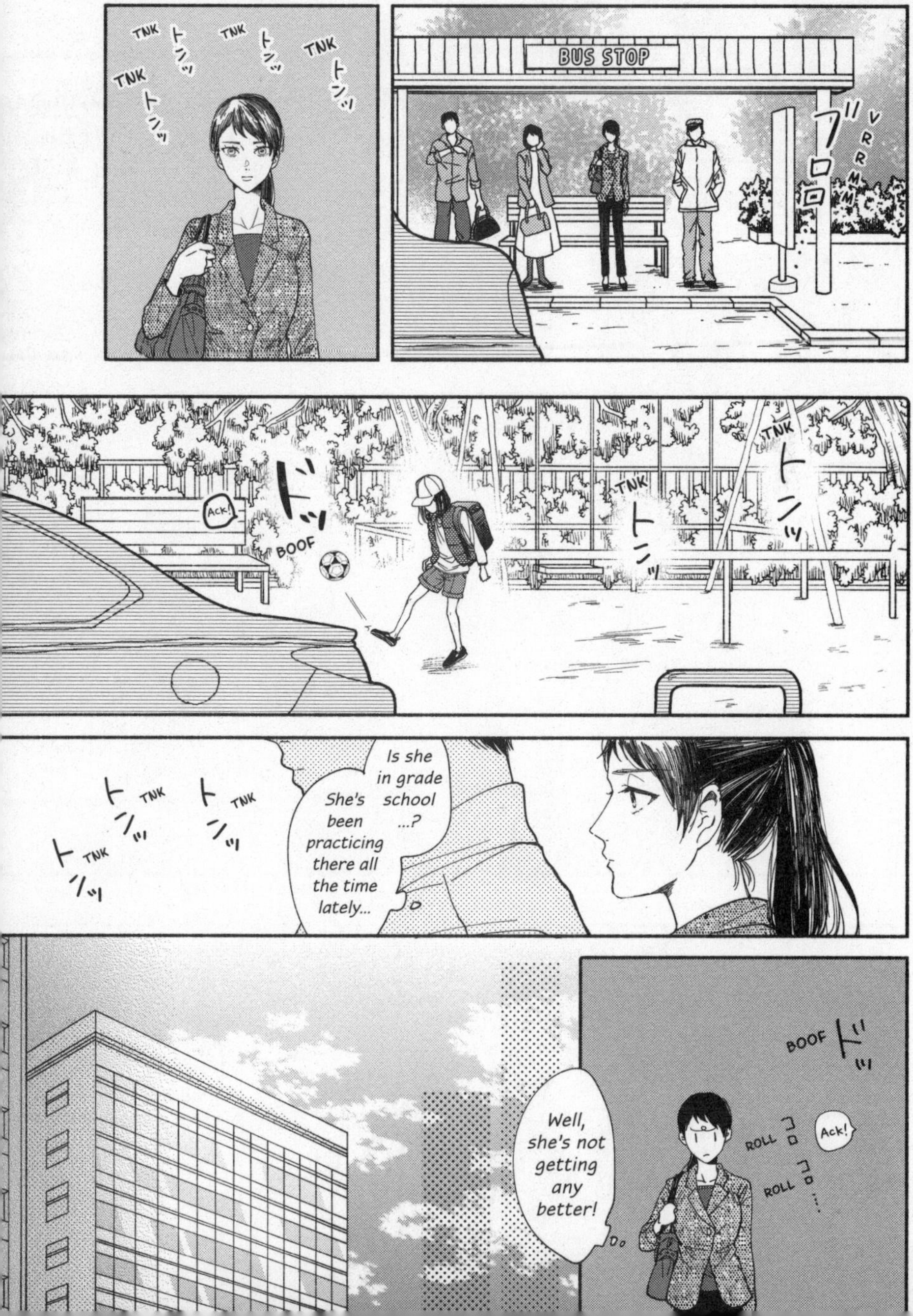
BUS STOP
ブロロロ VRRMM
TNK トンッ
TNK トンッ
TNK トンッ
TNK トンッ
TNK トンッ
TNK トンッ
ドッ BOOF
Ack!
Is she in grade school ...?
She's been practicing there all the time lately...
TNK トンッ
TNK トンッ
TNK トンッ
BOOF ドッ
Ack!
ROLL コロ
ROLL コロ...
Well, she's not getting any better!

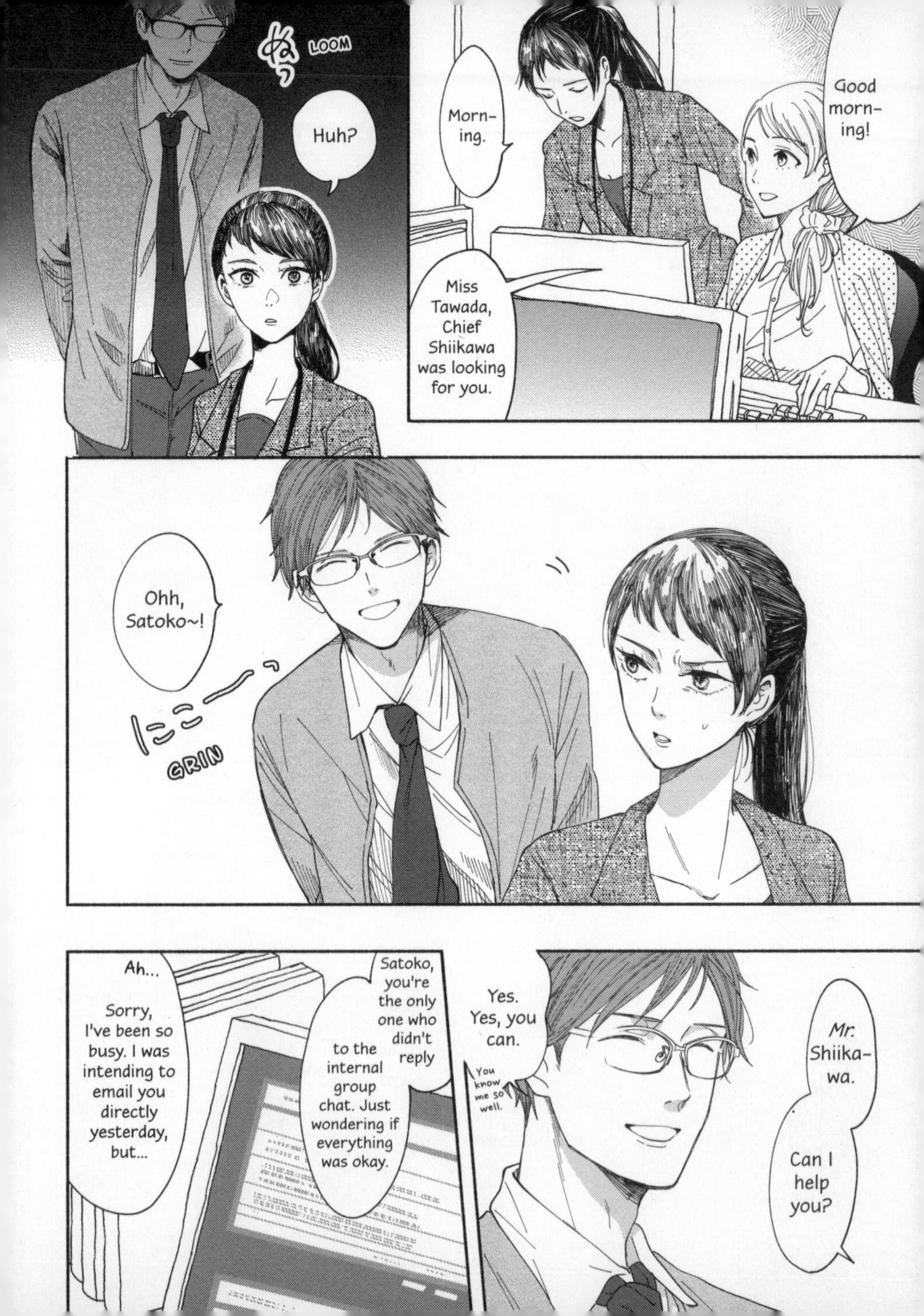
Good morning!
Morning.
Miss Tawada, Chief Shiikawa was looking for you.
LOOM
Huh?
Ohh, Satoko~!
GRIN
Mr. Shiikawa.
Can I help you?
Yes. Yes, you can.
You know me so well.
Satoko, you're the only one who didn't reply to the internal group chat. Just wondering if everything was okay.
Ah... Sorry, I've been so busy. I was intending to email you directly yesterday, but...

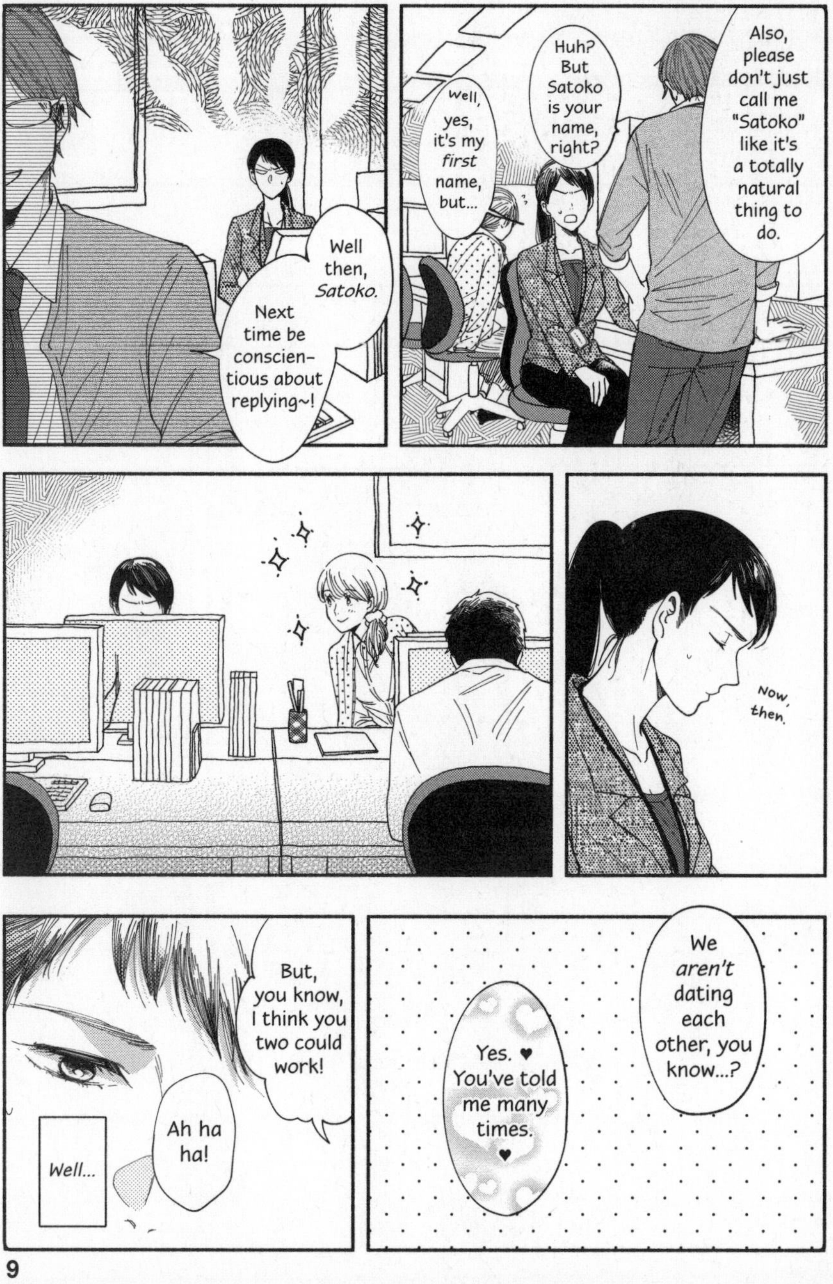
Also, please don't just call me "Satoko" like it's a totally natural thing to do.
Huh? But Satoko is your name, right?
Well, yes, it's my *first* name, but...
Well then, *Satoko.*
Next time be conscien-tious about replying~!
Now, then.
We *aren't* dating each other, you know...?
Yes. ♥ You've told me many times. ♥
But, you know, I think you two could work!
Ah ha ha!
Well...

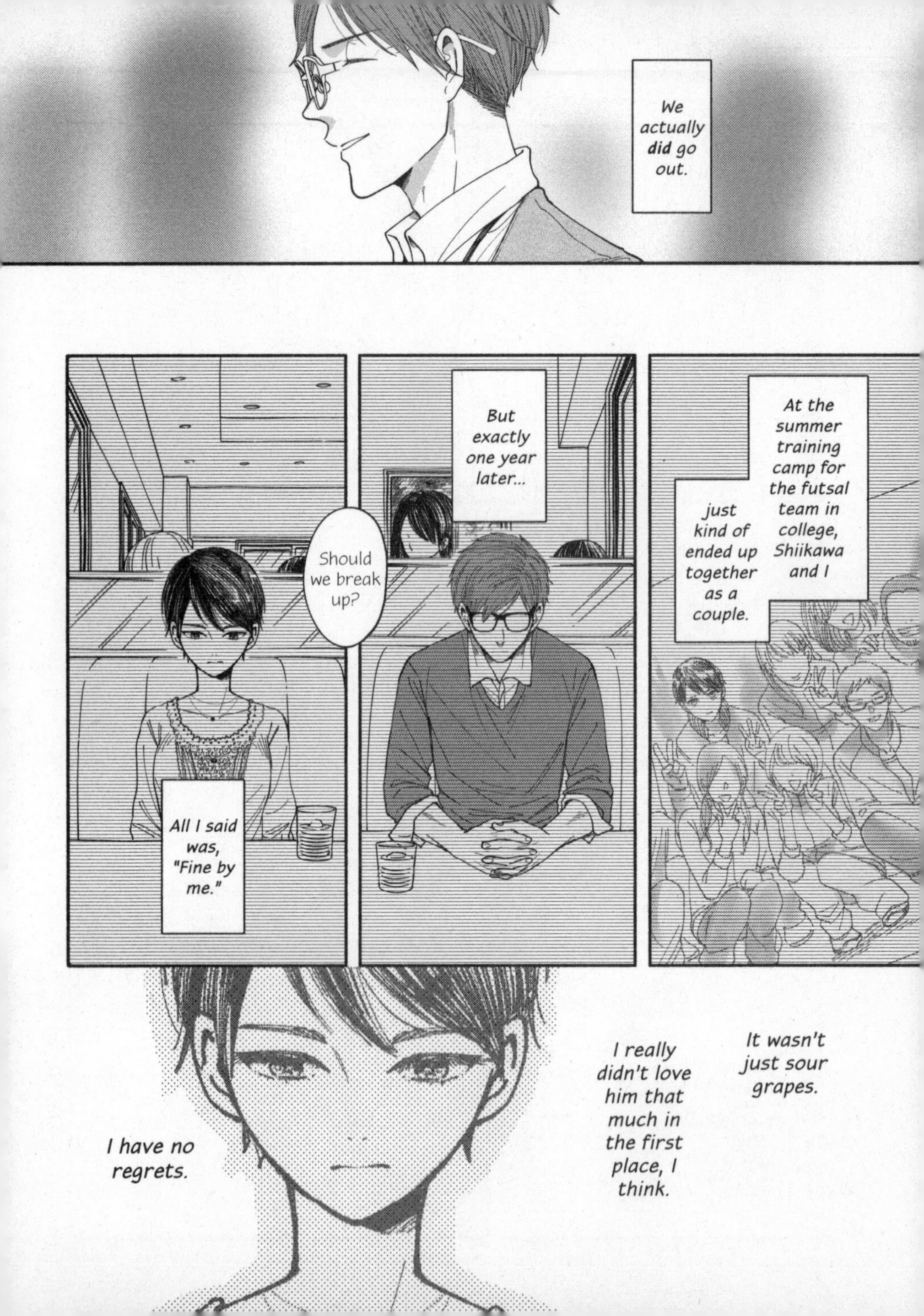
We actually **did** go out.
At the summer training camp for the futsal team in college, Shiikawa and I
just kind of ended up together as a couple.
But exactly one year later...
Should we break up?
All I said was, "Fine by me."
It wasn't just sour grapes.
I really didn't love him that much in the first place, I think.
I have no regrets.

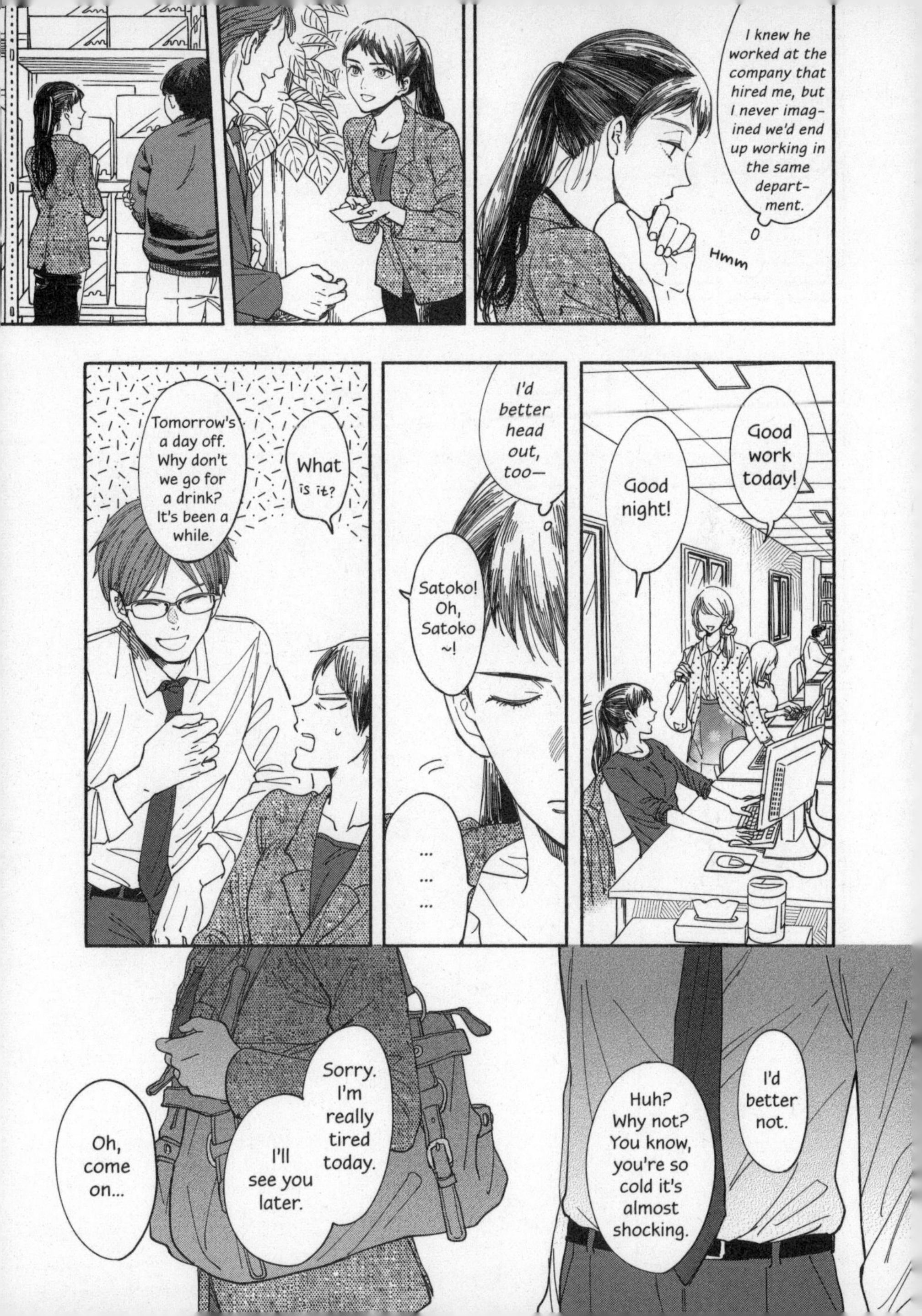
I knew he worked at the company that hired me, but I never imagined we'd end up working in the same department.
Hmm
Good work today!
Good night!
I'd better head out, too—
Satoko! Oh, Satoko ~!
... ...
What is it?
Tomorrow's a day off. Why don't we go for a drink? It's been a while.
I'd better not.
Huh? Why not? You know, you're so cold it's almost shocking.
Sorry. I'm really tired today.
I'll see you later.
Oh, come on...

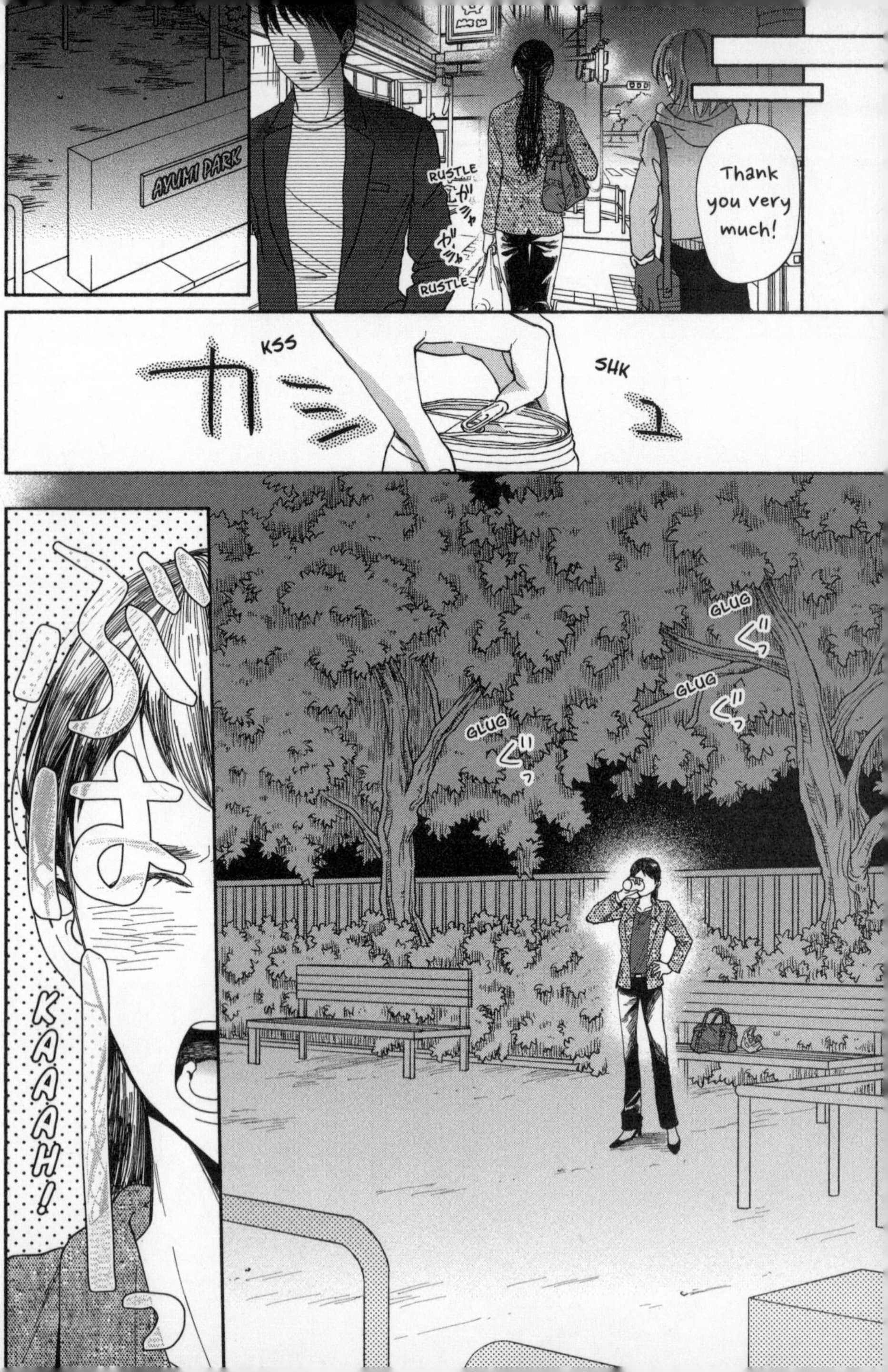

Thank you very much!
RUSTLE
ガリ
ジャ
ガリ
ジャ
RUSTLE
AYUMI PARK
SHK
ユ
KSS
カ
GLUG
ぐっ
GLUG
ぐっ
GLUG
ぐっ
ぷはっ
KAAAAH!

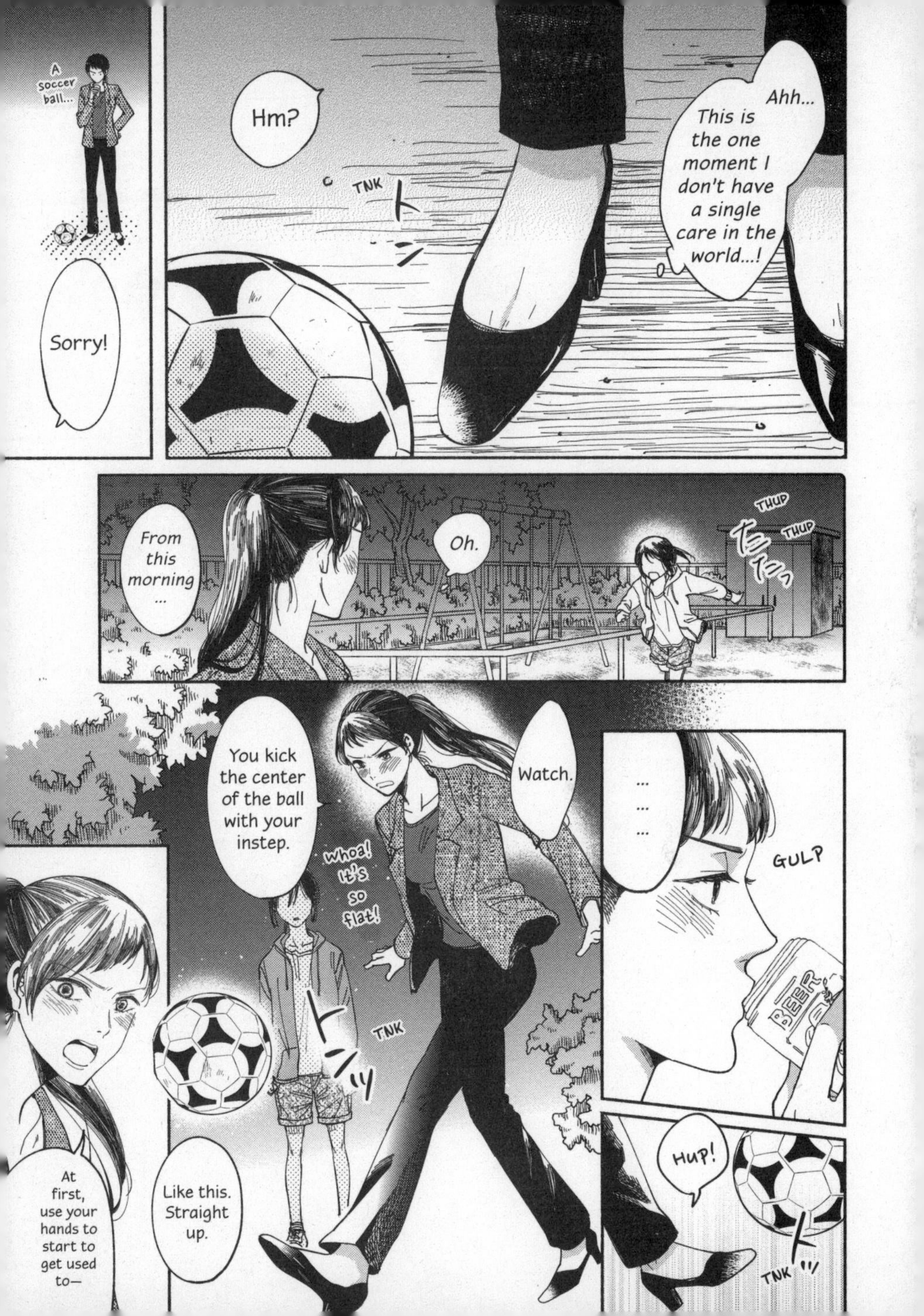

Ahh... This is the one moment I don't have a single care in the world...!
Hm?
TNK
A soccer ball...
Sorry!
THUP THUP
Oh.
From this morning ...
... ...
GULP
Hup!
TNK
Watch.
You kick the center of the ball with your instep.
whoa! it's so flat!
TNK
Like this. Straight up.
At first, use your hands to start to get used to—

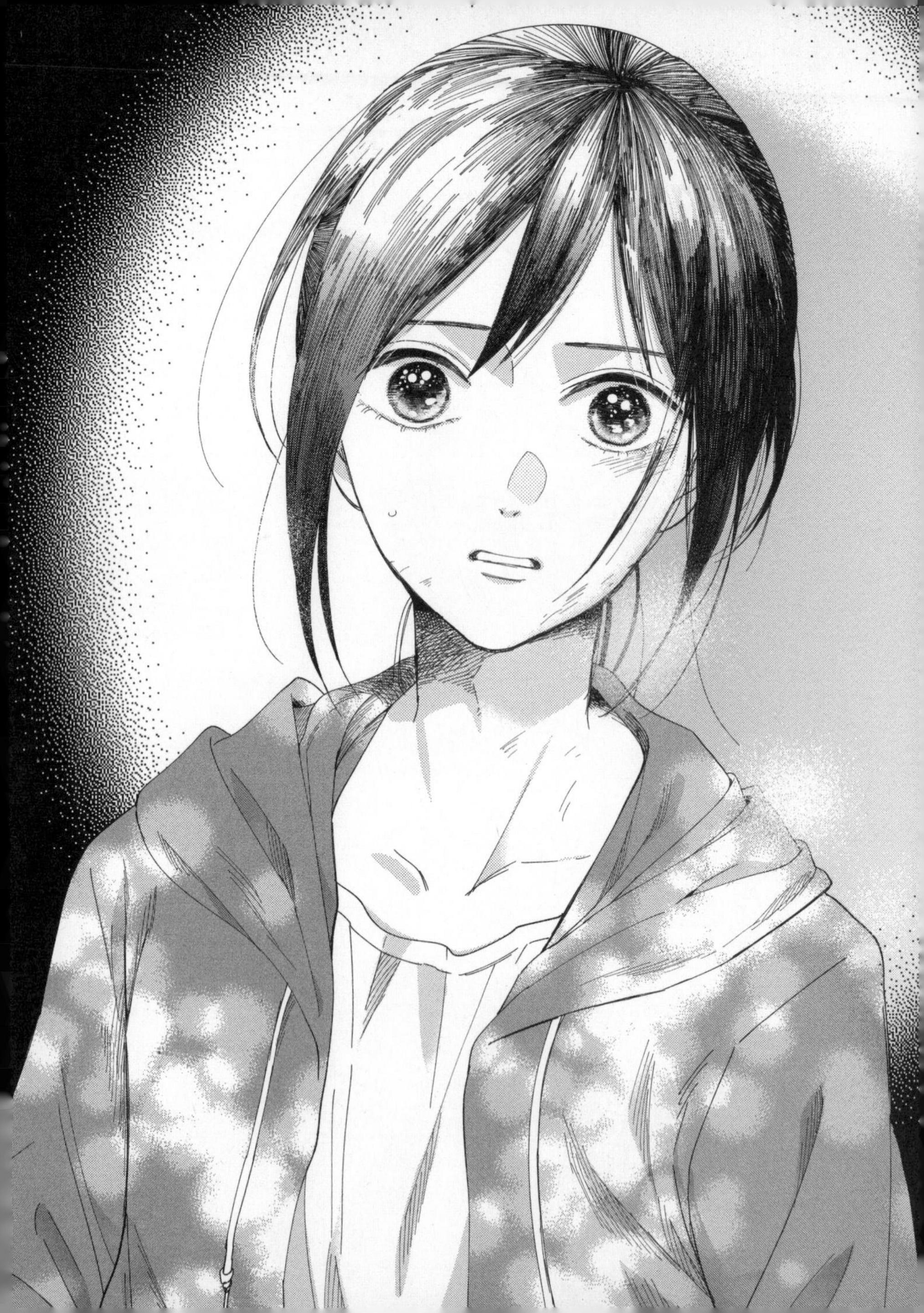

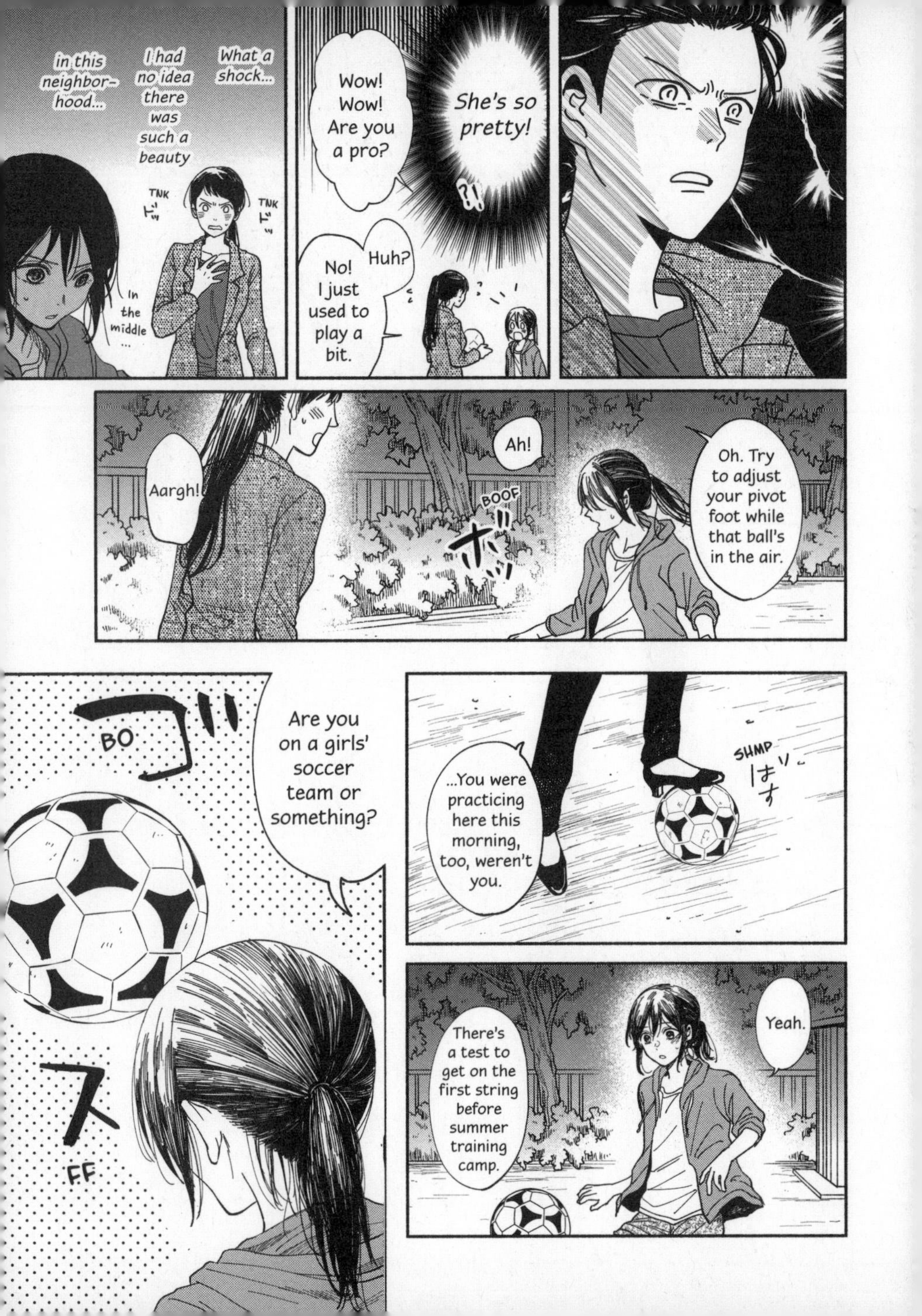

She's so pretty!
Wow! Wow! Are you a pro?
?!
Huh?
No! I just used to play a bit.
What a shock...
I had no idea there was such a beauty
in this neighbor-hood...
TNK
TNK
In the middle ...
Oh. Try to adjust your pivot foot while that ball's in the air.
Ah!
BOOF
Aargh!
SHMP
...You were practicing here this morning, too, weren't you.
Yeah.
There's a test to get on the first string before summer training camp.
Are you on a girls' soccer team or something?
BO
FF

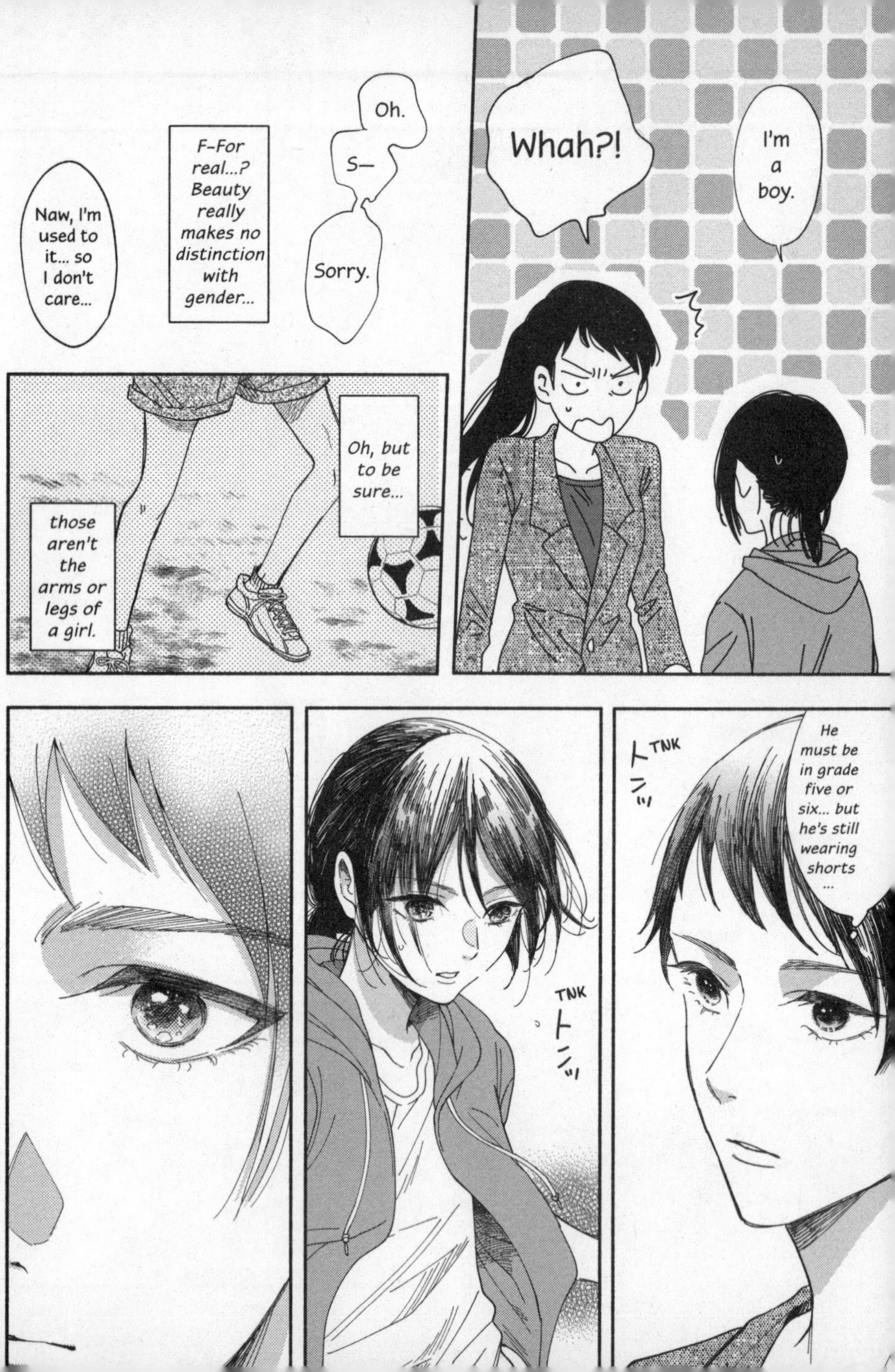
I'm a boy.
Whah?!
Oh. S— Sorry.
F-For real...? Beauty really makes no distinction with gender...
Naw, I'm used to it... so I don't care...
Oh, but to be sure...
those aren't the arms or legs of a girl.
TNK
He must be in grade five or six... but he's still wearing shorts ...
TNK

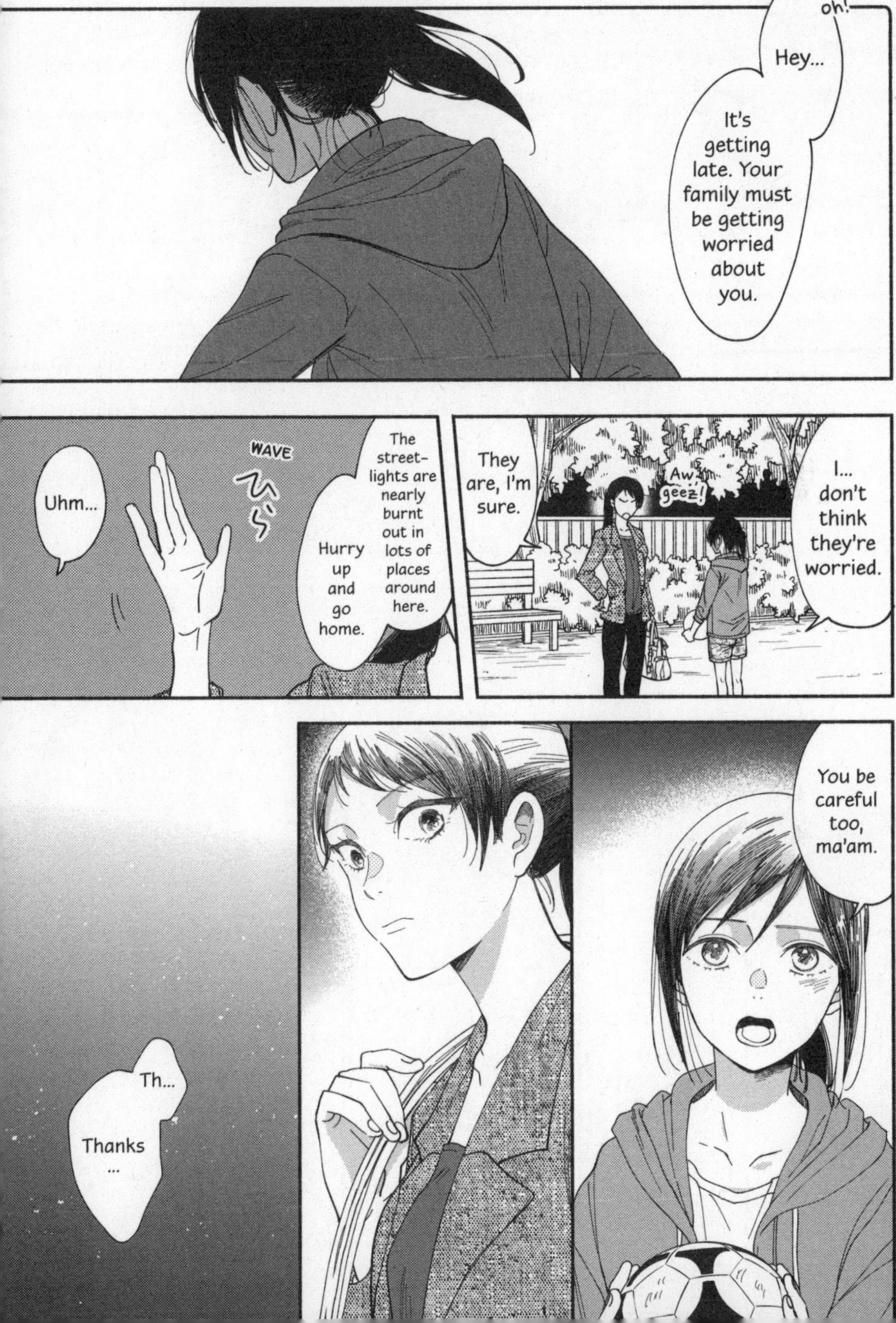
oh!
Hey...
It's getting late. Your family must be getting worried about you.
I... don't think they're worried.
Aw geez!
They are, I'm sure.
The street-lights are nearly burnt out in lots of places around here.
Hurry up and go home.
WAVE
Uhm...
You be careful too, ma'am.
Th...
Thanks ...

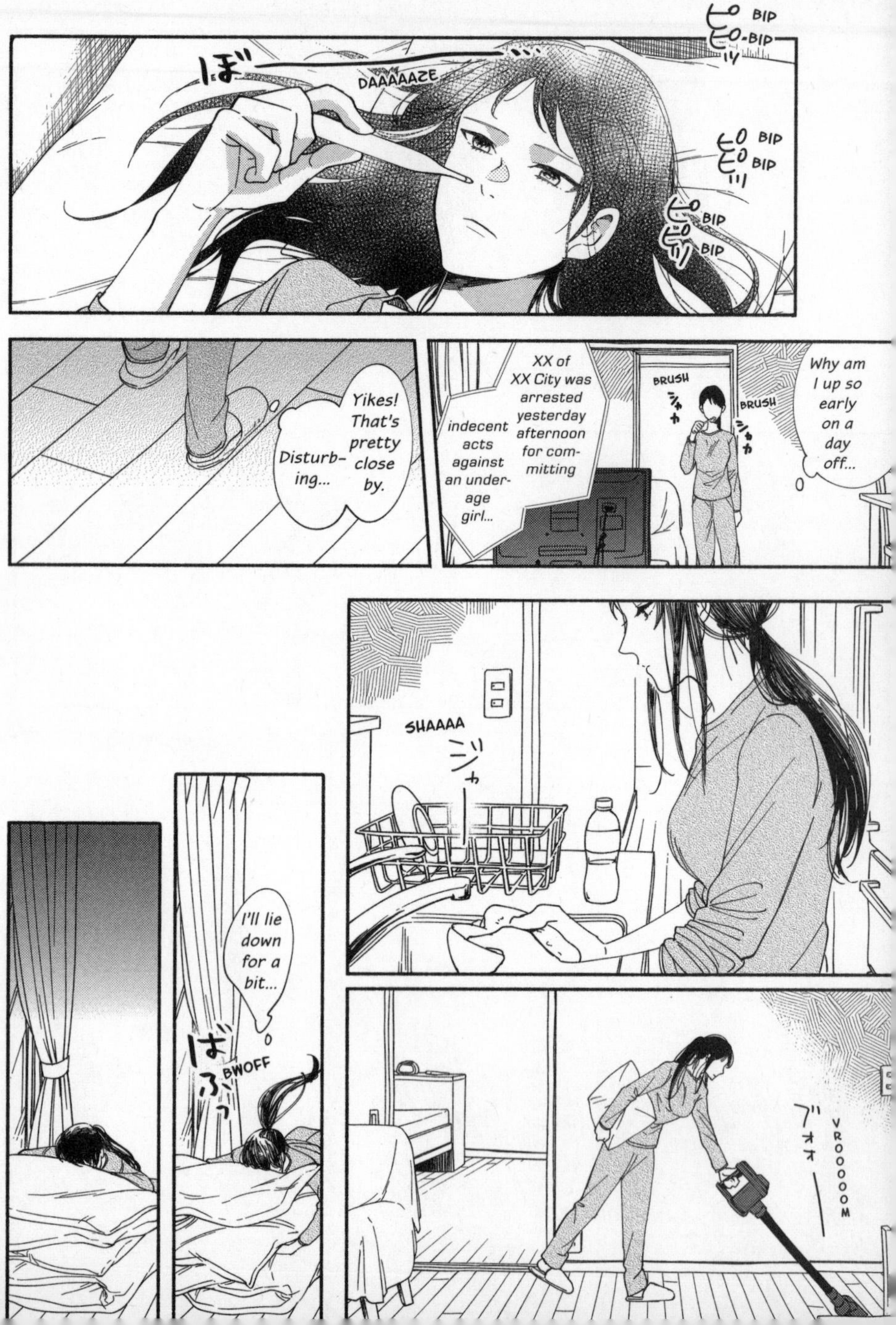
ピピッ BIP BIP
ピピッ BIP BIP
ピピッ BIP BIP
ぼーっ DAAAAAZE
シャカ BRUSH
シャカ BRUSH
Why am I up so early on a day off...
XX of XX City was arrested yesterday afternoon for com-mitting indecent acts against an under-age girl...
Yikes! That's pretty close by.
Disturb-ing...
ジャー SHAAAA
ブオオー VROOOOOOM
I'll lie down for a bit...
ばふっ BWOFF

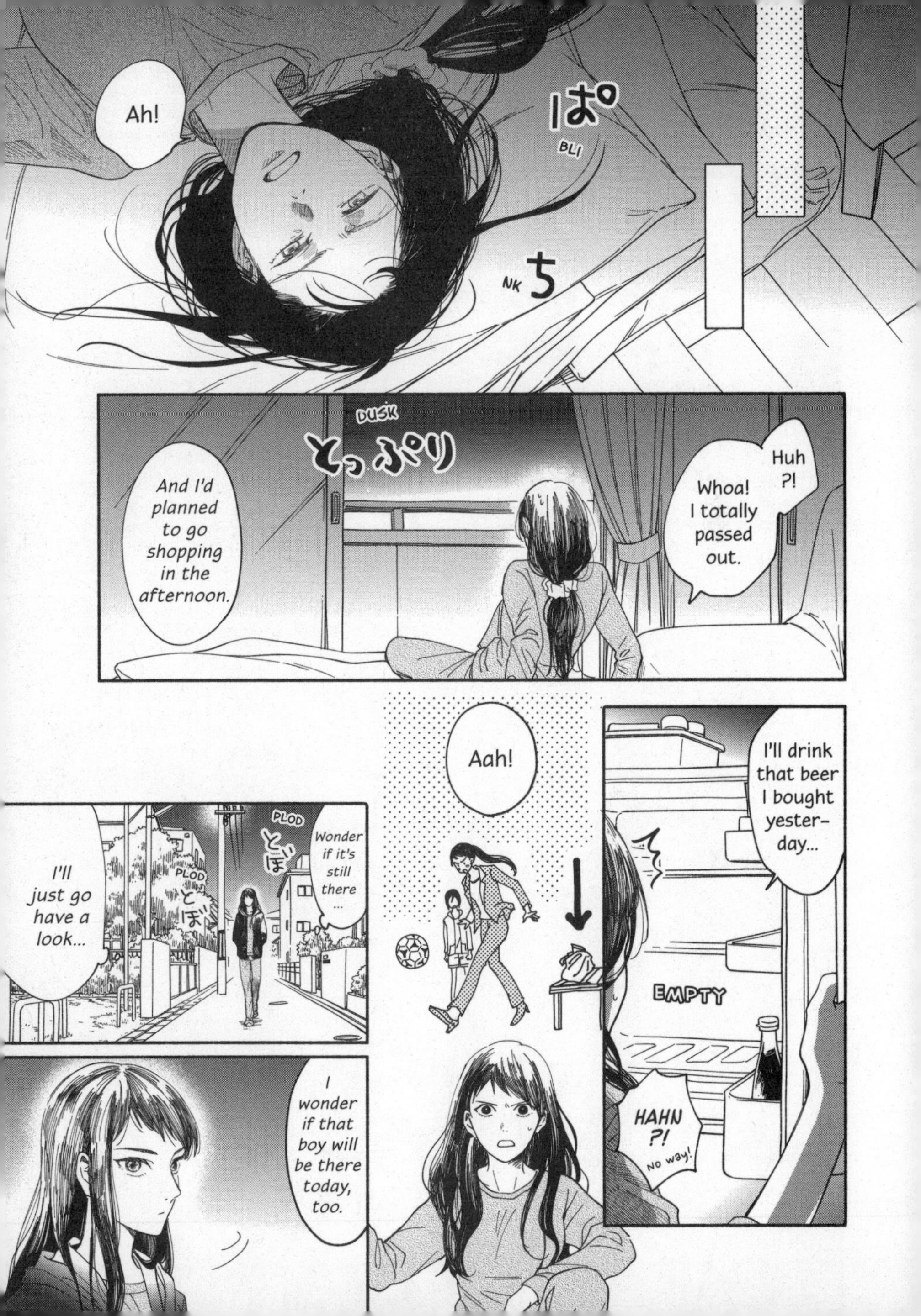

Ah!
ぱ
BLI
ち
NK
Huh ?!
Whoa! I totally passed out.
とっぷり
DUSK
And I'd planned to go shopping in the afternoon.
I'll drink that beer I bought yester-day...
EMPTY
HAHN ?!
No way!
Aah!
I wonder if that boy will be there today, too.
Wonder if it's still there ...
とぼ
PLOD
とぼ
PLOD
I'll just go have a look...

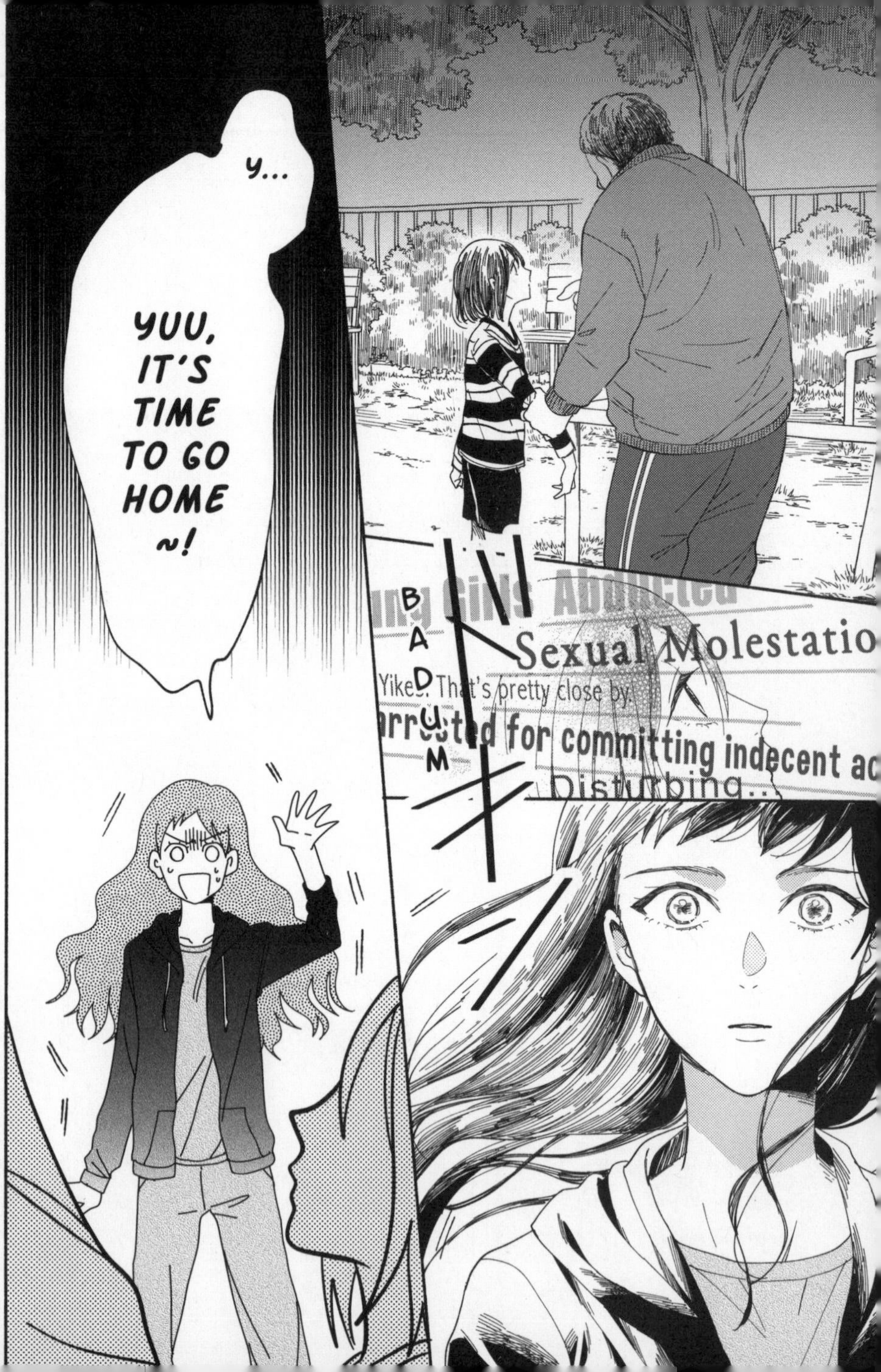

Young Girls Abducted
Sexual Molestatio
Yikes. That's pretty close by.
arrested for committing indecent ac
Disturbing..
BADUM
Y...
YUU, IT'S TIME TO GO HOME ~!

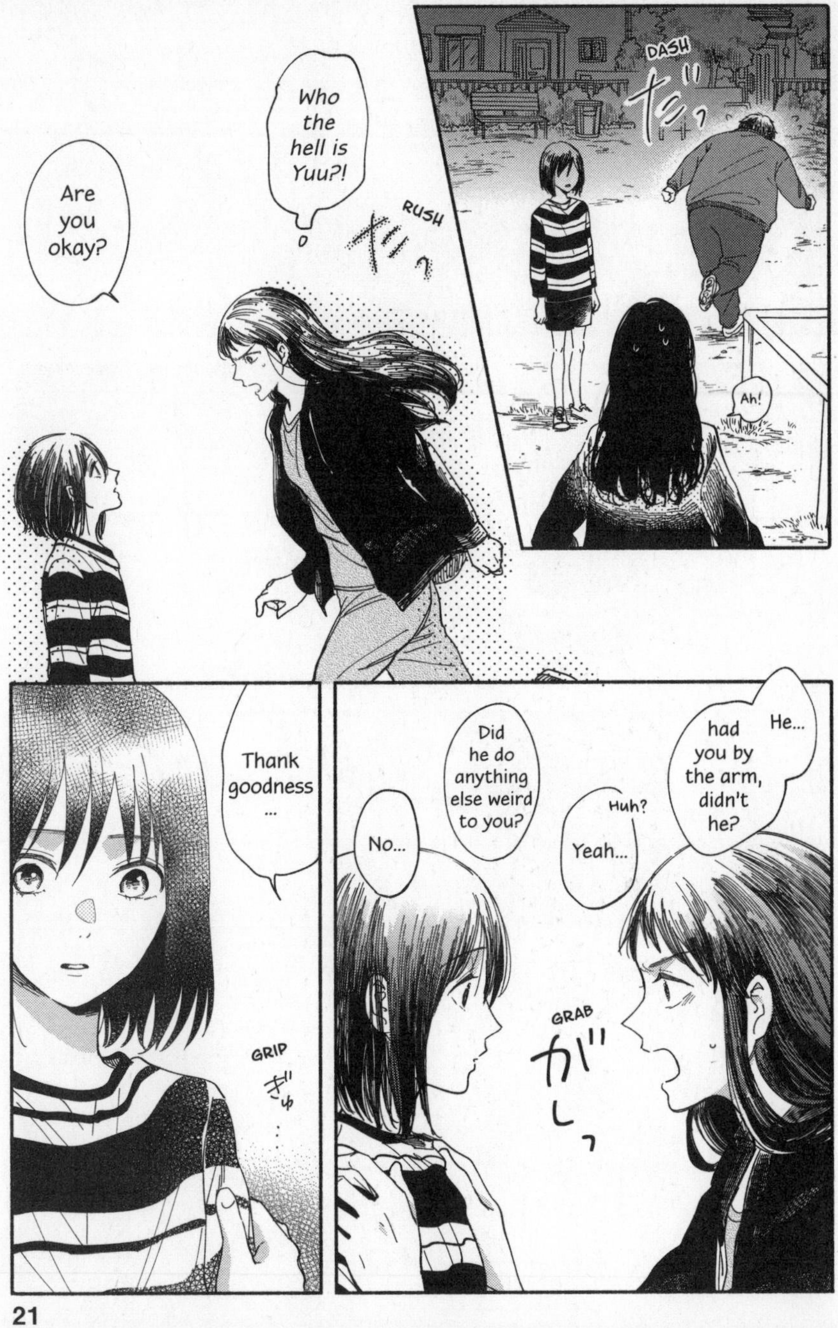
DASH
ダッ
Ah!
Who the hell is Yuu?!
RUSH
ダッ
Are you okay?
He...
had you by the arm, didn't he?
Huh?
Yeah...
Did he do anything else weird to you?
No...
GRAB
がしっ
Thank goodness ...
GRIP
ぎゅ

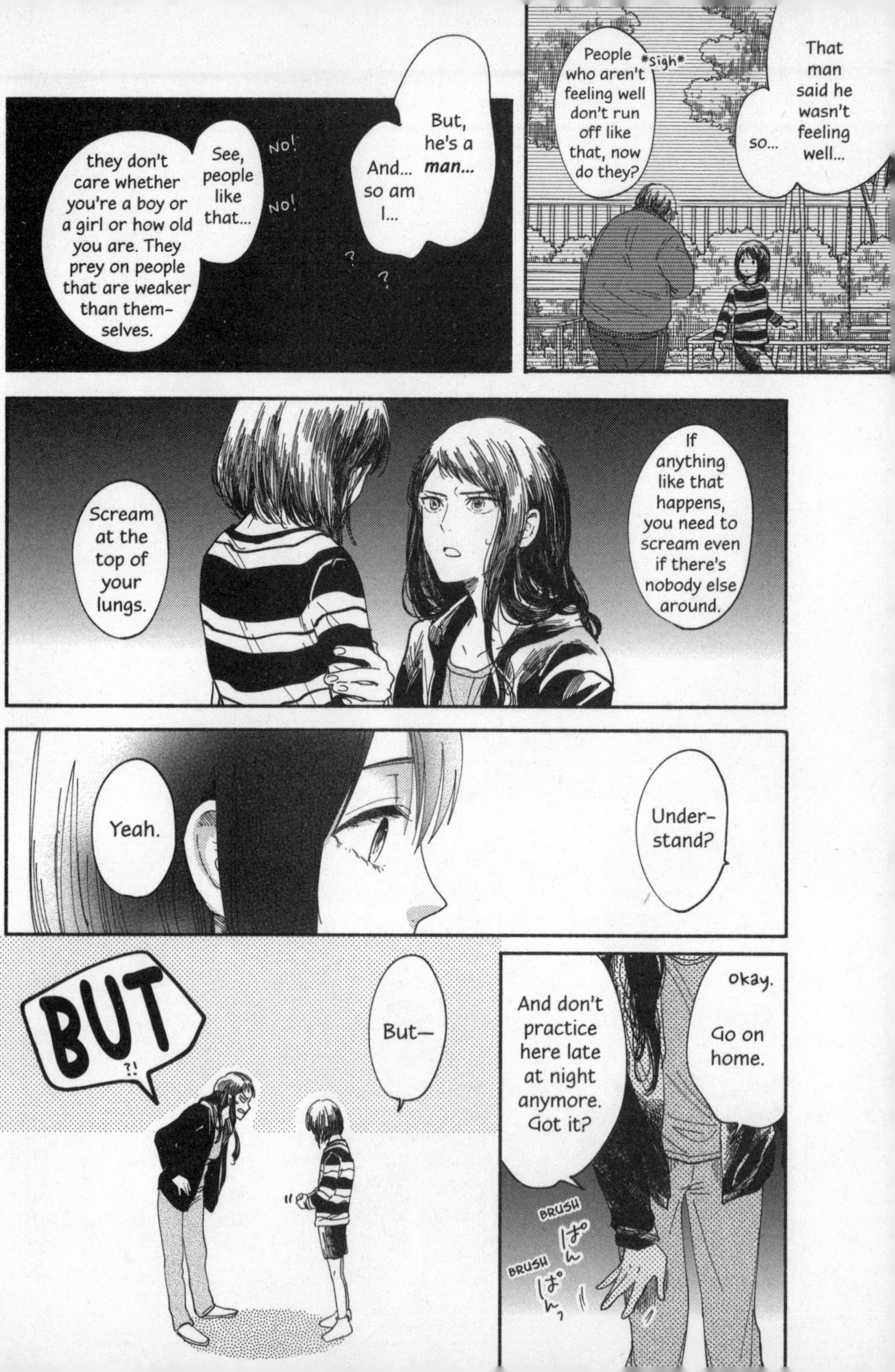
That man said he wasn't feeling well...
so...
People who aren't feeling well don't run off like that, now do they?
sigh
But, he's a *man*...
And... so am I...
?
?
See, people like that...
No!
No!
they don't care whether you're a boy or a girl or how old you are. They prey on people that are weaker than themselves.
If anything like that happens, you need to scream even if there's nobody else around.
Scream at the top of your lungs.
Understand?
Yeah.
Okay.
Go on home.
And don't practice here late at night anymore. Got it?
BRUSH
ぱん
BRUSH
ぱんっ
But—
BUT
?!

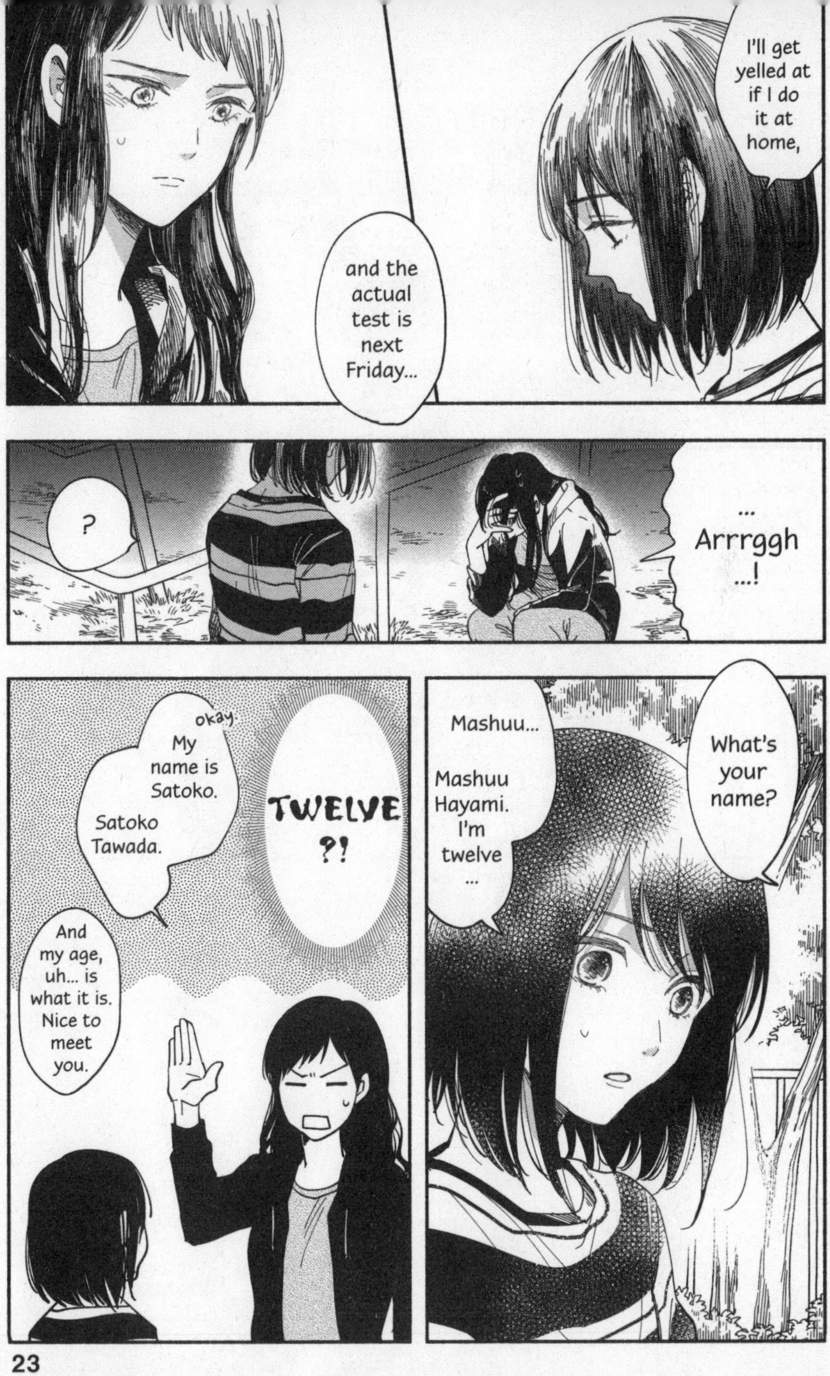
I'll get yelled at if I do it at home,
and the actual test is next Friday...
... Arrrggh ...!
?
What's your name?
Mashuu...
Mashuu Hayami. I'm twelve ...
TWELVE ?!
okay.
My name is Satoko. Satoko Tawada.
And my age, uh... is what it is. Nice to meet you.

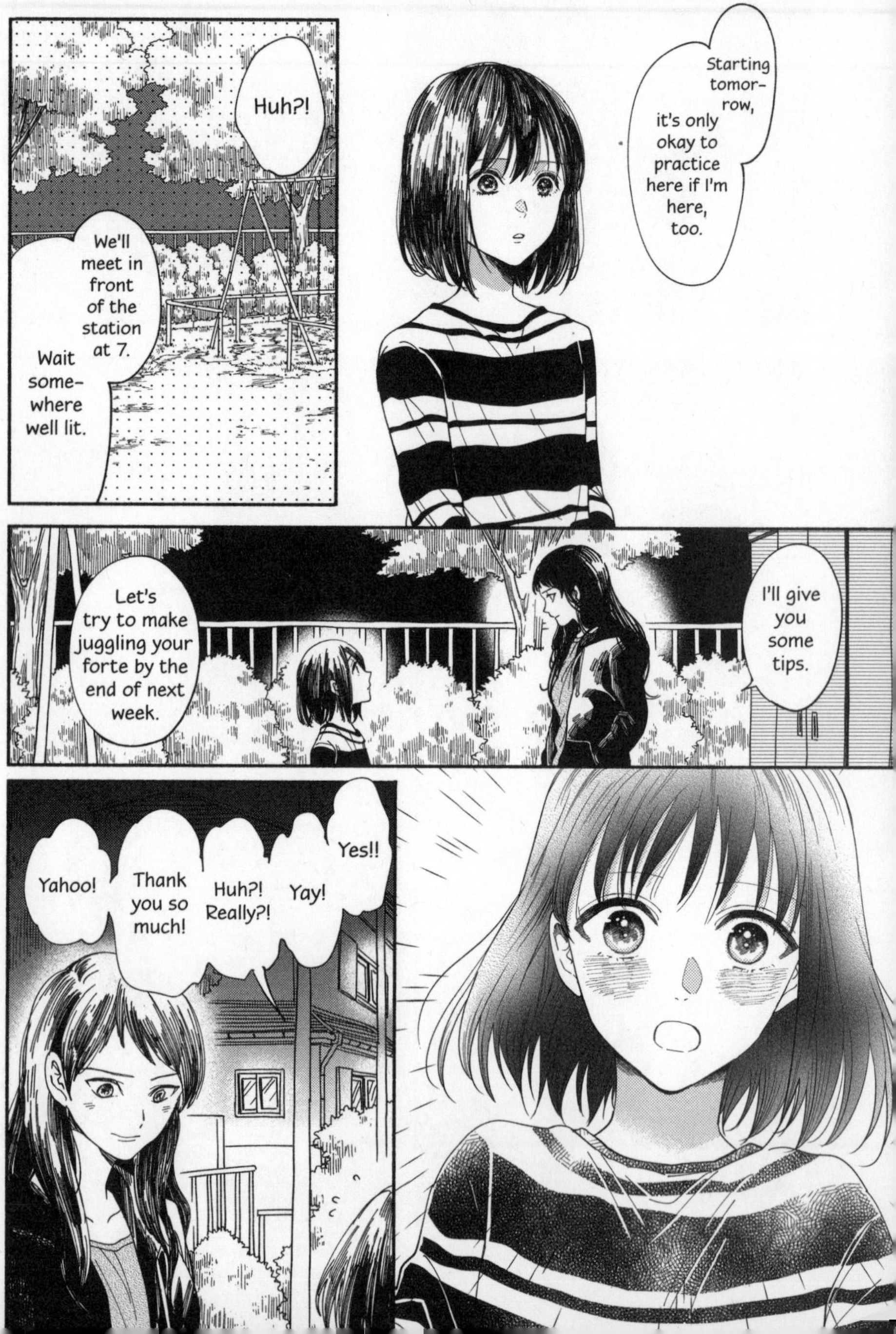
Starting tomorrow, it's only okay to practice here if I'm here, too.
Huh?!
We'll meet in front of the station at 7.
Wait somewhere well lit.
I'll give you some tips.
Let's try to make juggling your forte by the end of next week.
Yes!!
Yay!
Huh?! Really?!
Thank you so much!
Yahoo!

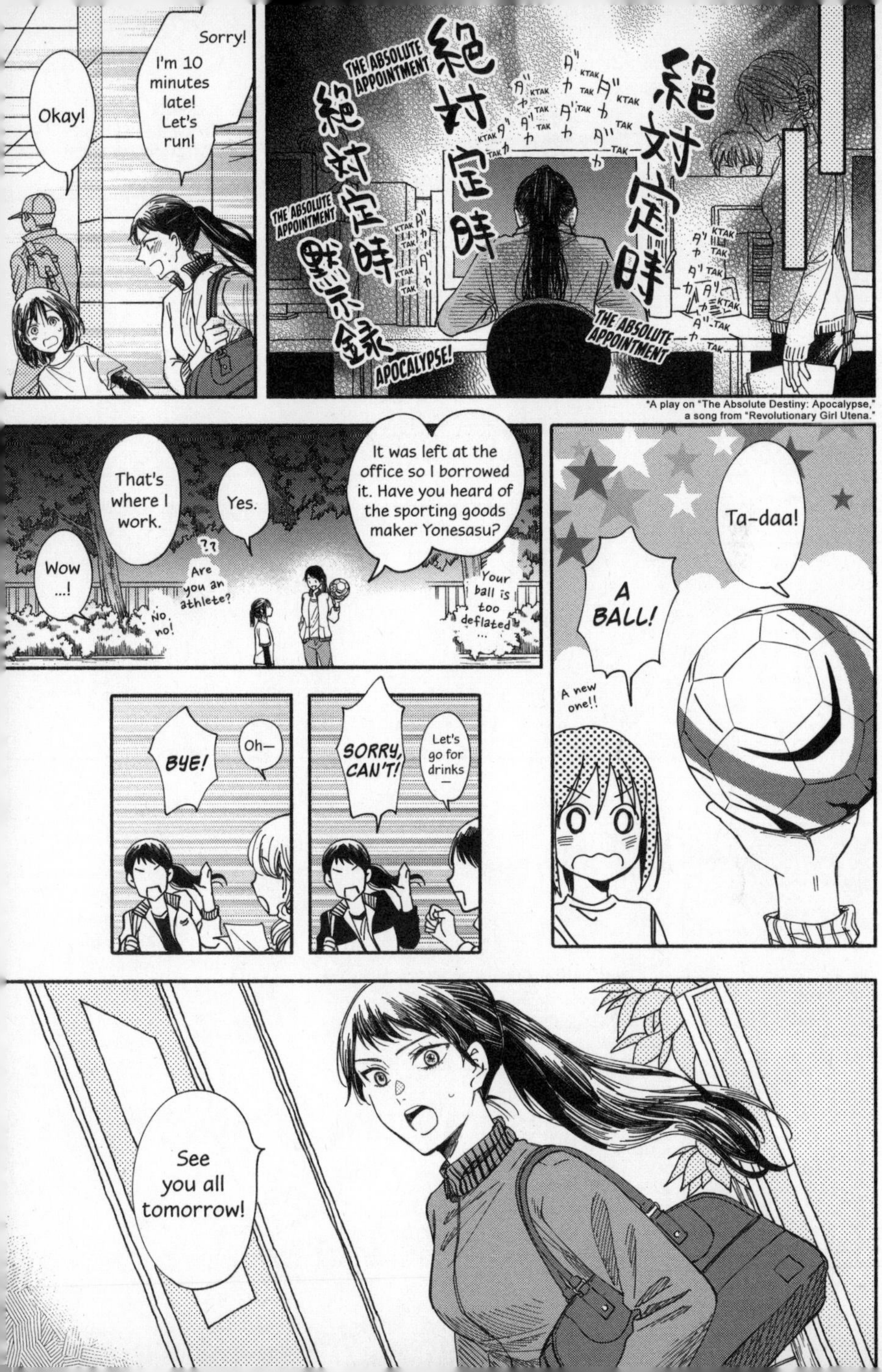
絶対定時
THE ABSOLUTE APPOINTMENT
KTAK TAK
絶対定時
THE ABSOLUTE APPOINTMENT
絶対定時黙示録
THE ABSOLUTE APPOINTMENT
APOCALYPSE!
Sorry! I'm 10 minutes late! Let's run!
Okay!
Ta-daa!
A BALL!
A new one!!
Your ball is too deflated ...
It was left at the office so I borrowed it. Have you heard of the sporting goods maker Yonesasu?
Yes.
Are you an athlete?
??
That's where I work.
No no!
Wow ...!
Let's go for drinks—
SORRY, CAN'T!
Oh—
BYE!
See you all tomorrow!

*A play on "The Absolute Destiny: Apocalypse," a song from "Revolutionary Girl Utena."

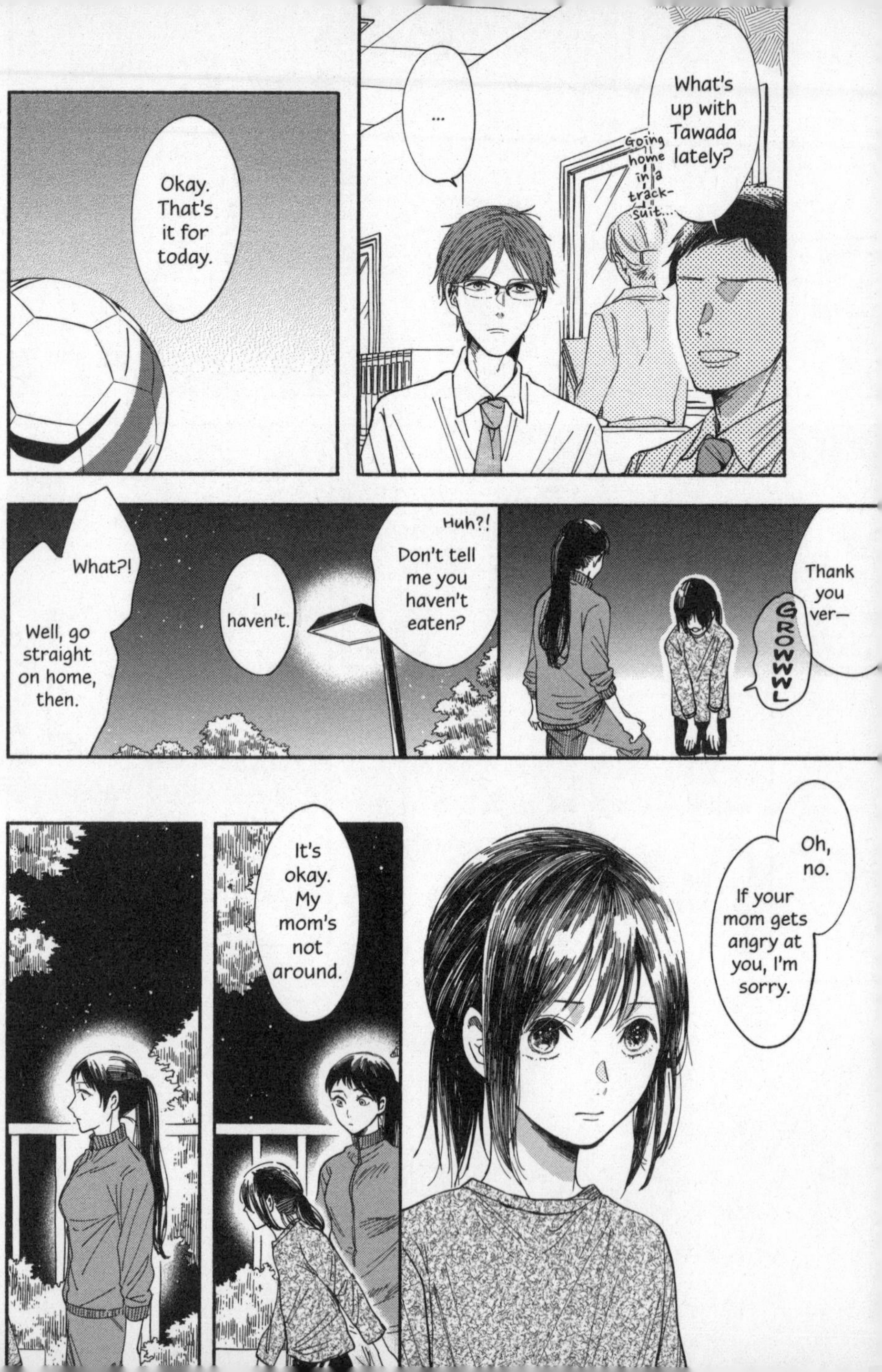
What's up with Tawada lately?
Going home in a track-suit...
...
Okay. That's it for today.
Thank you ver—
GROWWWL
Huh?!
Don't tell me you haven't eaten?
I haven't.
What?!
Well, go straight on home, then.
Oh, no.
If your mom gets angry at you, I'm sorry.
It's okay. My mom's not around.

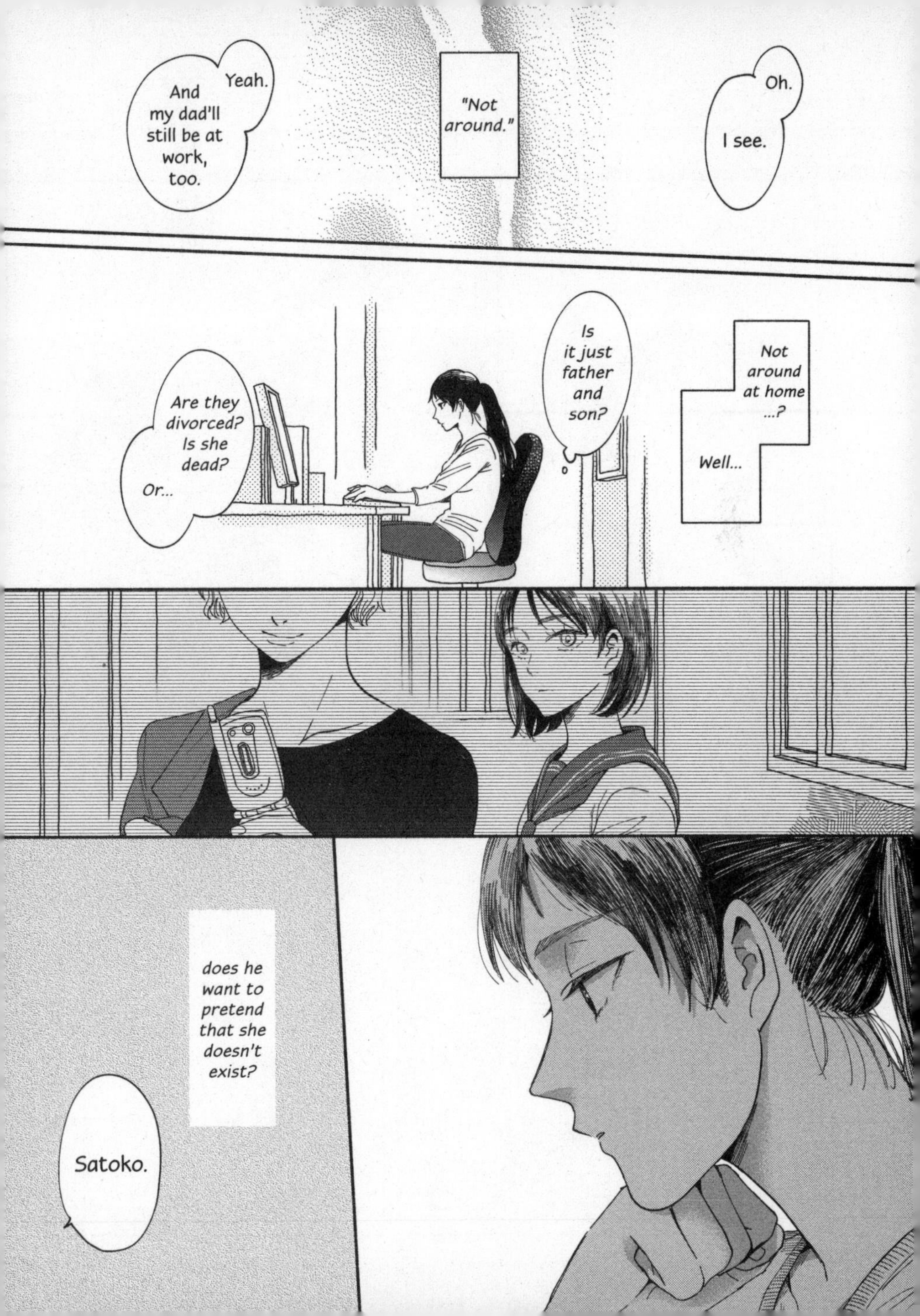

Oh. I see.
"Not around."
Yeah. And my dad'll still be at work, too.
Not around at home ...? Well...
Is it just father and son?
Are they divorced? Is she dead? Or...
does he want to pretend that she doesn't exist?
Satoko.

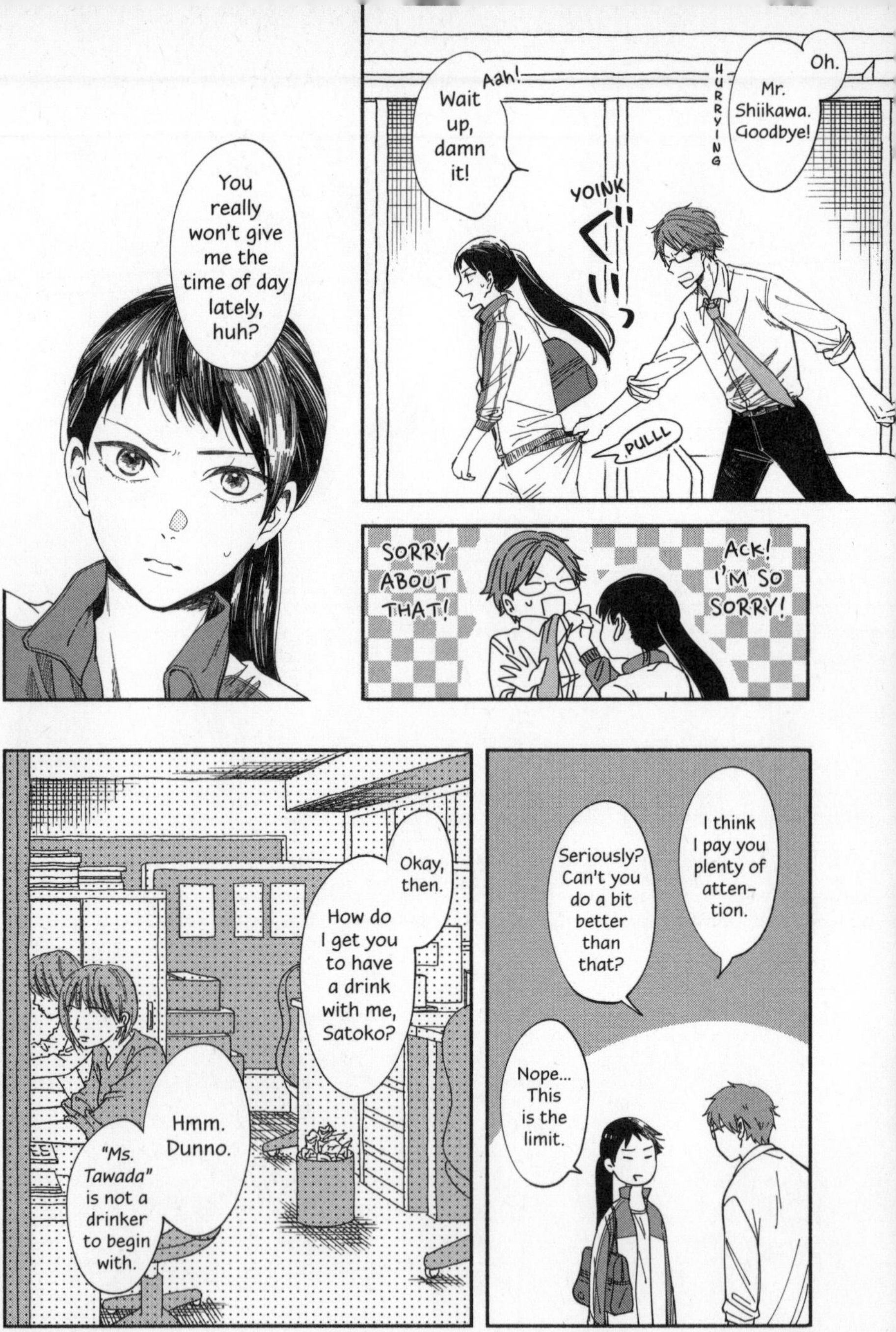
Oh. Mr. Shiikawa. Goodbye!
HURRYING
Aah! Wait up, damn it!
YOINK
PULLL
Ack! I'M SO SORRY!
SORRY ABOUT THAT!
You really won't give me the time of day lately, huh?
I think I pay you plenty of attention.
Seriously? Can't you do a bit better than that?
Nope... This is the limit.
Okay, then.
How do I get you to have a drink with me, Satoko?
Hmm. Dunno.
"Ms. Tawada" is not a drinker to begin with.

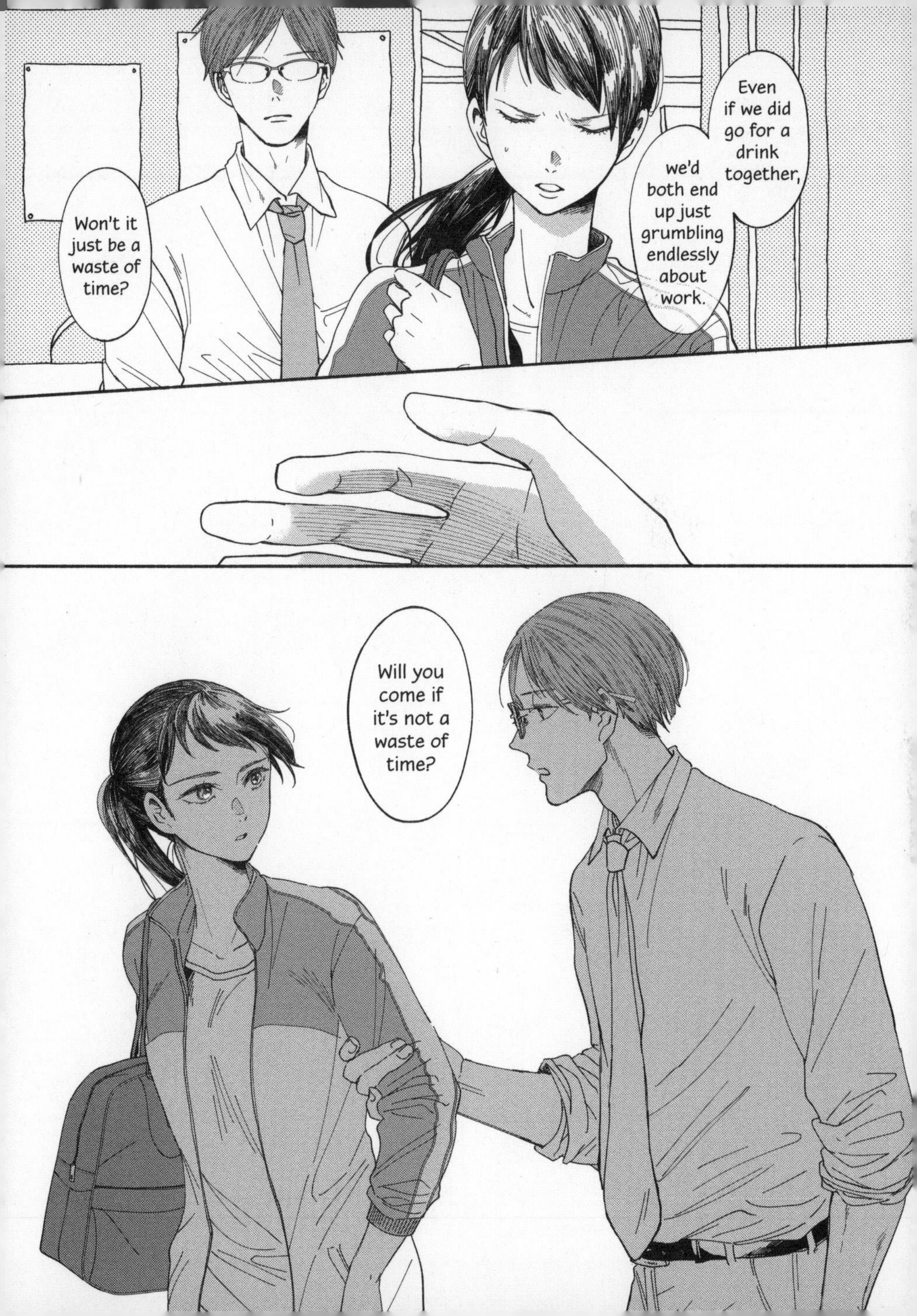
Even if we did go for a drink together,
we'd both end up just grumbling endlessly about work.
Won't it just be a waste of time?
Will you come if it's not a waste of time?

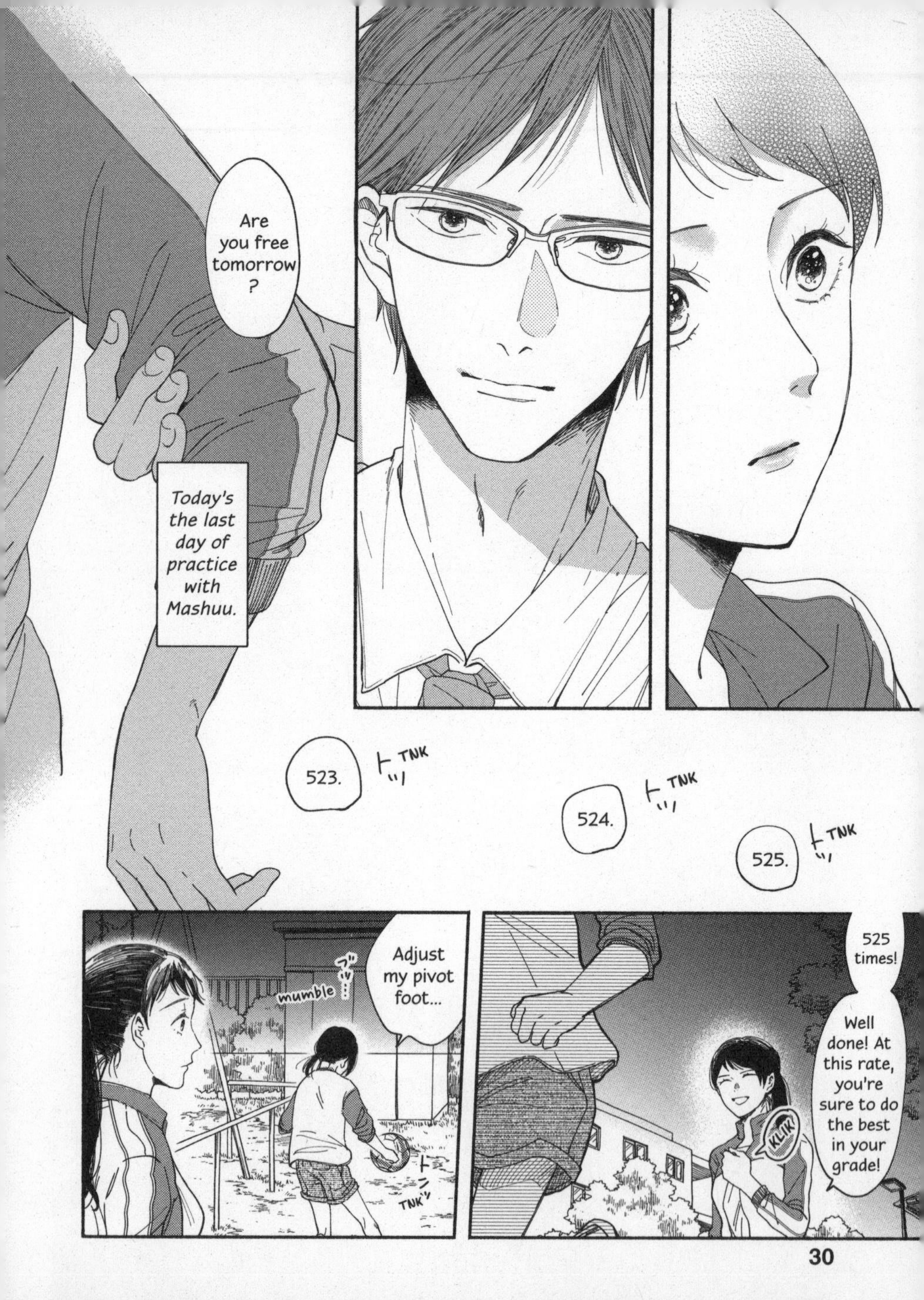
Are you free tomorrow ?
Today's the last day of practice with Mashuu.
523.
TNK
524.
TNK
525.
TNK
525 times!
Well done! At this rate, you're sure to do the best in your grade!
KLIK!
Adjust my pivot foot...
mumble
TNK

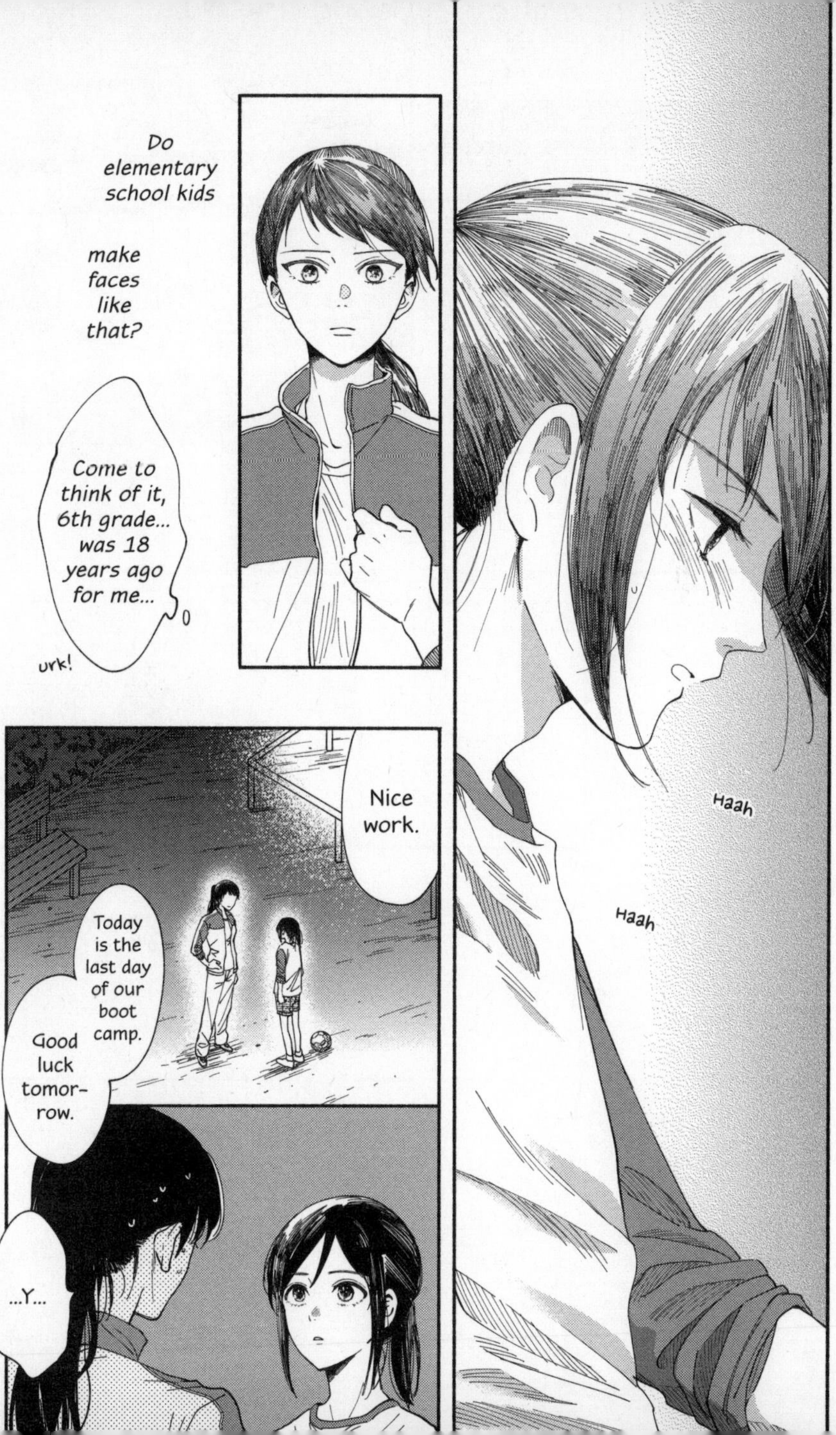
Haah
Haah
Do elementary school kids
make faces like that?
Come to think of it, 6th grade... was 18 years ago for me...
urk!
Nice work.
Today is the last day of our boot camp.
Good luck tomor-row.
...Y...

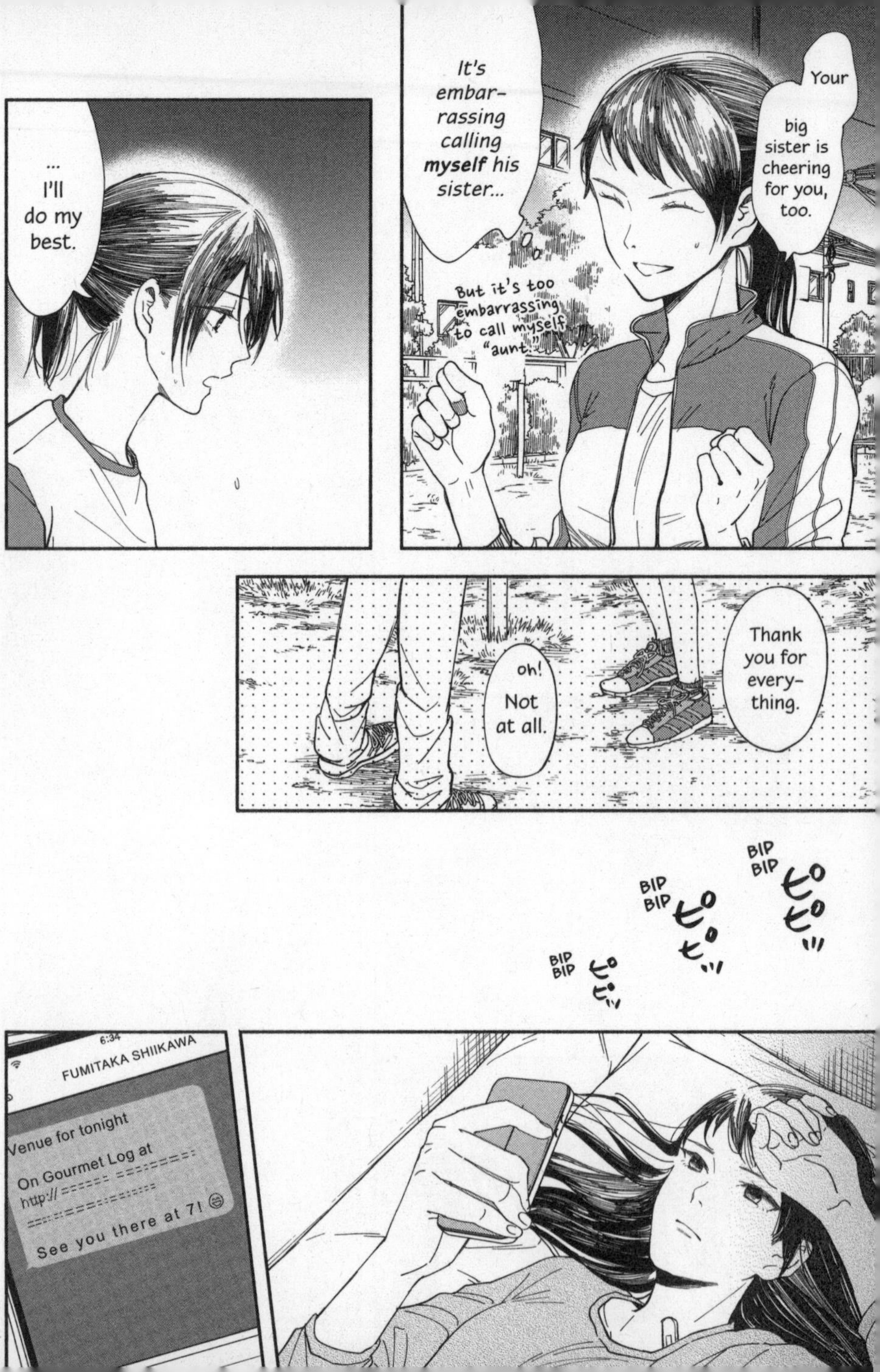
Your big sister is cheering for you, too.
It's embarrassing calling **myself** his sister...
But it's too embarrassing to call myself "aunt."
... I'll do my best.
Thank you for everything.
oh! Not at all.
BIP BIP ピピッ
BIP BIP ピピッ
BIP BIP ピピッ
6:34
FUMITAKA SHIIKAWA
Venue for tonight
On Gourmet Log at
See you there at 7!

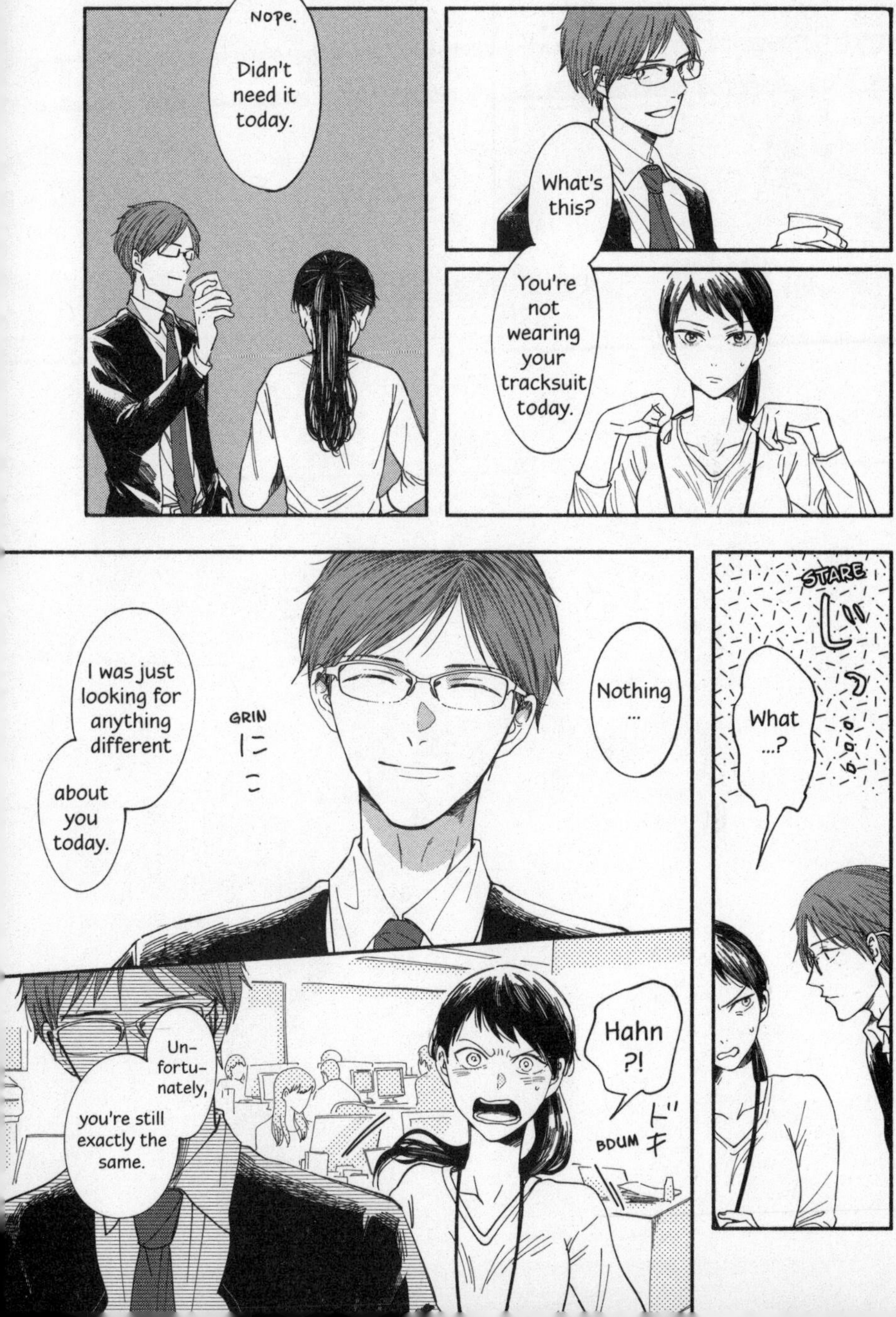

What's this?
You're not wearing your tracksuit today.
Nope.
Didn't need it today.
STARE
What ...?
Nothing ...
I was just looking for anything different
about you today.
GRIN
にこ
Hahn ?!
BDUM
Un-fortu-nately,
you're still exactly the same.

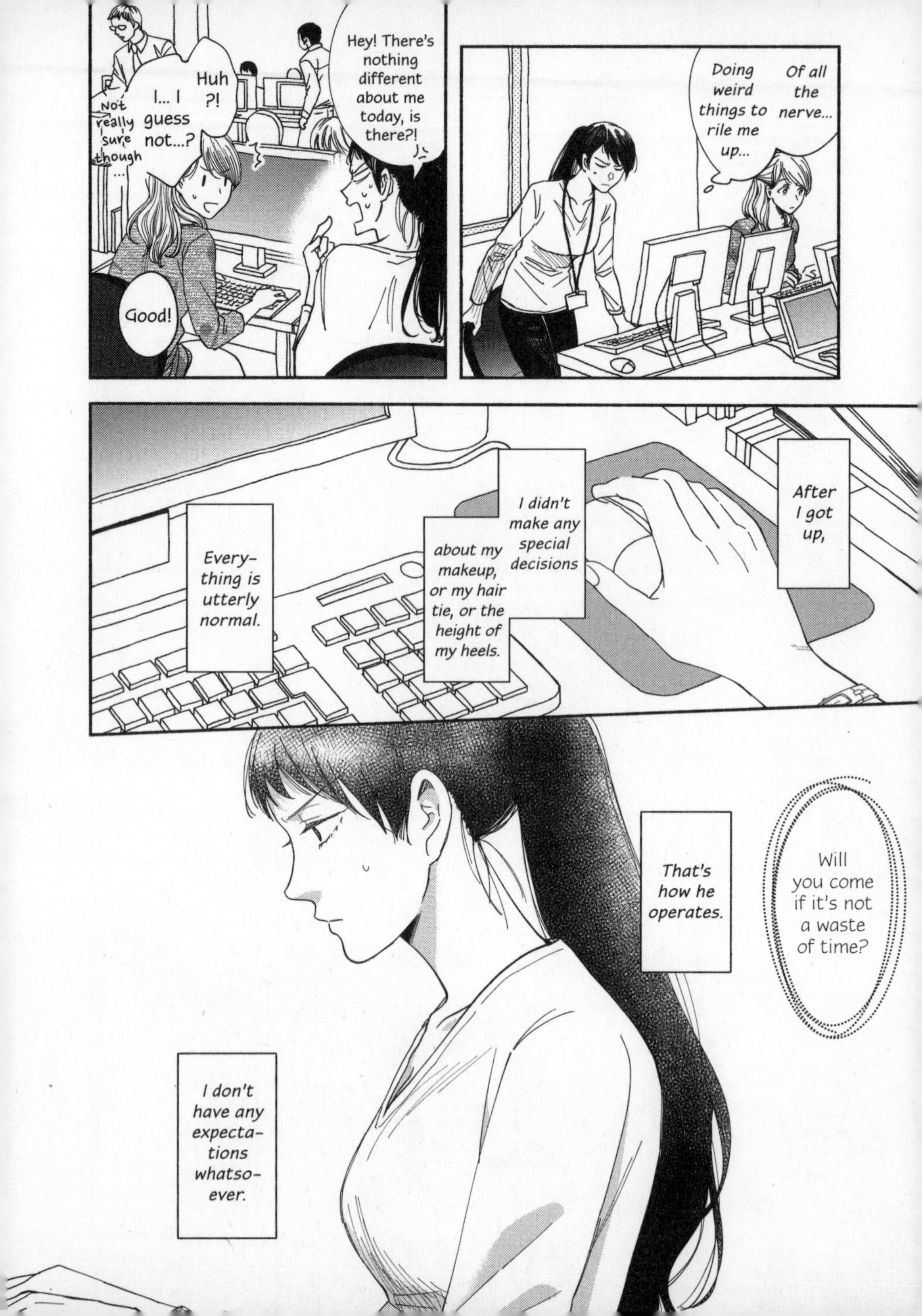

Of all the nerve...
Doing weird things to rile me up...
Hey! There's nothing different about me today, is there?!
Huh ?!
I... I guess not...?
Not really sure though ...
Good!
After I got up,
I didn't make any special decisions
about my makeup, or my hair tie, or the height of my heels.
Everything is utterly normal.
Will you come if it's not a waste of time?
That's how he operates.
I don't have any expectations whatsoever.

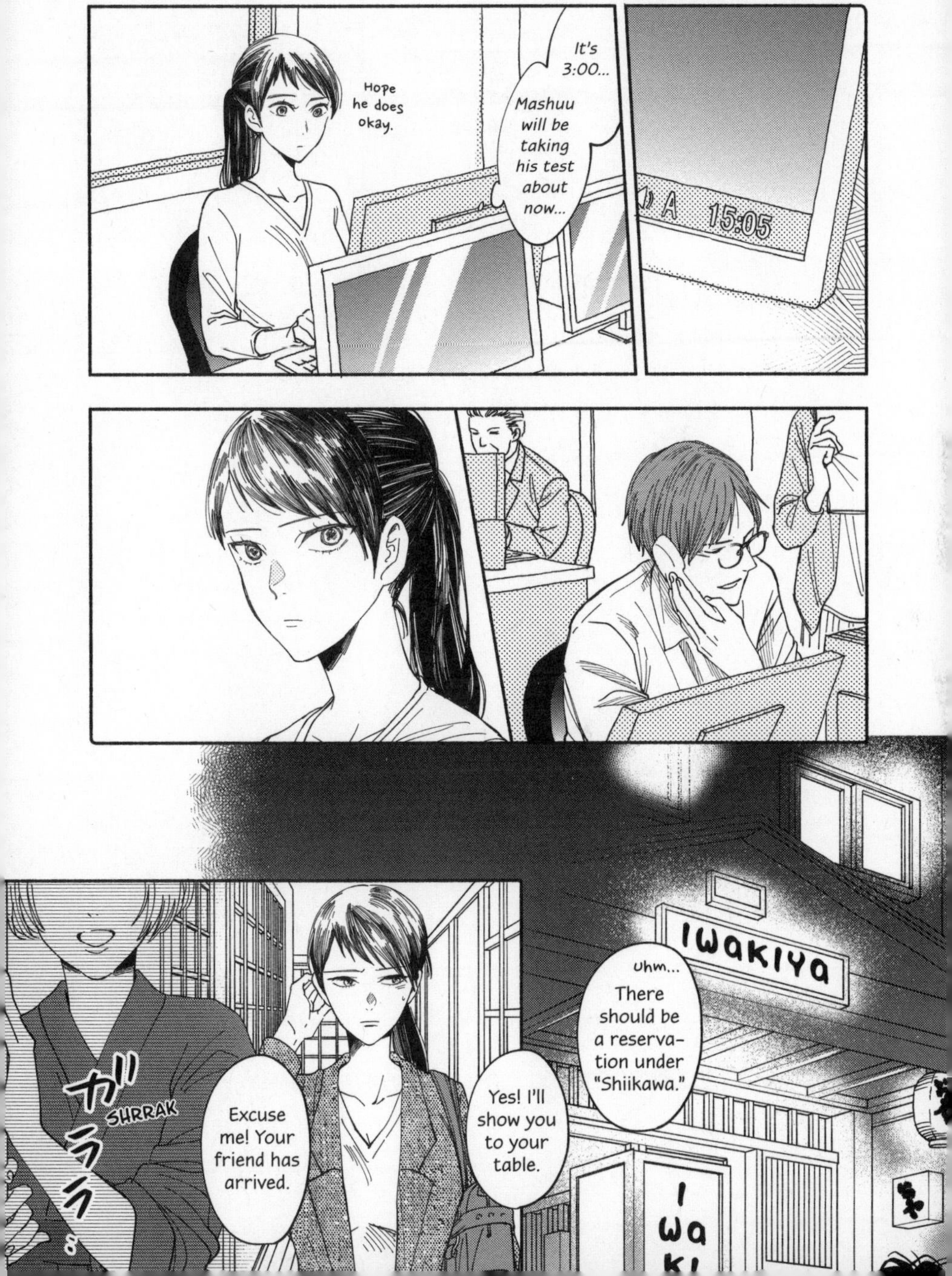
15:05
It's 3:00...
Mashuu will be taking his test about now...
Hope he does okay.
IWAKIYA
Iwa ki
Uhm... There should be a reservation under "Shiikawa."
Yes! I'll show you to your table.
ガラ
SHRRAK
Excuse me! Your friend has arrived.

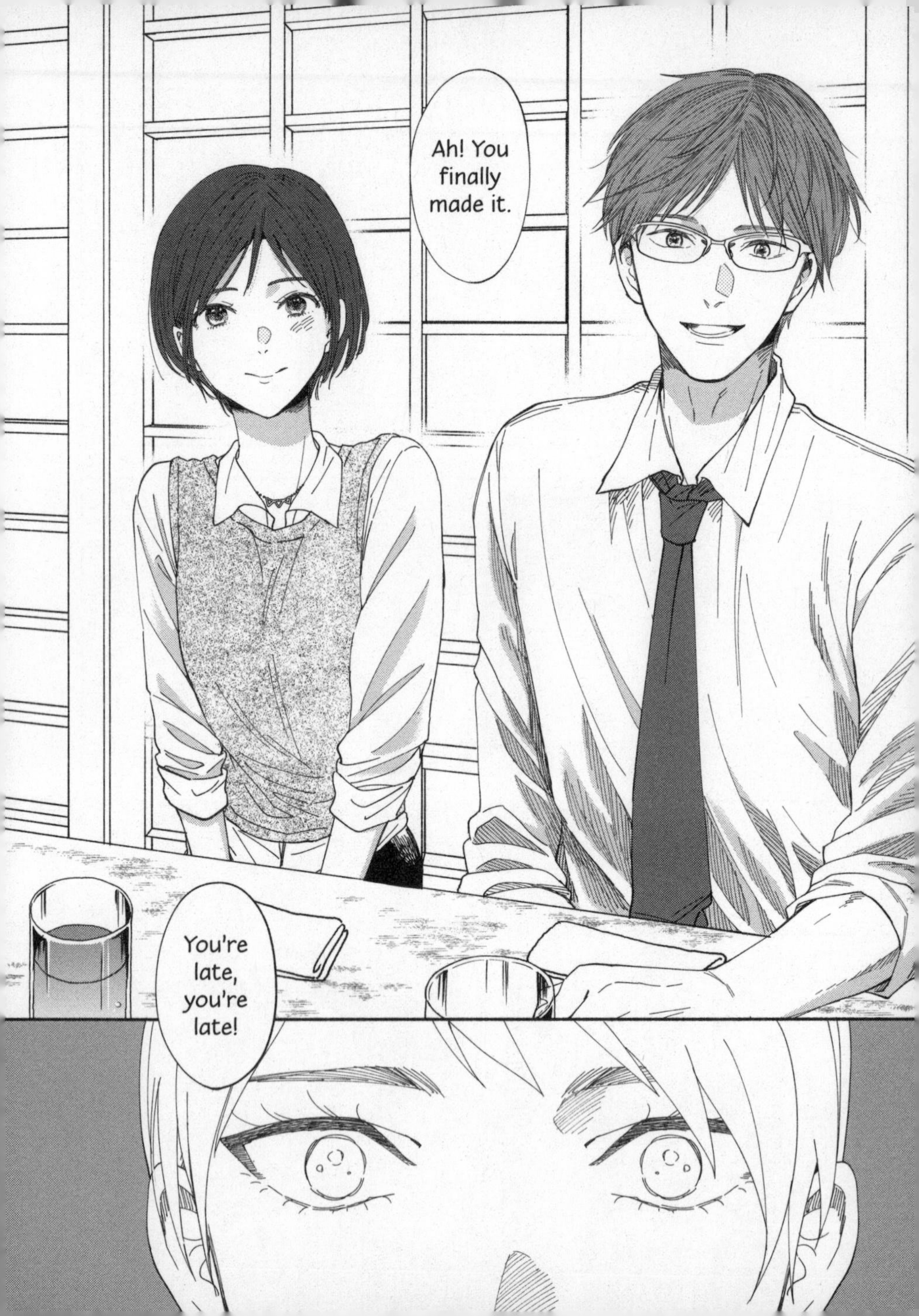
Ah! You finally made it.
You're late, you're late!

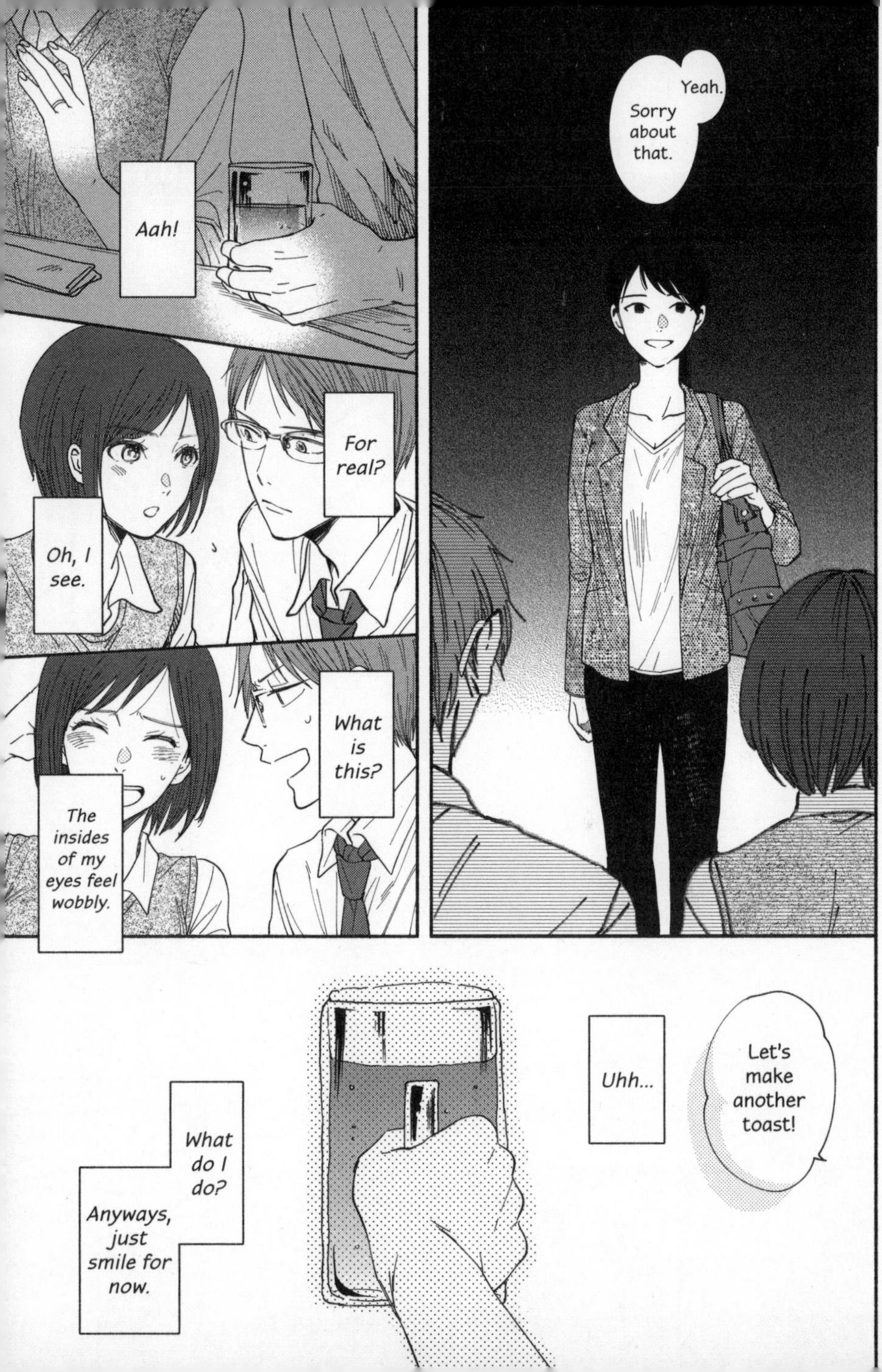
Yeah.
Sorry about that.
Aah!
For real?
Oh, I see.
What is this?
The insides of my eyes feel wobbly.
Let's make another toast!
Uhh...
What do I do?
Anyways, just smile for now.

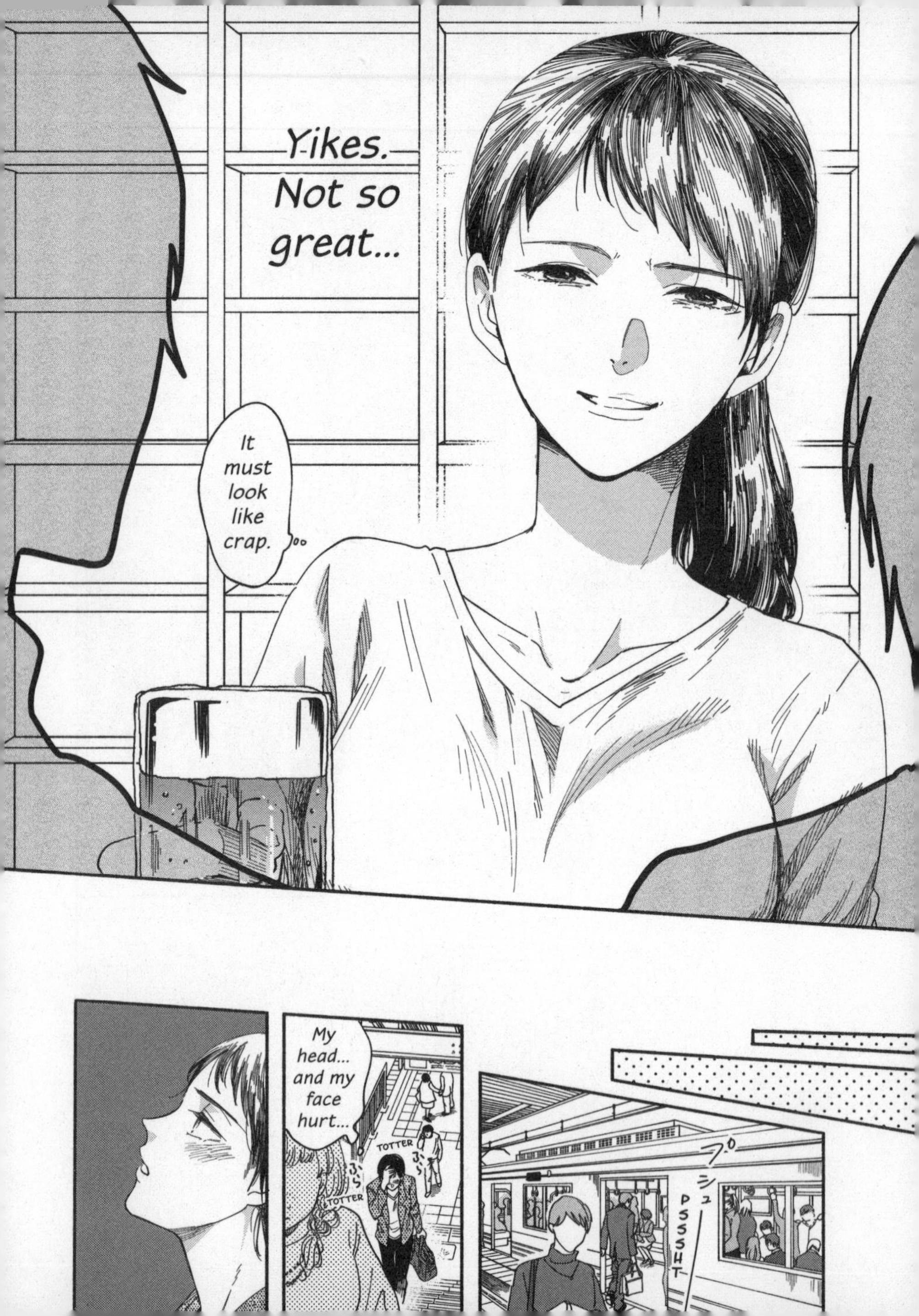
Yikes. Not so great...
It must look like crap.
PSSSHT
My head... and my face hurt...
TOTTER
TOTTER

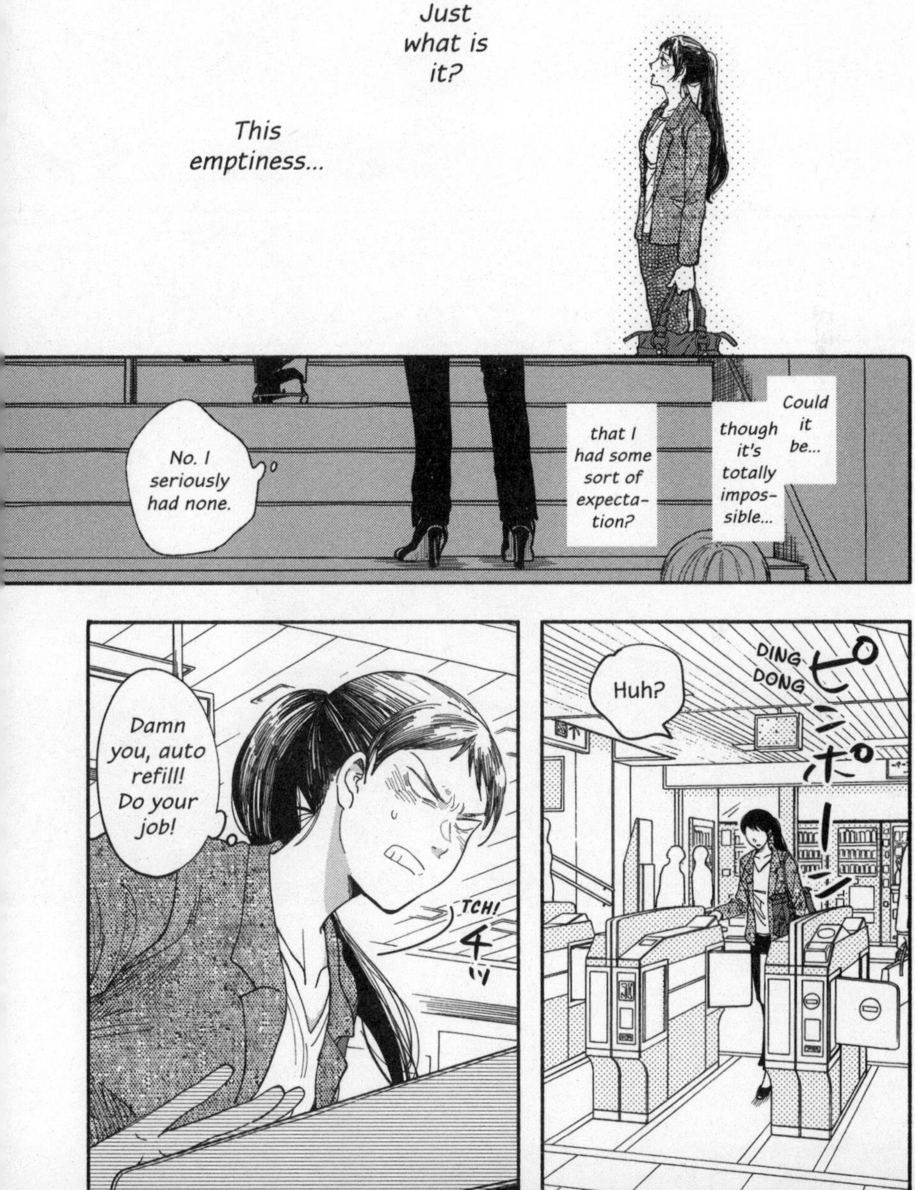
Just what is it?
This emptiness...
Could it be...
though it's totally impossible...
that I had some sort of expectation?
No. I seriously had none.
DING DONG
Huh?
Damn you, auto refill! Do your job!
TCH!

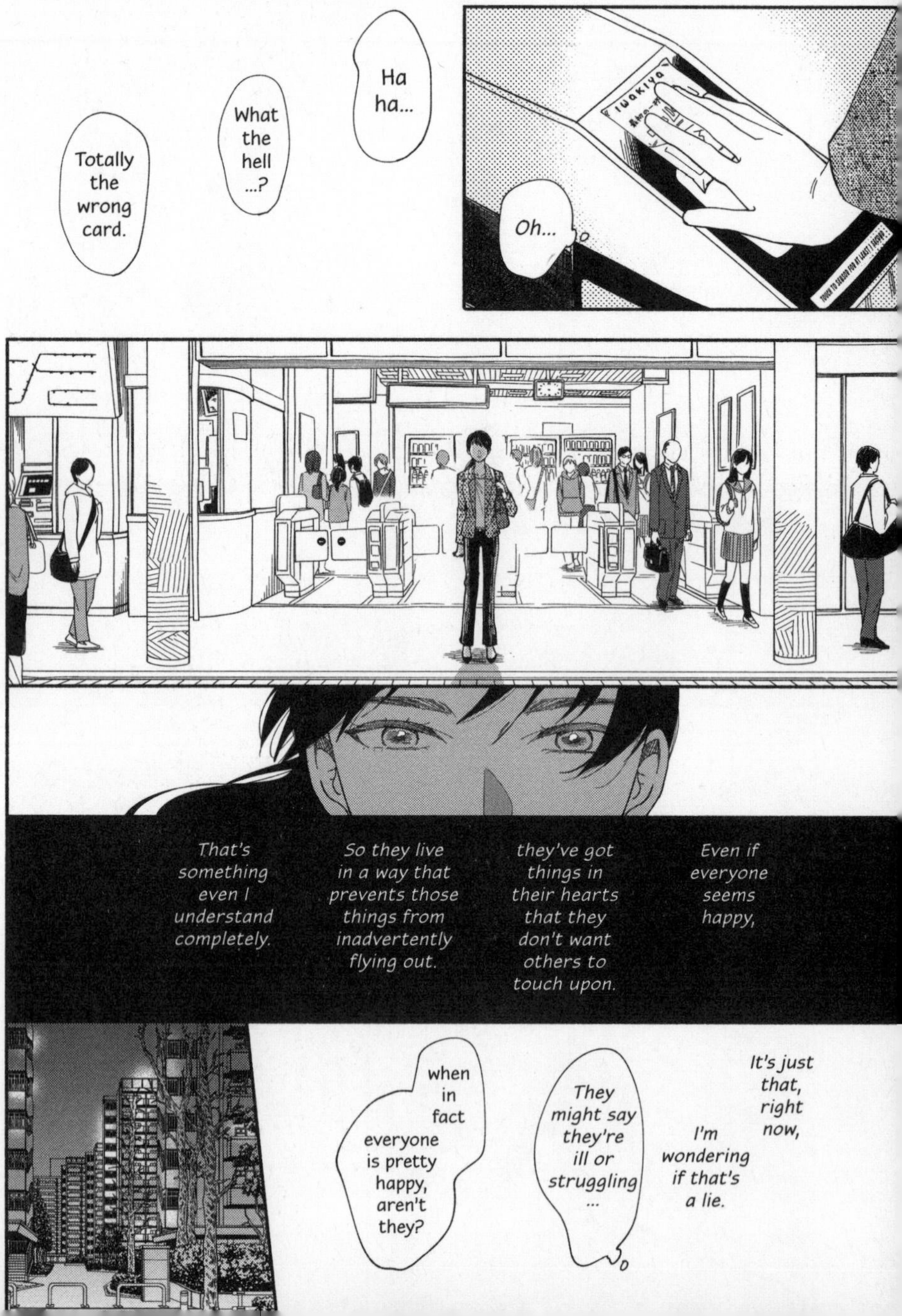
Oh...
Ha ha...
What the hell ...?
Totally the wrong card.
Even if everyone seems happy,
they've got things in their hearts that they don't want others to touch upon.
So they live in a way that prevents those things from inadvertently flying out.
That's something even I understand completely.
It's just that, right now,
I'm wondering if that's a lie.
They might say they're ill or struggling ...
when in fact everyone is pretty happy, aren't they?

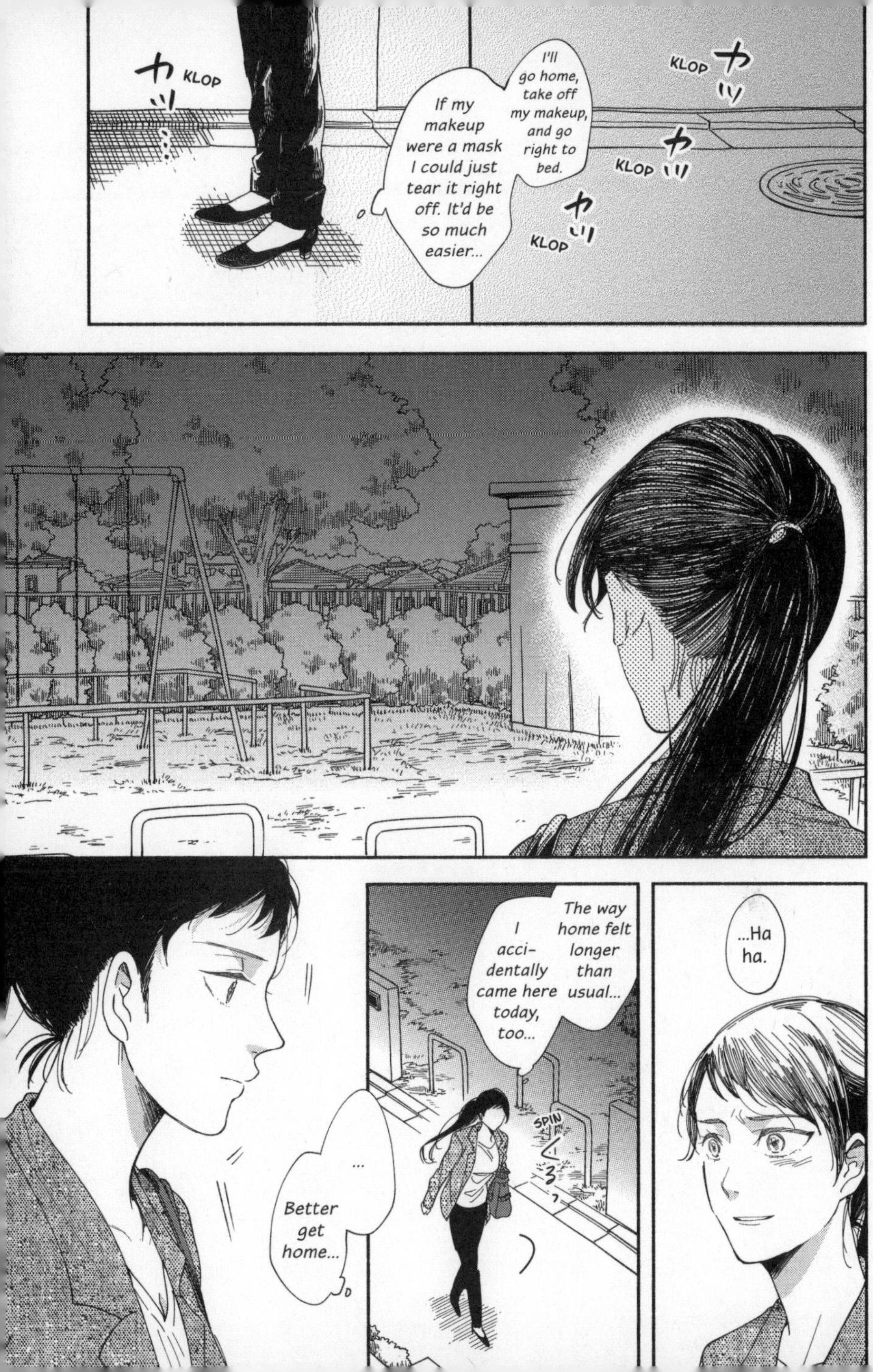
KLOP カッ
KLOP カッ
KLOP カッ
I'll go home, take off my makeup, and go right to bed.
If my makeup were a mask I could just tear it right off. It'd be so much easier...
カッ KLOP
...Ha ha.
The way home felt longer than usual...
I accidentally came here today, too...
SPIN くるっ
...
Better get home...

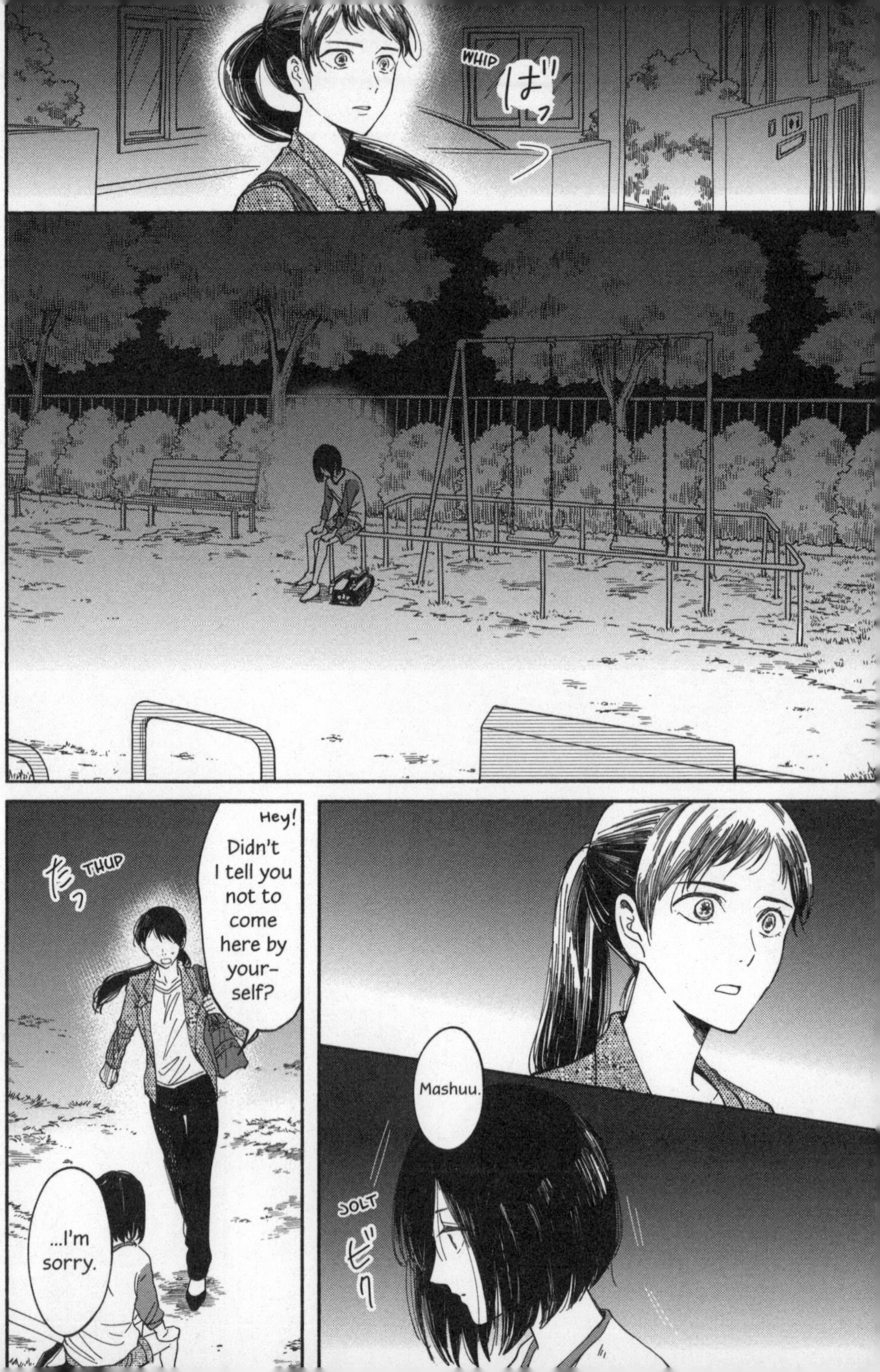
WHIP
ばっ
Mashuu.
JOLT
ビク
THUP
たっ
Hey! Didn't I tell you not to come here by yourself?
...I'm sorry.

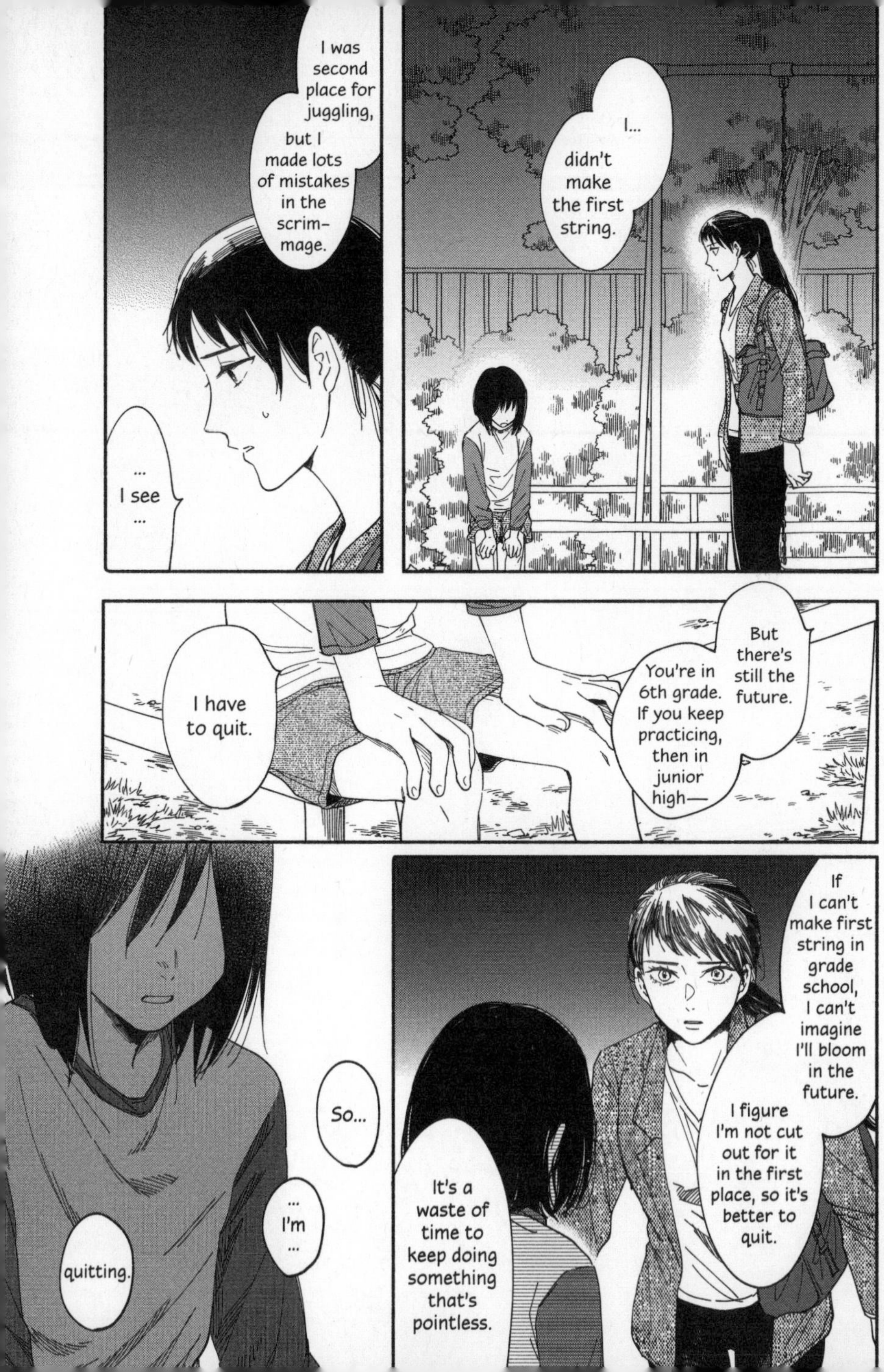
I... didn't make the first string.
I was second place for juggling,
but I made lots of mistakes in the scrim-mage.
... I see ...
But there's still the future.
You're in 6th grade. If you keep practicing, then in junior high—
I have to quit.
If I can't make first string in grade school, I can't imagine I'll bloom in the future.
I figure I'm not cut out for it in the first place, so it's better to quit.
It's a waste of time to keep doing something that's pointless.
So...
... I'm ...
quitting.

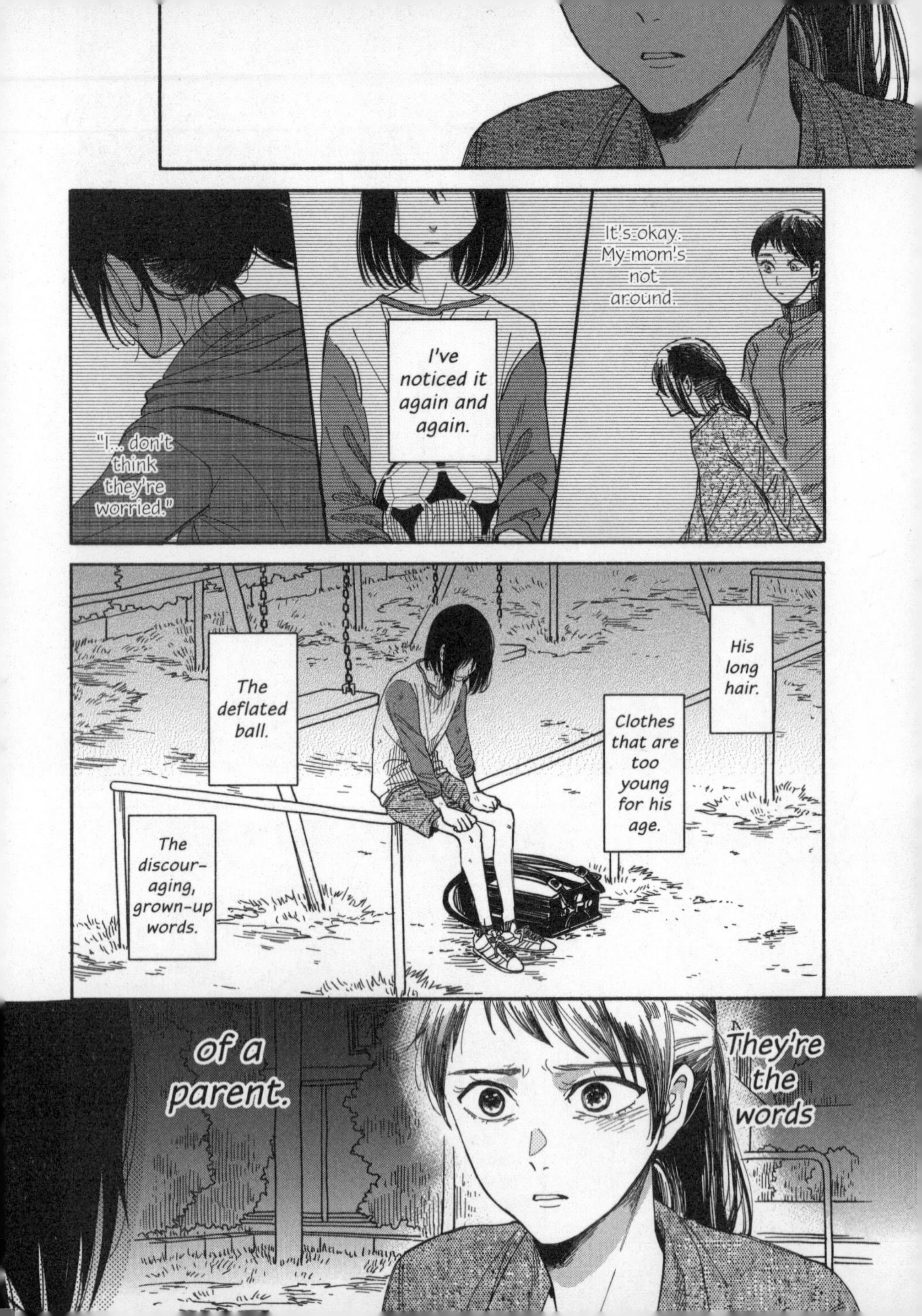
It's okay. My mom's not around.
I've noticed it again and again.
"I... don't think they're worried."
His long hair.
Clothes that are too young for his age.
The deflated ball.
The discouraging, grown-up words.
They're the words
of a parent.

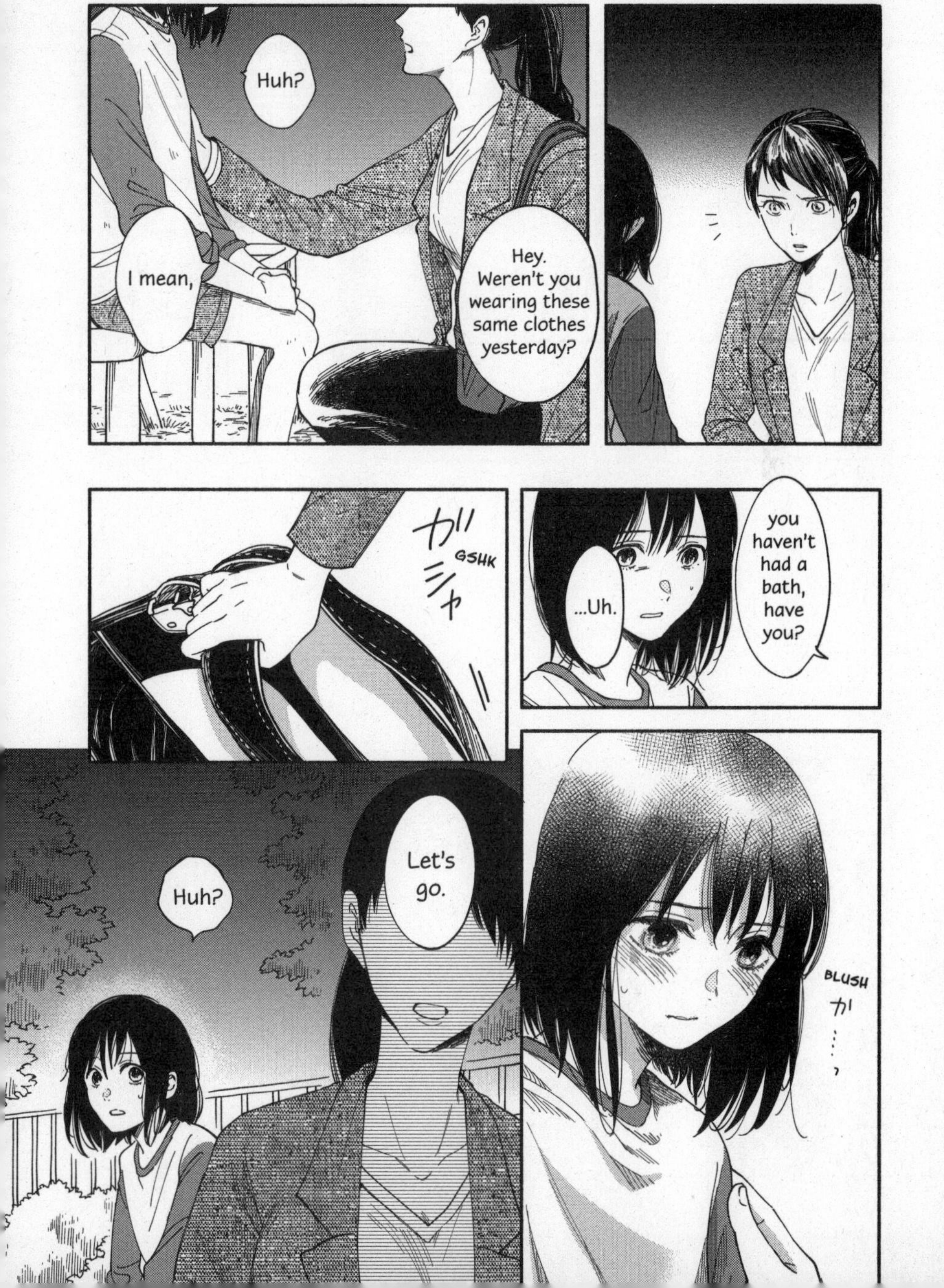
Hey. Weren't you wearing these same clothes yesterday?
Huh?
I mean,
you haven't had a bath, have you?
...Uh.
GSHK
BLUSH
Let's go.
Huh?

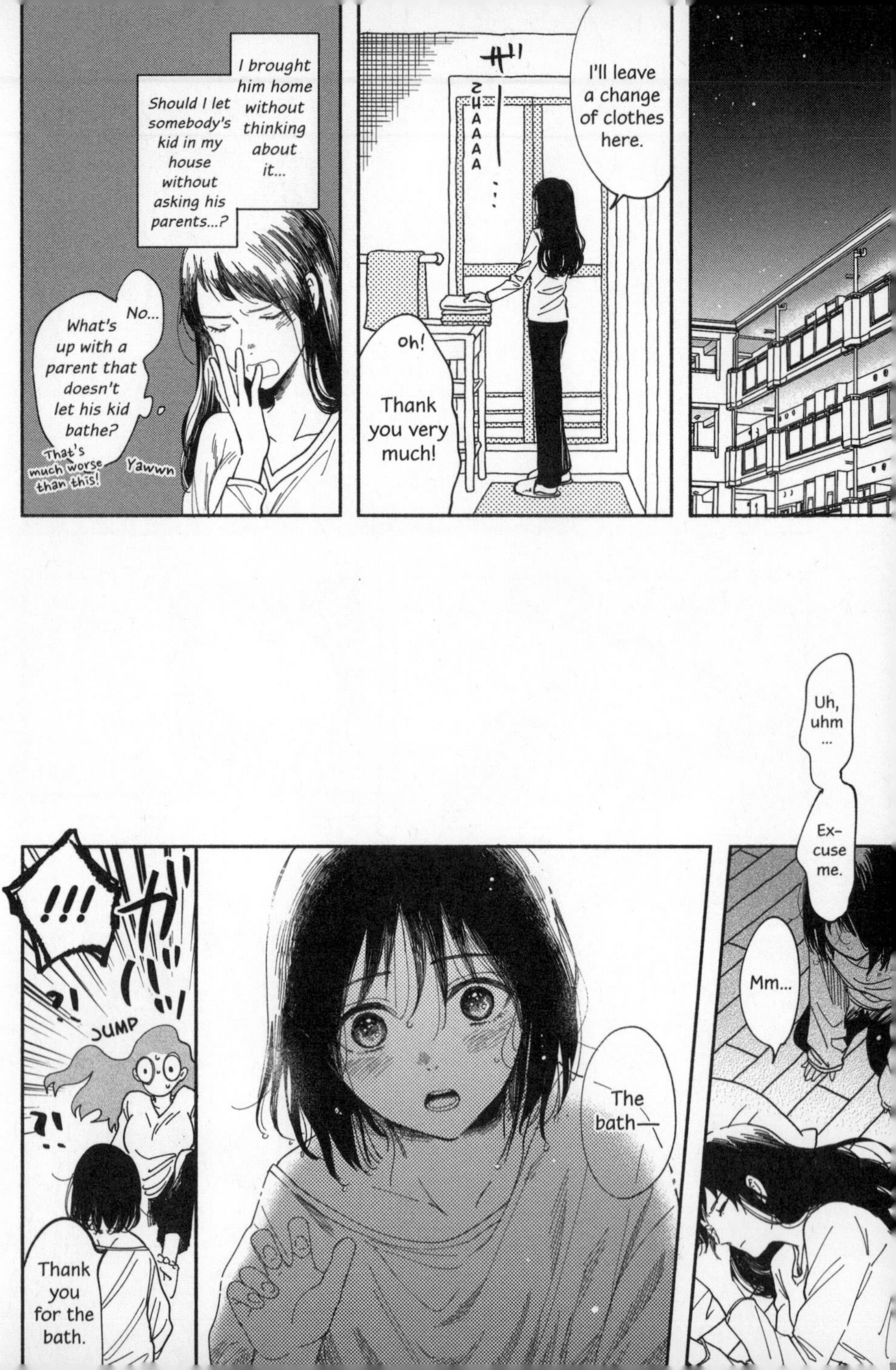
ZHAAAA
I'll leave a change of clothes here.
Oh!
Thank you very much!
I brought him home without thinking about it...
Should I let somebody's kid in my house without asking his parents...?
No... What's up with a parent that doesn't let his kid bathe?
That's much worse than this!
Yawwn
Uh, uhm...
Excuse me.
Mm...
The bath—
!!!
JUMP
?!
?!
Thank you for the bath.

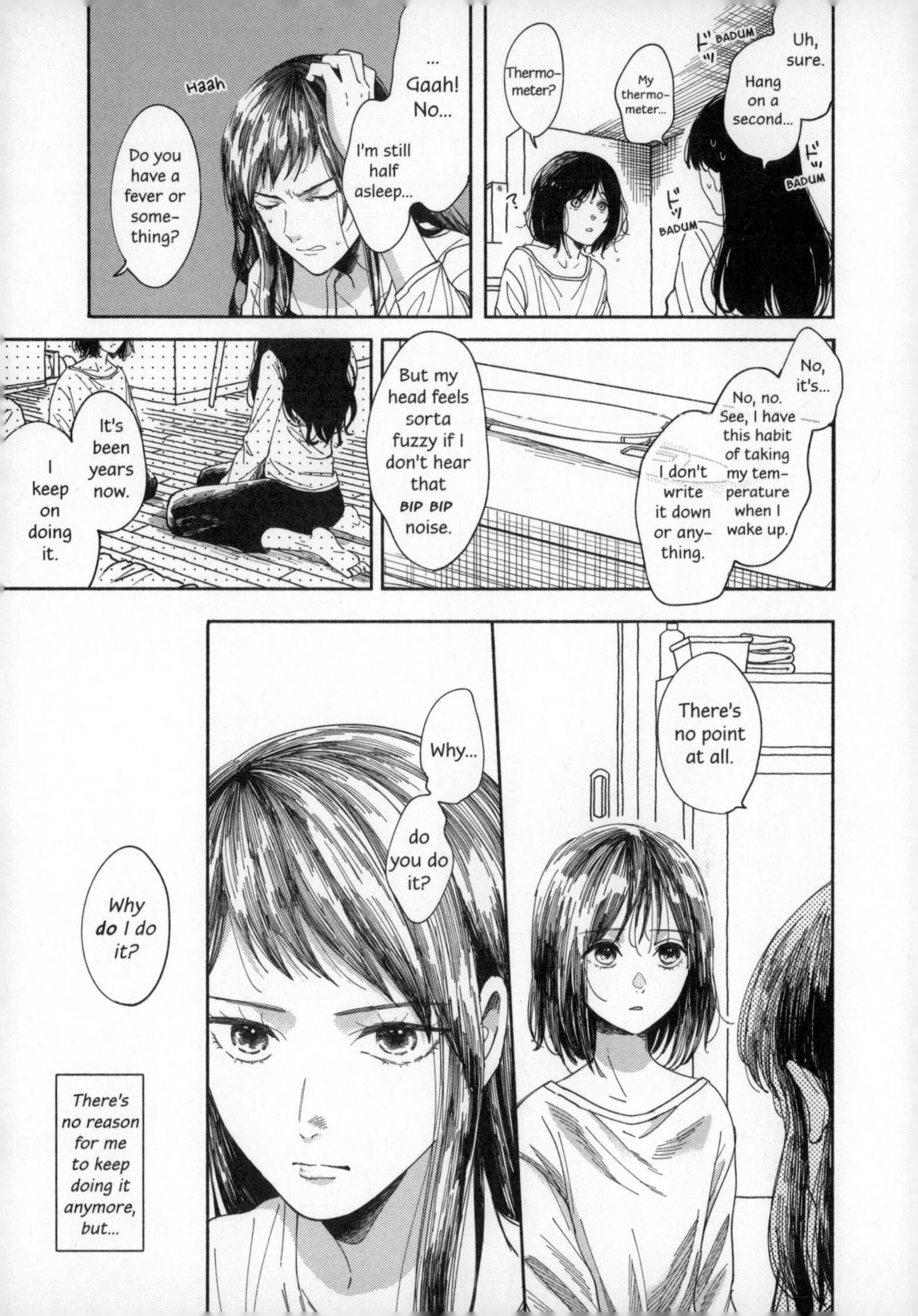

Uh, sure.
Hang on a second...
ドッ BADUM
ドッ BADUM
ドッ BADUM
My thermometer...
Thermometer?
?
... Gaah! No...
I'm still half asleep...
Haah
Do you have a fever or something?
No, it's...
No, no. See, I have this habit of taking my temperature when I wake up.
I don't write it down or anything.
But my head feels sorta fuzzy if I don't hear that BIP BIP noise.
It's been years now.
I keep on doing it.
There's no point at all.
Why...
do you do it?
Why do I do it?
There's no reason for me to keep doing it anymore, but...

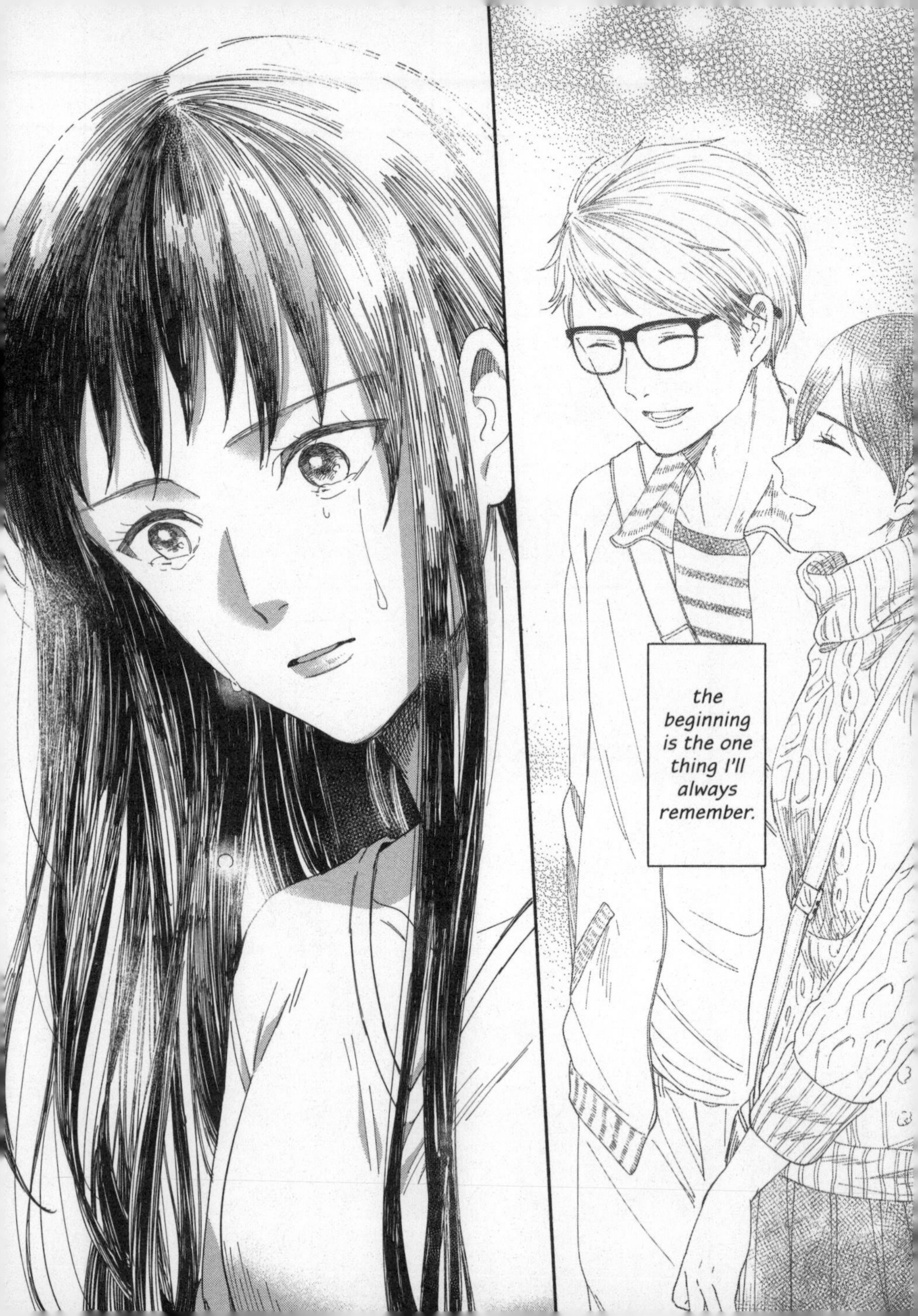
the beginning is the one thing I'll always remember.

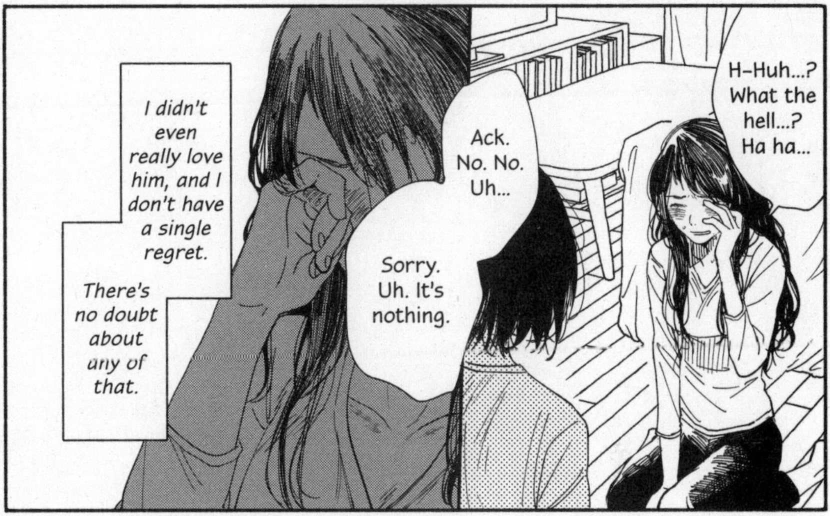
H-Huh...? What the hell...? Ha ha...
Ack. No. No. Uh...
Sorry. Uh. It's nothing.
I didn't even really love him, and I don't have a single regret.
There's no doubt about any of that.

I just got the idea into my head

that ever since then

he's been living his life with the same baggage that I have.

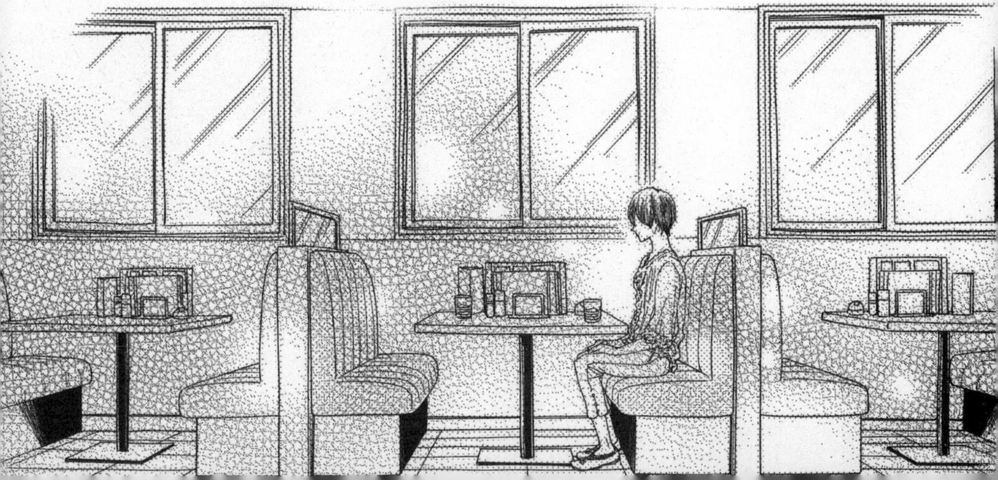

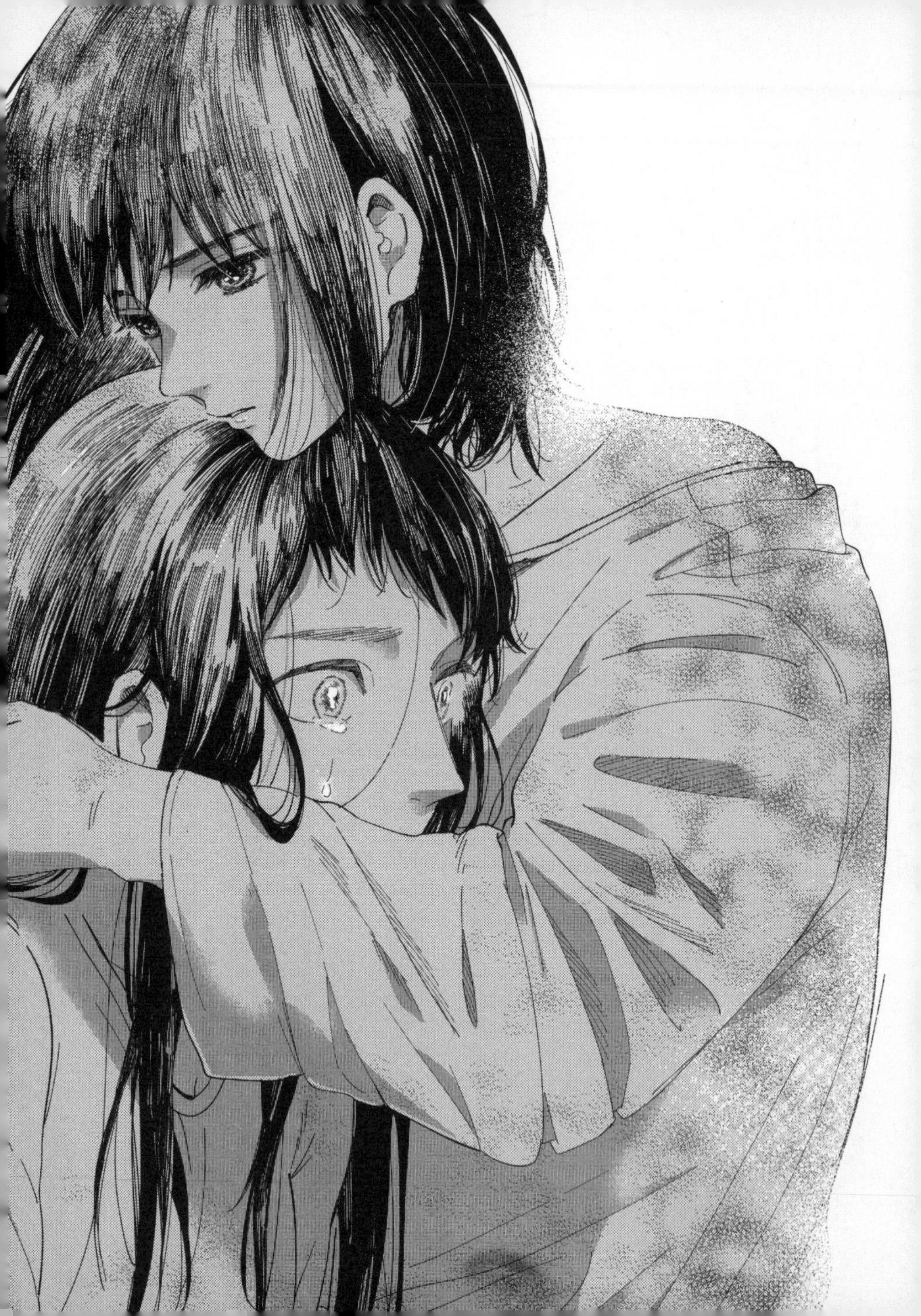

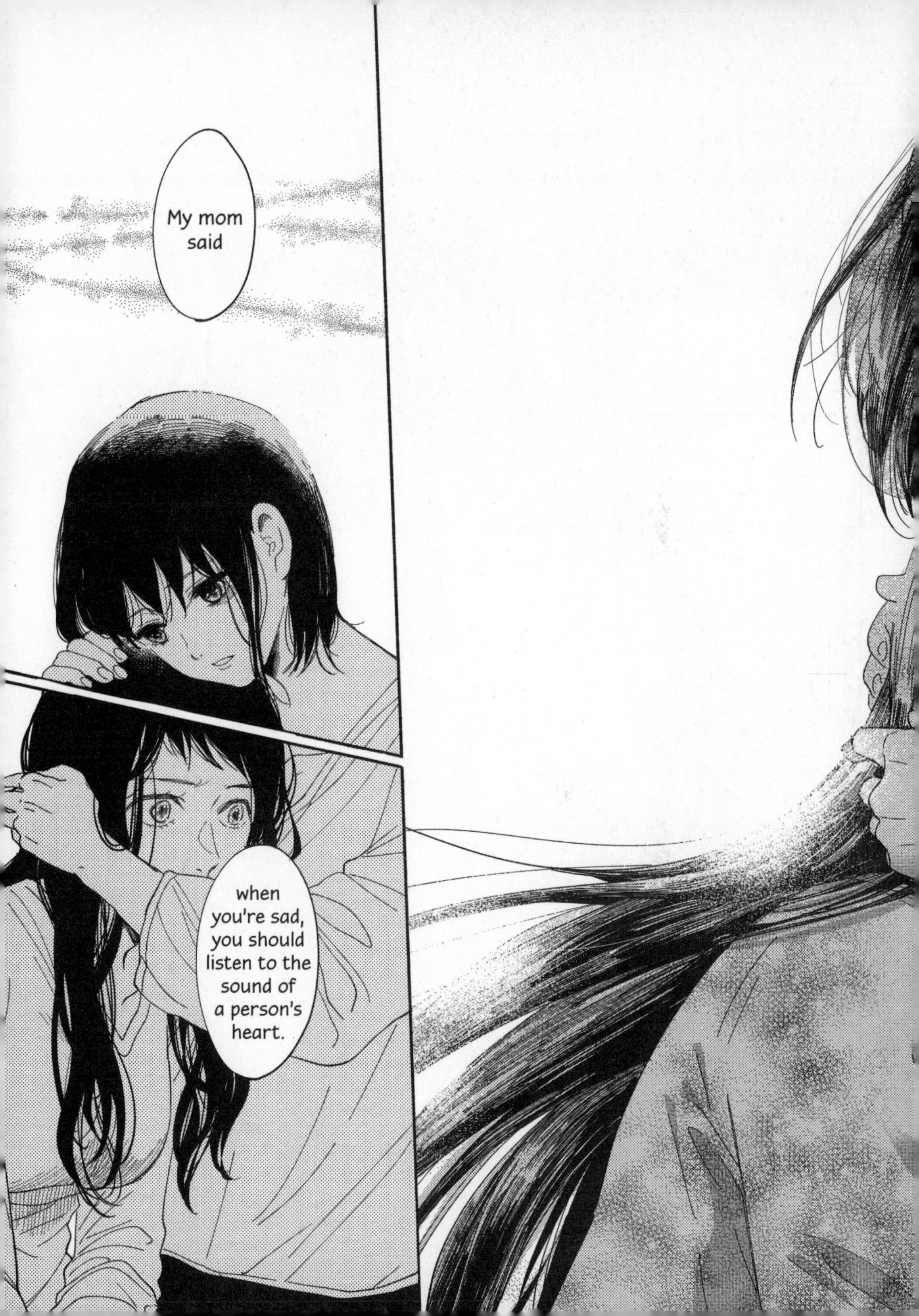
My mom said
when you're sad, you should listen to the sound of a person's heart.

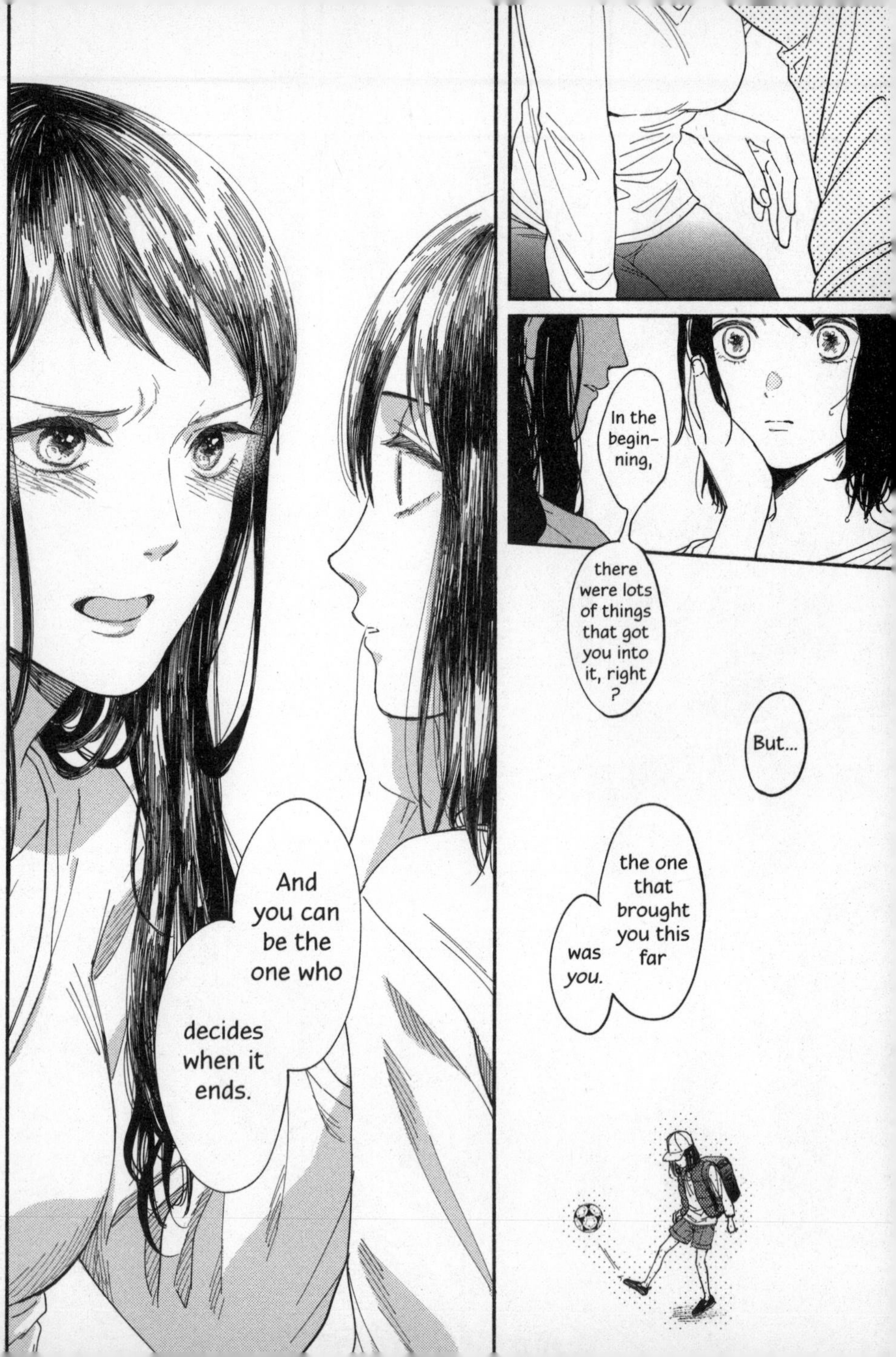
In the beginning,
there were lots of things that got you into it, right?
But...
the one that brought you this far was you.
And you can be the one who
decides when it ends.

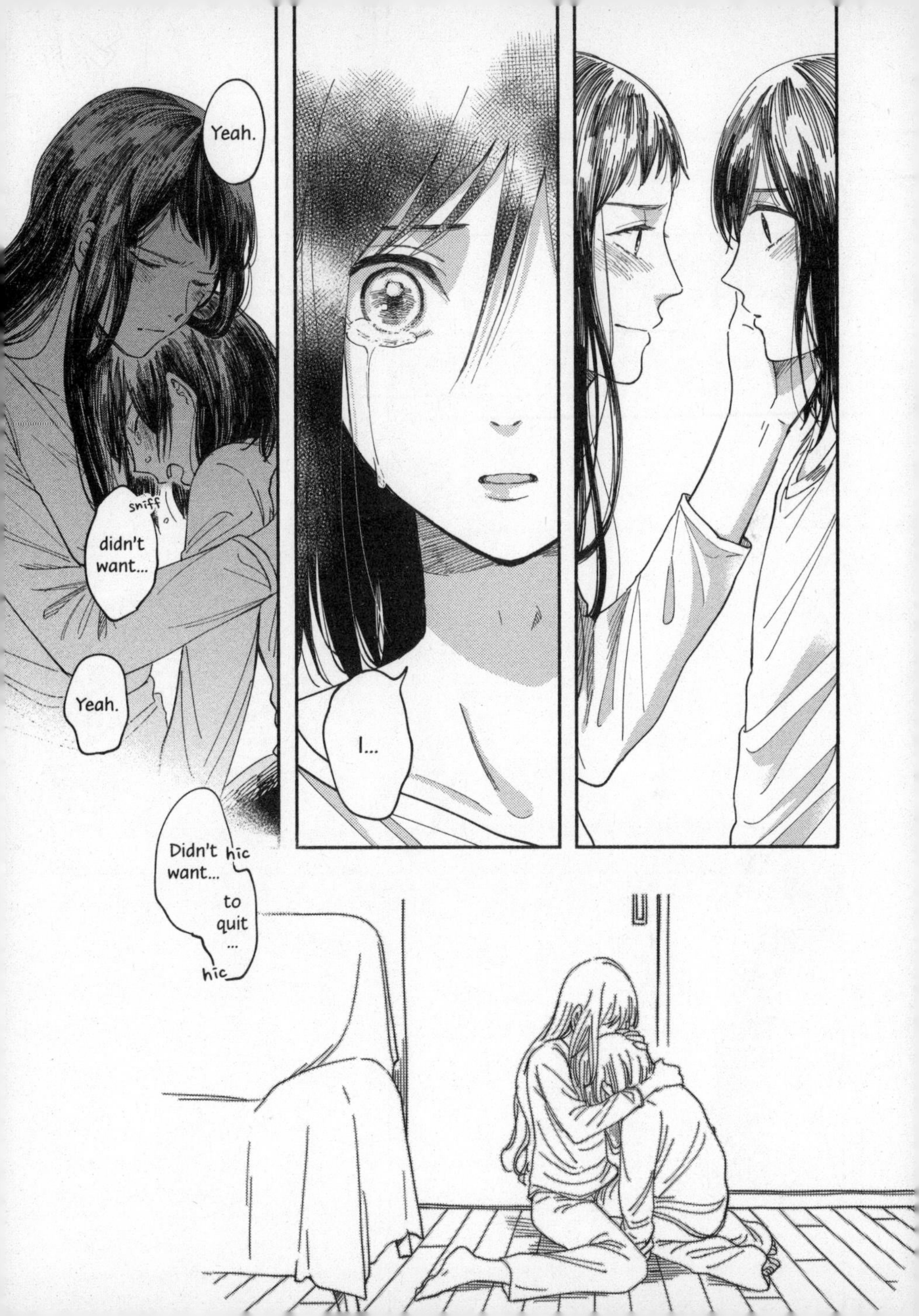

I...
Yeah.
sniff
didn't want...
Yeah.
Didn't hic want... to quit ... hic

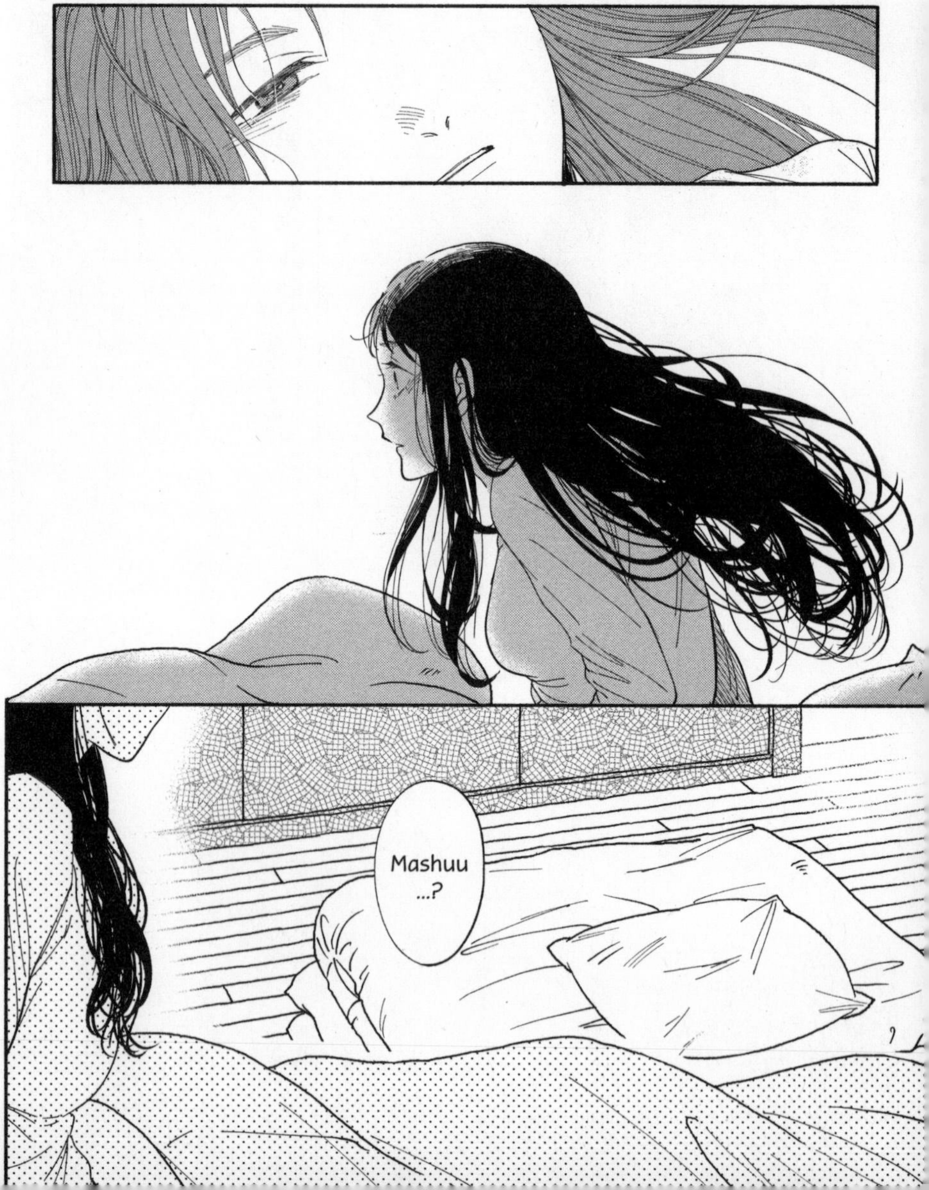
Mashuu
...?

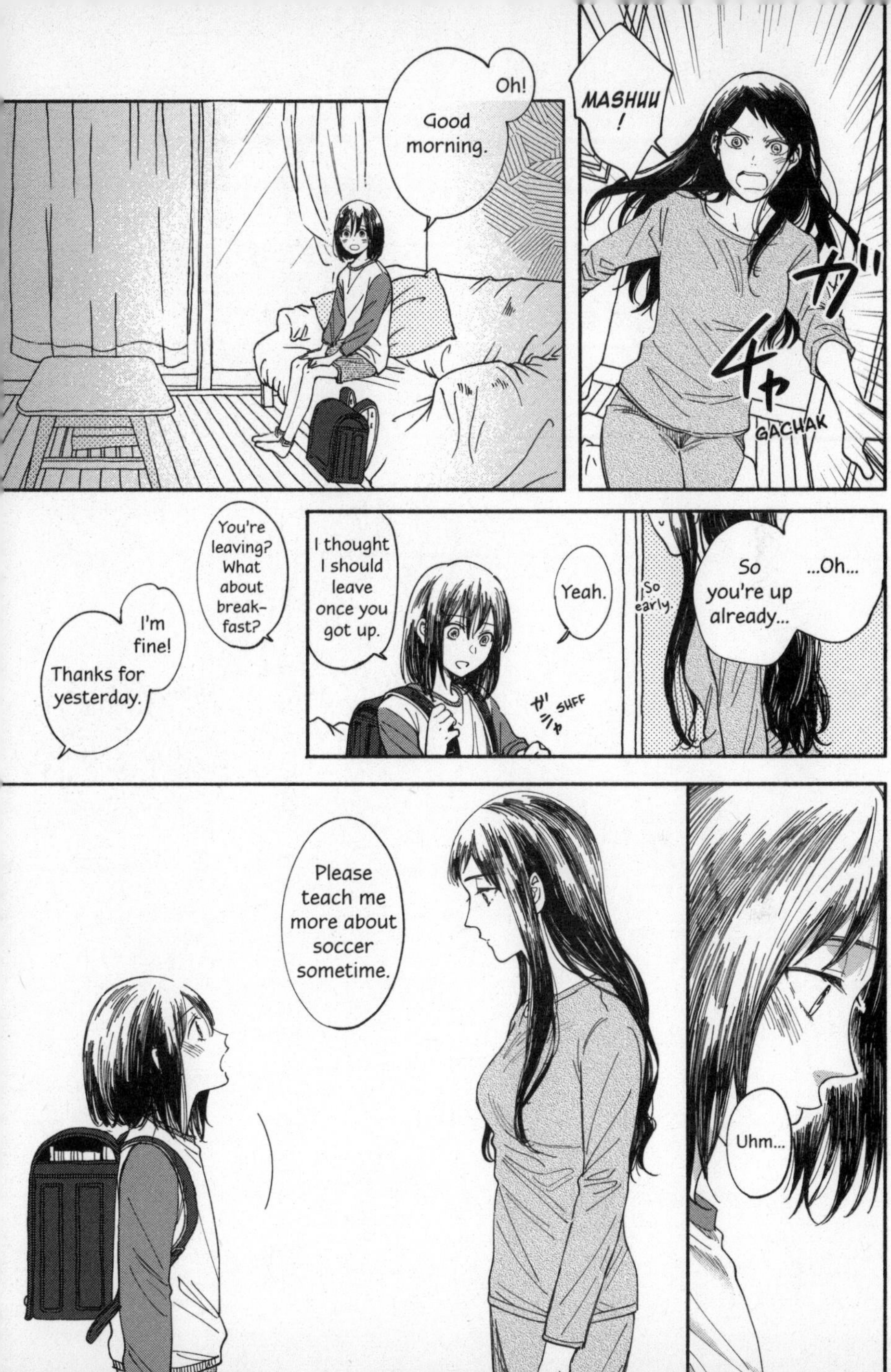
MASHUU!
ガチャ
GACHAK
Oh!
Good morning.
...Oh...
So you're up already...
So early.
Yeah.
I thought I should leave once you got up.
ガシャ
SHFF
You're leaving? What about breakfast?
I'm fine!
Thanks for yesterday.
Uhm...
Please teach me more about soccer sometime.

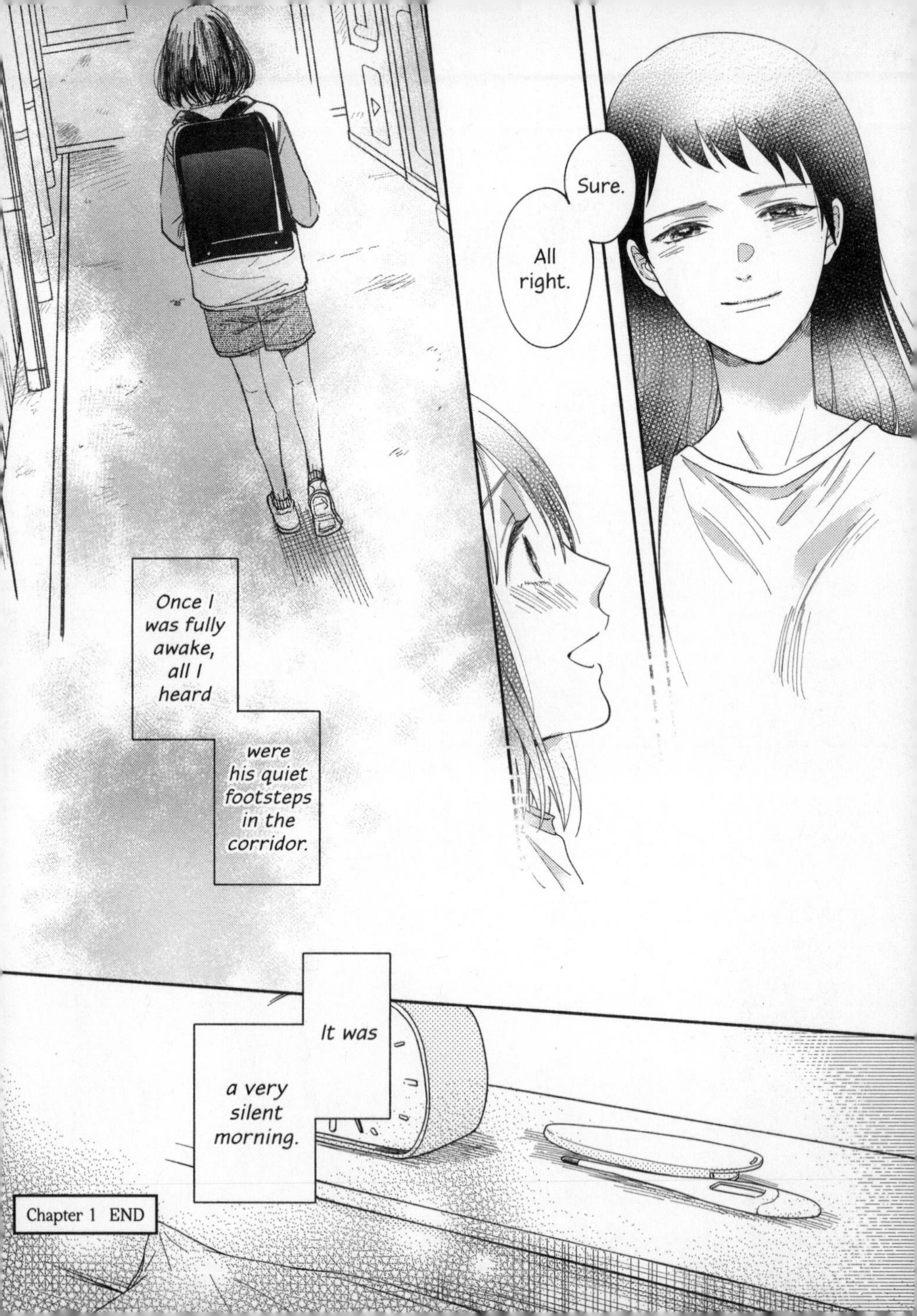
Sure.
All right.
Once I was fully awake, all I heard
were his quiet footsteps in the corridor.
It was
a very silent morning.
Chapter 1 END

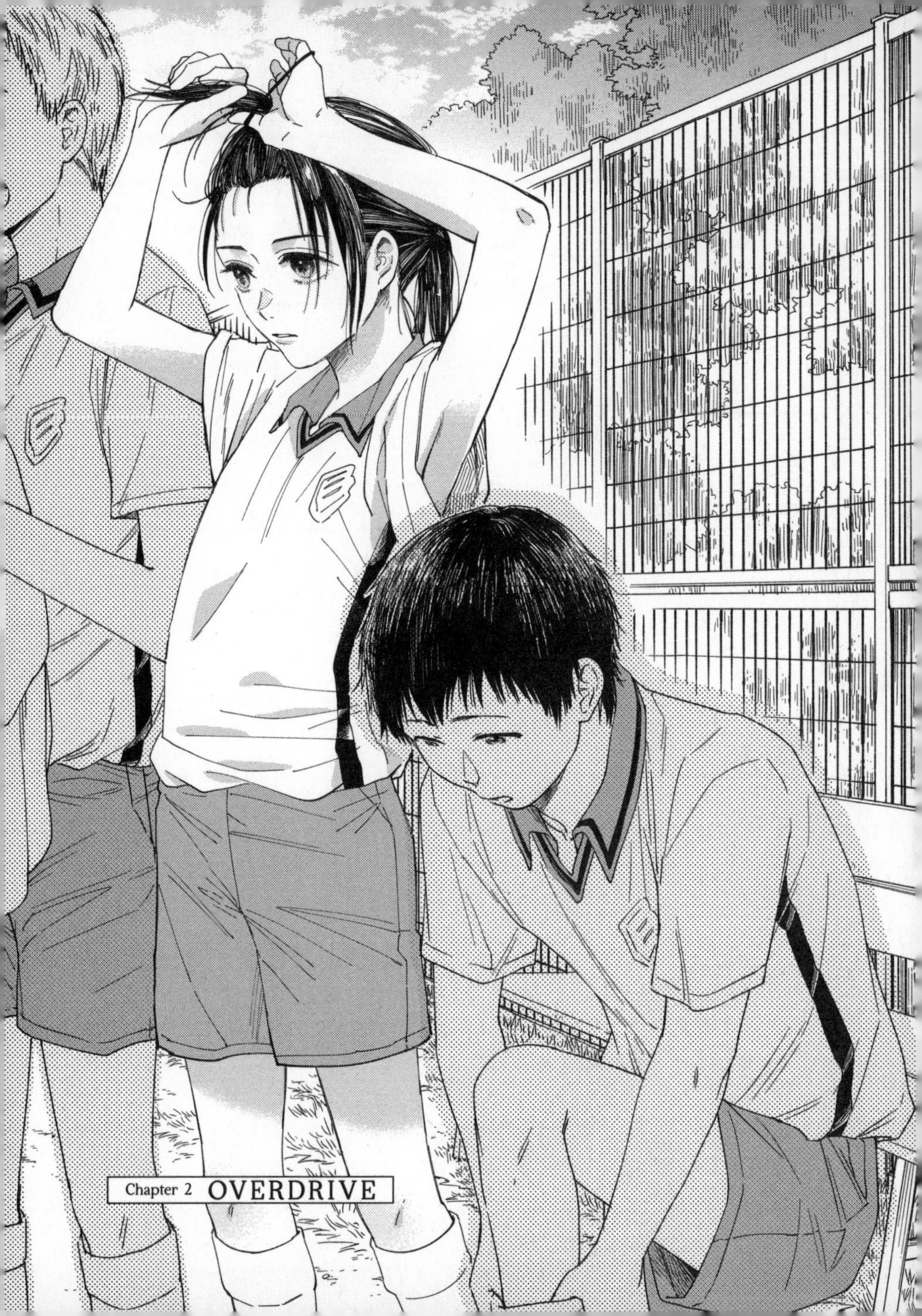
Chapter 2 OVERDRIVE

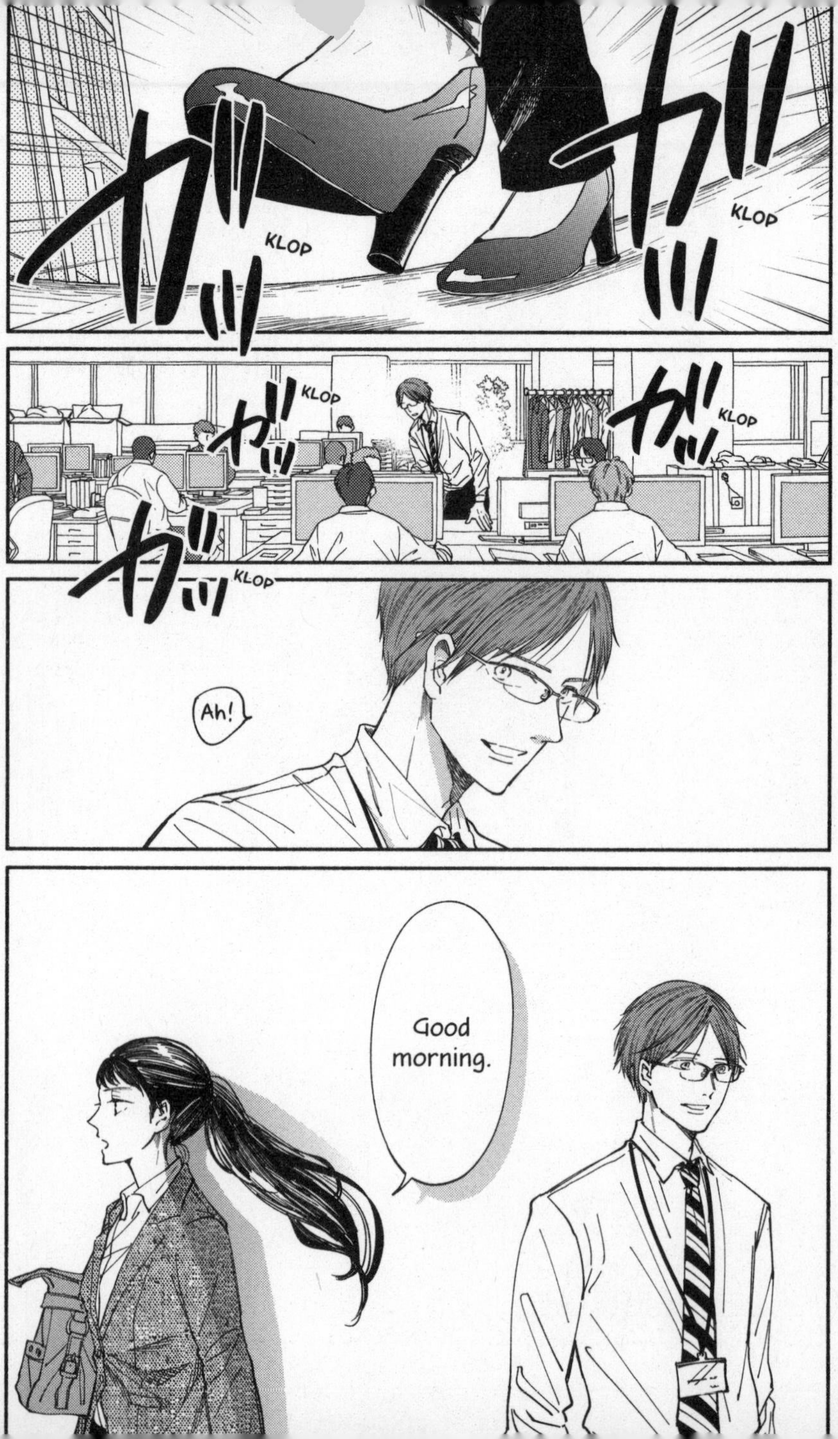
KLOP
KLOP
KLOP
KLOP
KLOP
Ah!
Good morning.

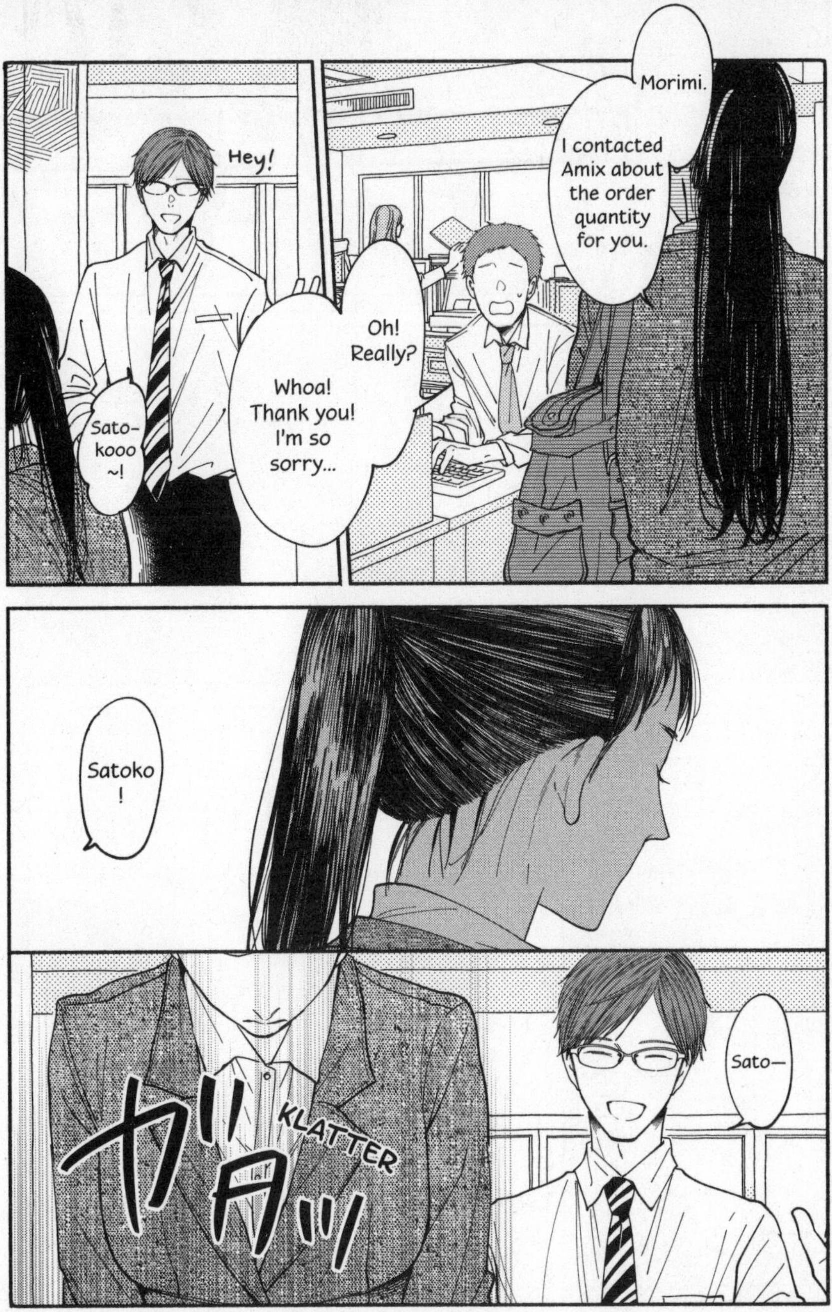
Morimi.
I contacted Amix about the order quantity for you.
Oh! Really?
Whoa! Thank you! I'm so sorry...
Hey!
Sato-kooo~!
Satoko!
Sato—
ガタッ
KLATTER

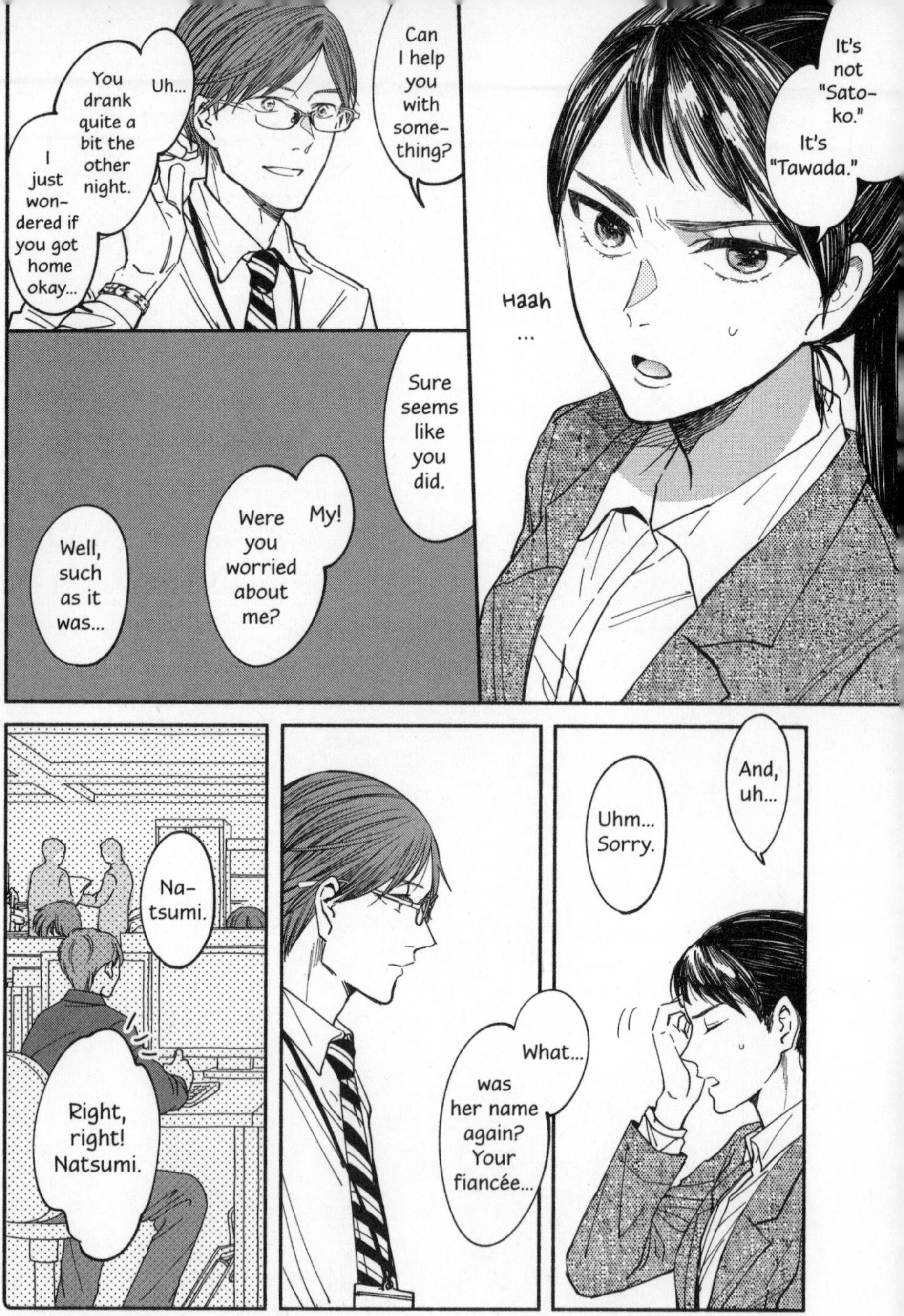
It's not "Sato-ko." It's "Tawada."
Haah ...
Can I help you with some-thing?
Uh...
You drank quite a bit the other night.
I just won-dered if you got home okay...
Sure seems like you did.
My!
Were you worried about me?
Well, such as it was...
And, uh...
Uhm... Sorry.
What...
was her name again? Your fiancée...
Na-tsumi.
Right, right! Natsumi.

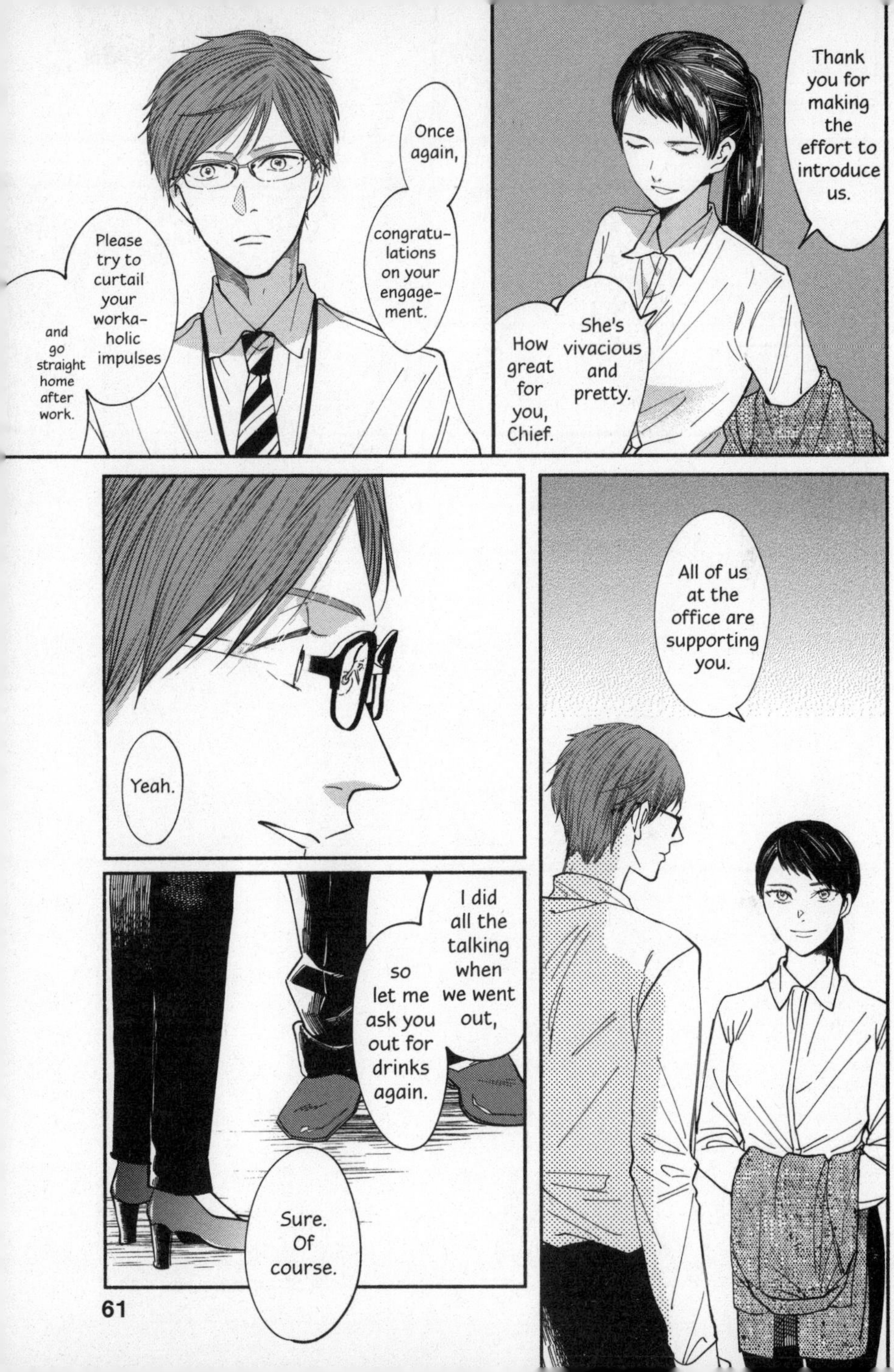
Thank you for making the effort to introduce us.
She's vivacious and pretty.
How great for you, Chief.
Once again,
congratulations on your engagement.
Please try to curtail your workaholic impulses
and go straight home after work.
All of us at the office are supporting you.
Yeah.
I did all the talking when we went out,
so let me ask you out for drinks again.
Sure. Of course.

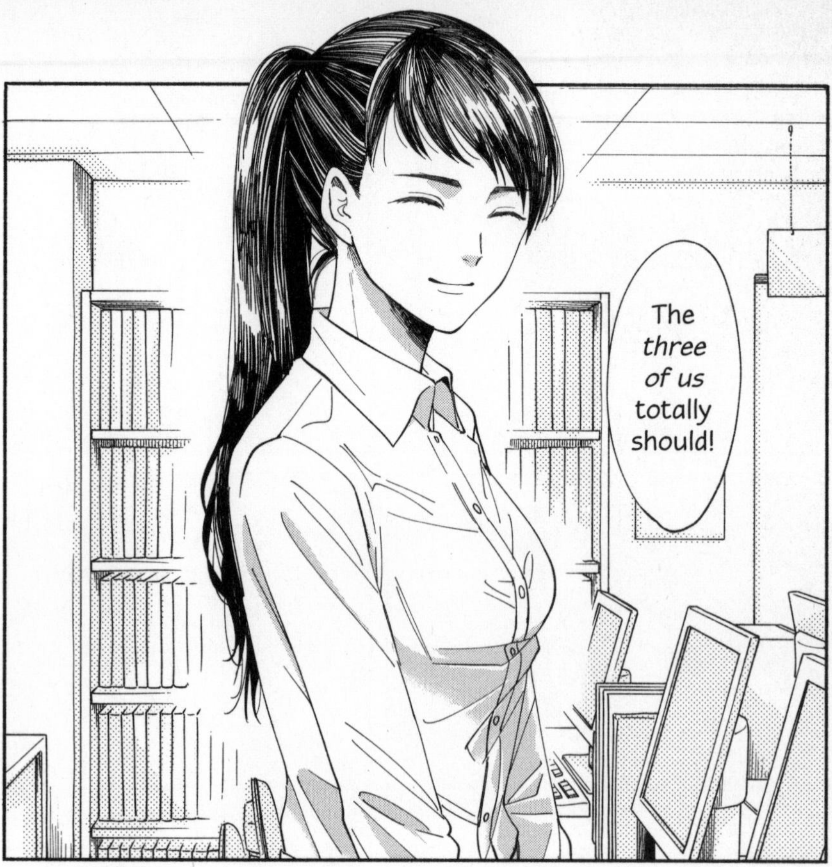
The *three* of us totally should!
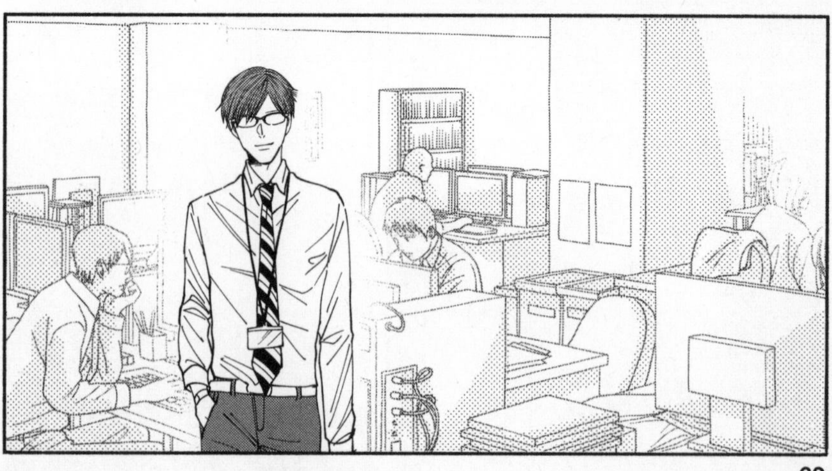

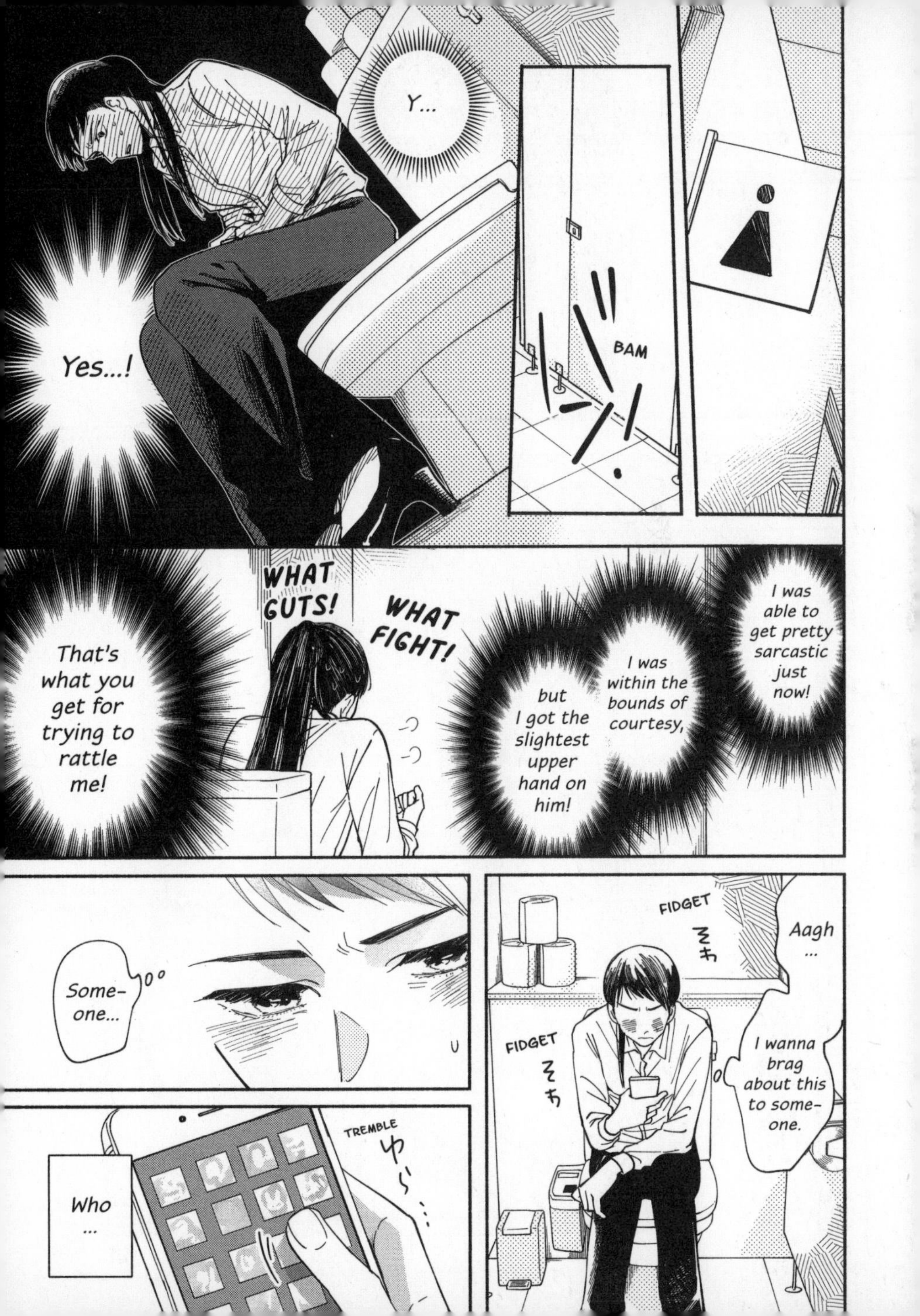

BAM
Y...
Yes...!
I was able to get pretty sarcastic just now!
I was within the bounds of courtesy,
but I got the slightest upper hand on him!
WHAT FIGHT!
WHAT GUTS!
That's what you get for trying to rattle me!
FIDGET
Aagh...
FIDGET
I wanna brag about this to some-one.
Some-one...
TREMBLE
ゆら
Who...

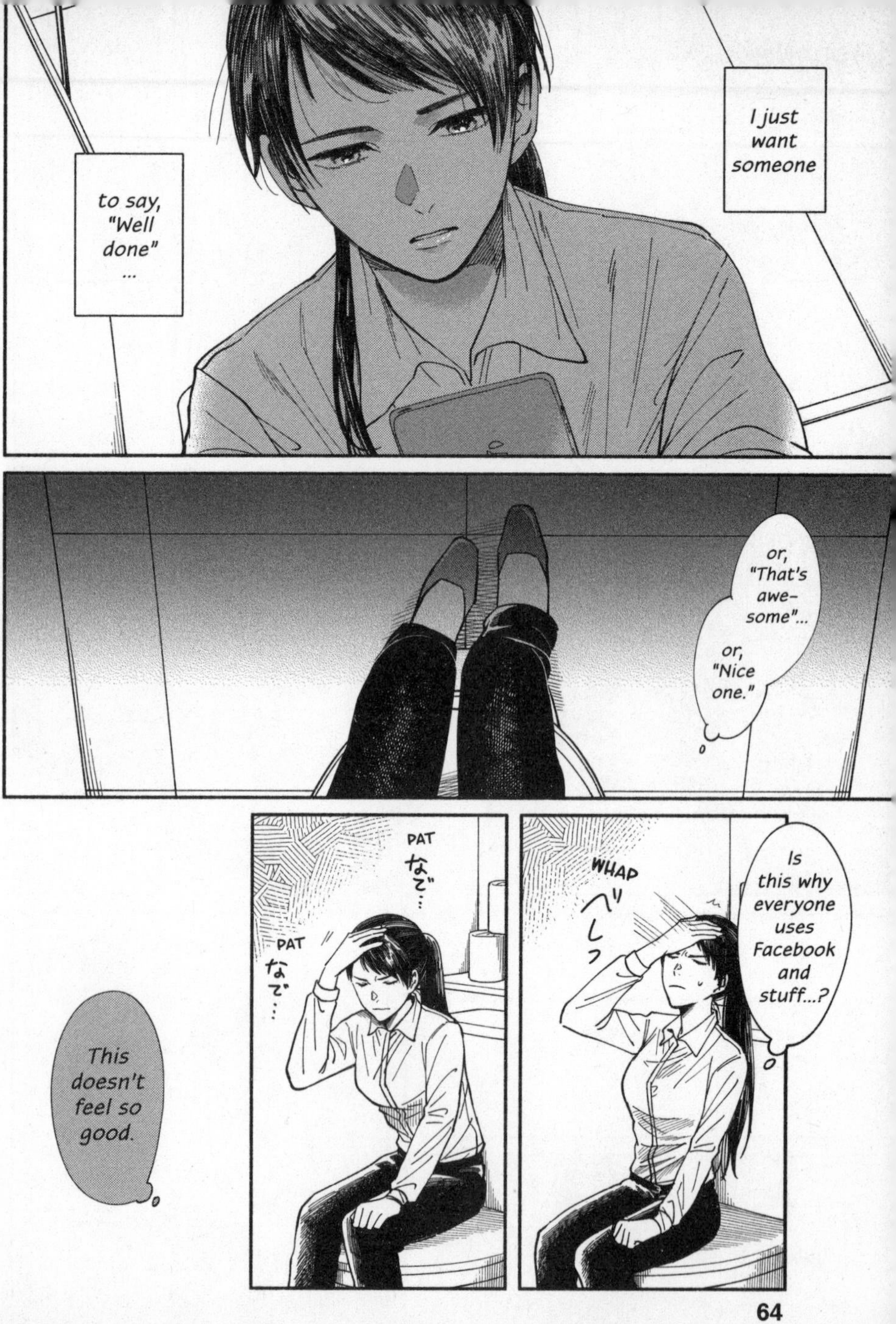
I just want someone
to say, "Well done" ...
or, "That's awe-some"...
or, "Nice one."
WHAP
べしっ
Is this why everyone uses Facebook and stuff...?
PAT
なで…
PAT
なで…
This doesn't feel so good.

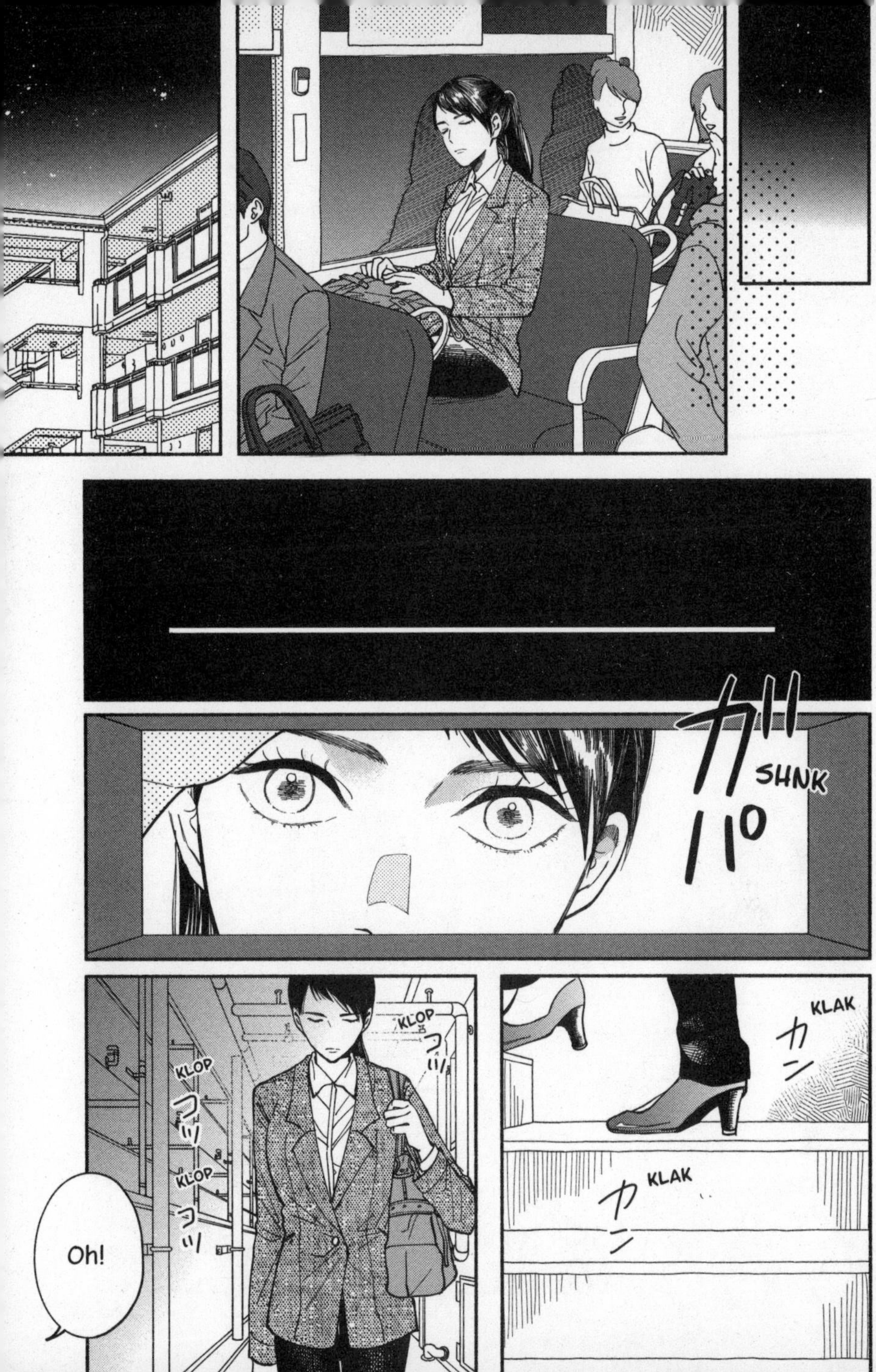
SHNK
ガバ
KLAK
カン
KLAK
カン
KLOP
コツ
KLOP
コツ
KLOP
コツ
Oh!

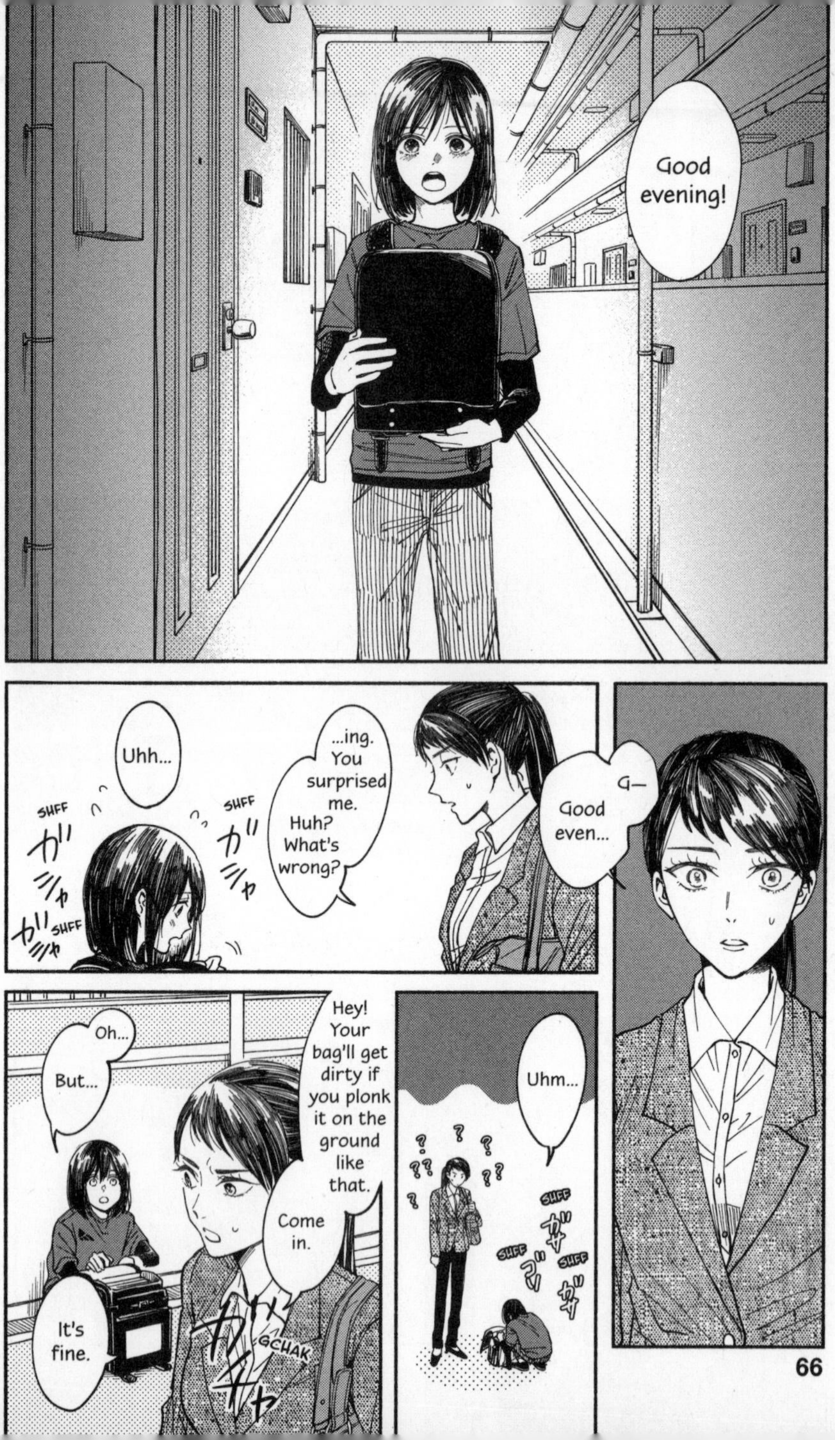
Good evening!
G— Good even...
...ing. You surprised me. Huh? What's wrong?
Uhh...
SHFF
SHFF
SHFF
Uhm...
SHFF
SHFF
SHFF
Hey! Your bag'll get dirty if you plonk it on the ground like that.
Come in.
Oh...
But...
It's fine.
GCHAK

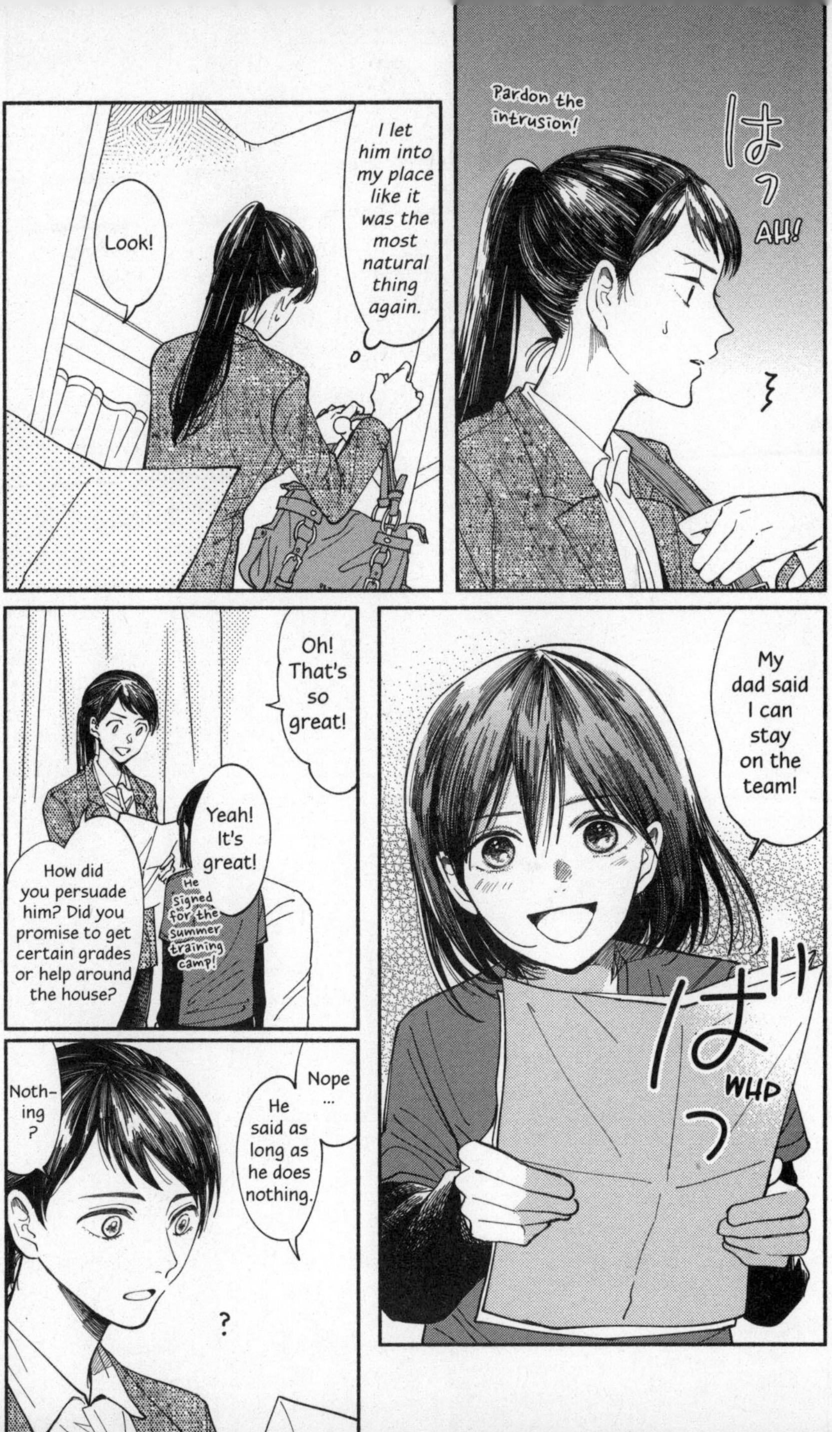
Pardon the intrusion!
はっ
AH!
I let him into my place like it was the most natural thing again.
Look!
My dad said I can stay on the team!
ばっ
WHP
Oh! That's so great!
Yeah! It's great!
He Signed for the summer training camp!
How did you persuade him? Did you promise to get certain grades or help around the house?
Nope ...
He said as long as he does nothing.
Nothing?
?

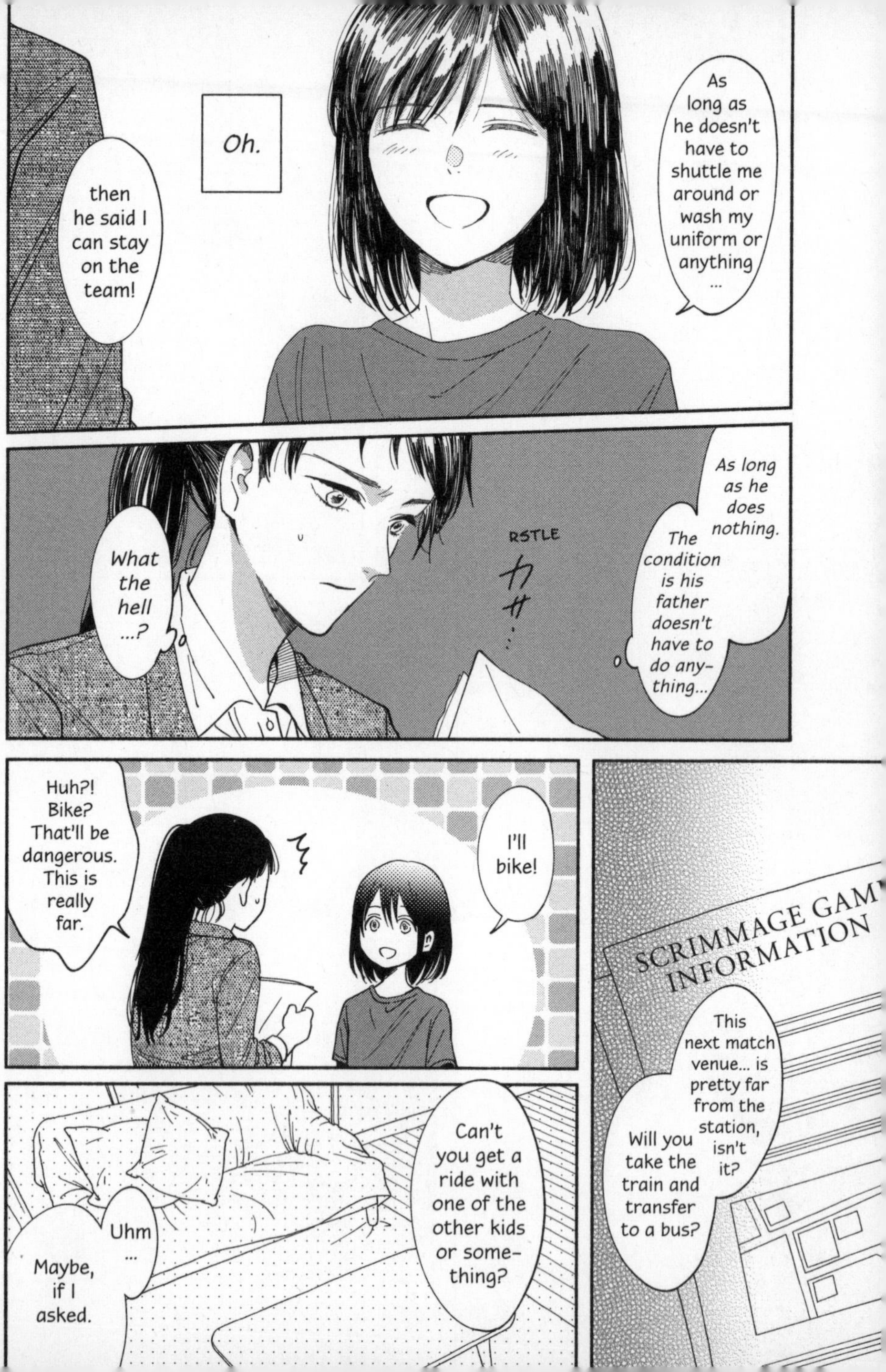
As long as he doesn't have to shuttle me around or wash my uniform or anything ...
Oh.
then he said I can stay on the team!
As long as he does nothing.
The condition is his father doesn't have to do anything...
RSTLE
カサ…
What the hell ...?
SCRIMMAGE GAM
INFORMATION
This next match venue... is pretty far from the station, isn't it?
Will you take the train and transfer to a bus?
I'll bike!
Huh?! Bike? That'll be dangerous. This is really far.
Can't you get a ride with one of the other kids or some-thing?
Uhm ...
Maybe, if I asked.

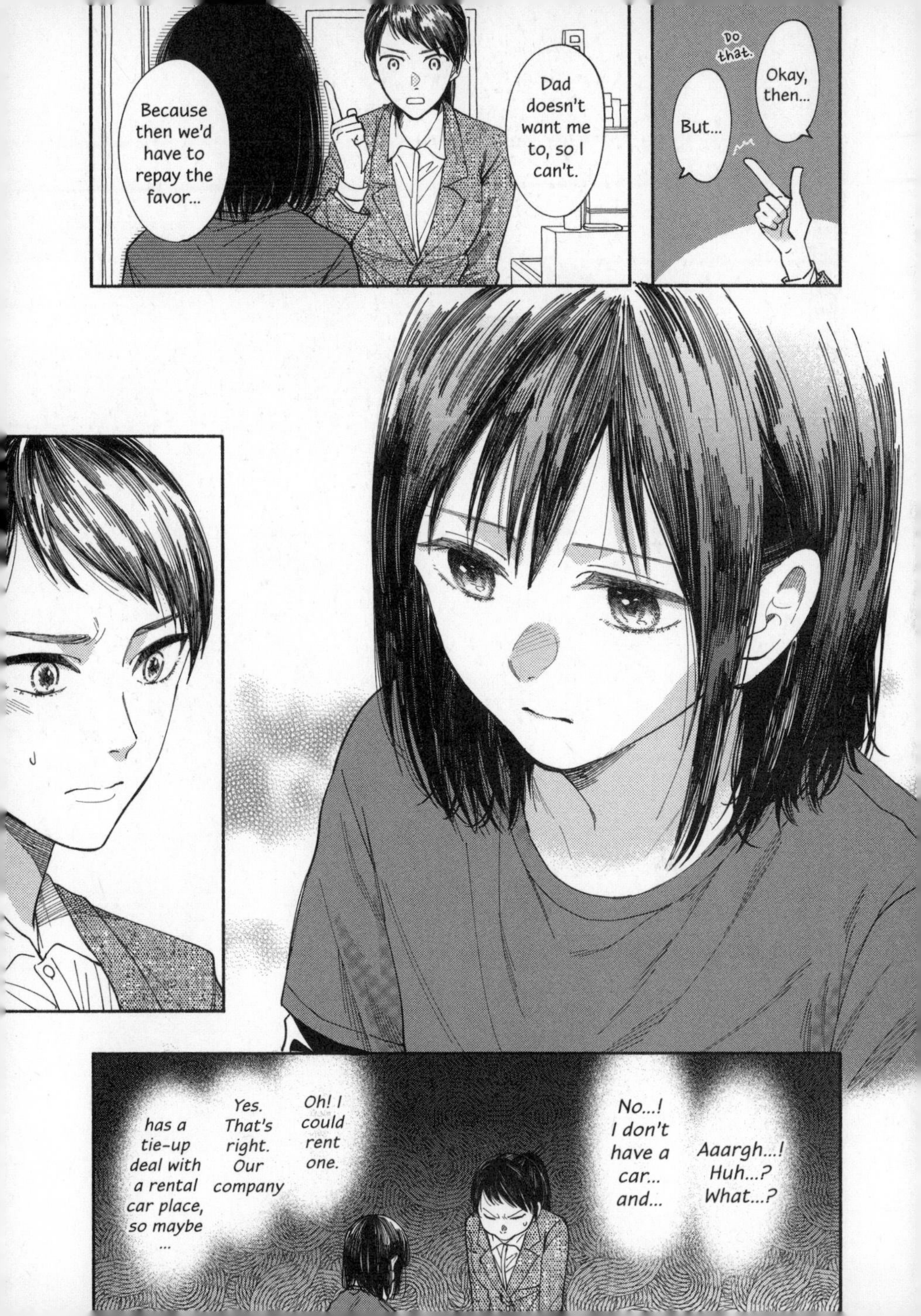
Okay, then...
Do that.
But...
Dad doesn't want me to, so I can't.
Because then we'd have to repay the favor...
Aaargh...! Huh...? What...?
No...! I don't have a car... and...
Oh! I could rent one.
Yes. That's right. Our company
has a tie-up deal with a rental car place, so maybe ...

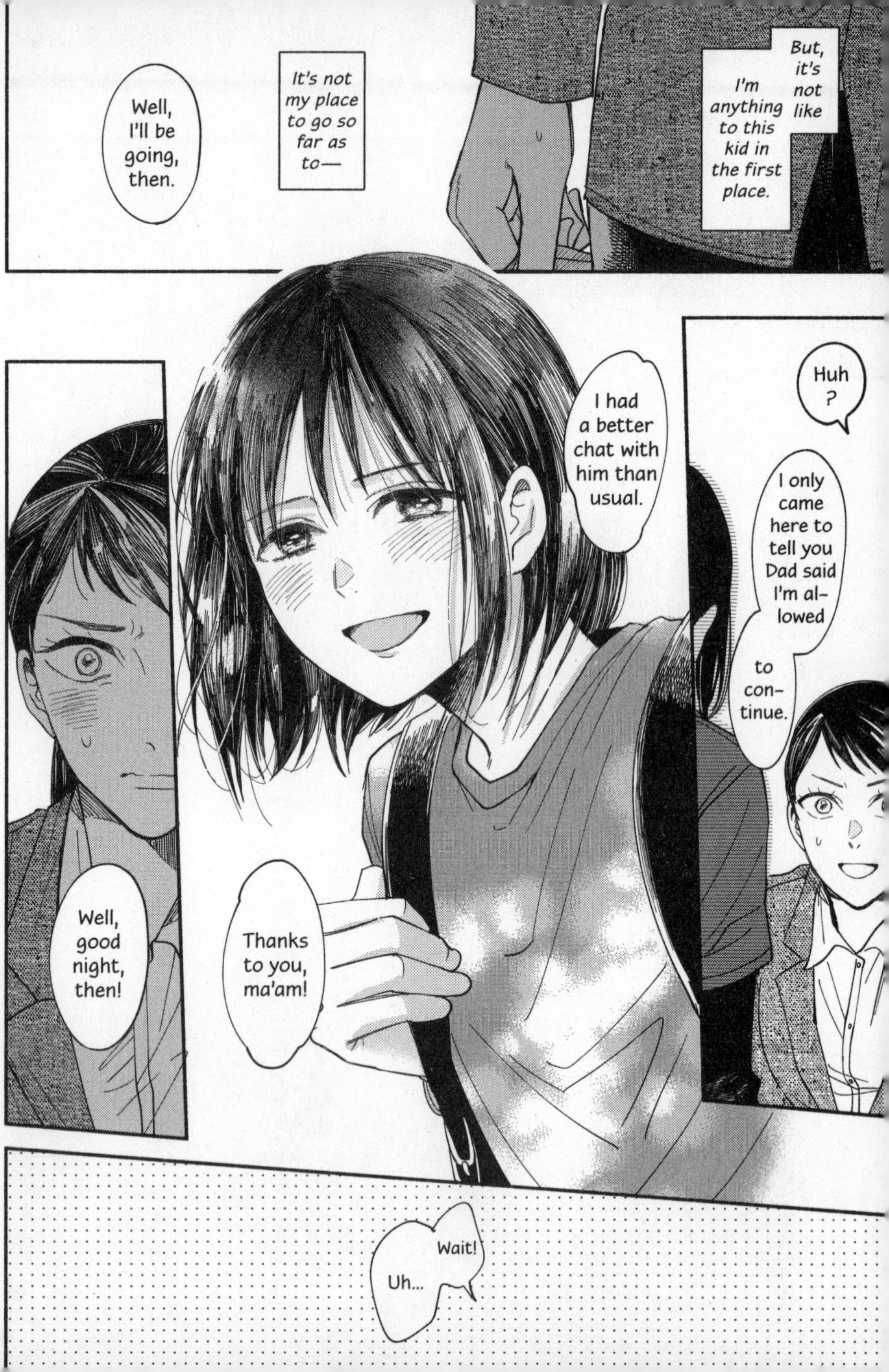
But, it's not like I'm anything to this kid in the first place.
It's not my place to go so far as to—
Well, I'll be going, then.
Huh?
I only came here to tell you Dad said I'm al-lowed
to con-tinue.
I had a better chat with him than usual.
Thanks to you, ma'am!
Well, good night, then!
Wait!
Uh...

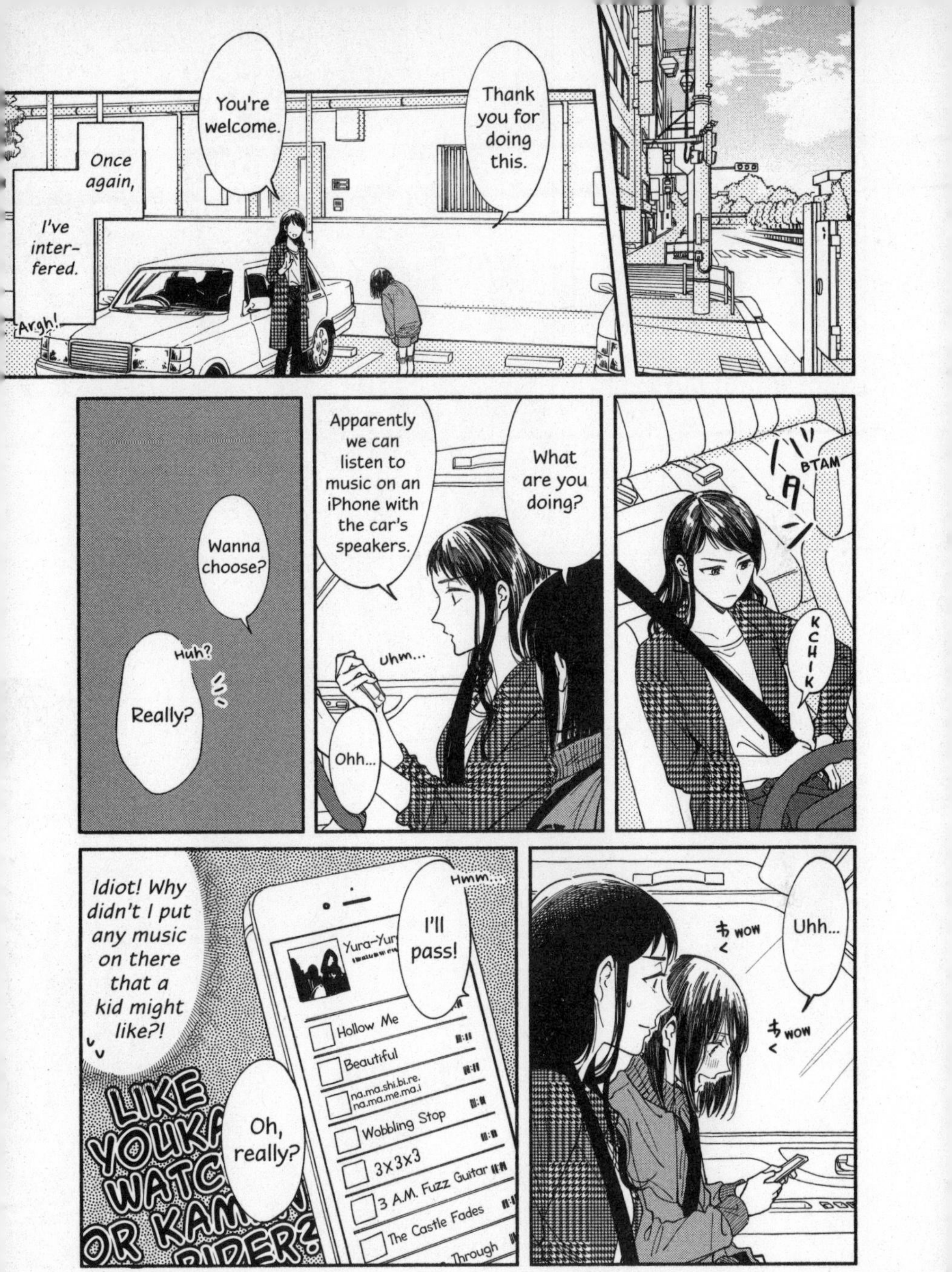
Thank you for doing this.
You're welcome.
Once again, I've interfered.
Argh!
BTAM
KCHIK
What are you doing?
Apparently we can listen to music on an iPhone with the car's speakers.
Uhm...
Ohh...
Wanna choose?
Huh?
Really?
Uhh...
WOW
WOW
Hmm...
I'll pass!
Idiot! Why didn't I put any music on there that a kid might like?!
Oh, really?
Hollow Me
Beautiful
na.ma.shi.bi.re. na.ma.me.ma.i
Wobbling Stop
3X3X3
3 A.M. Fuzz Guitar
The Castle Fades
Through
LIKE

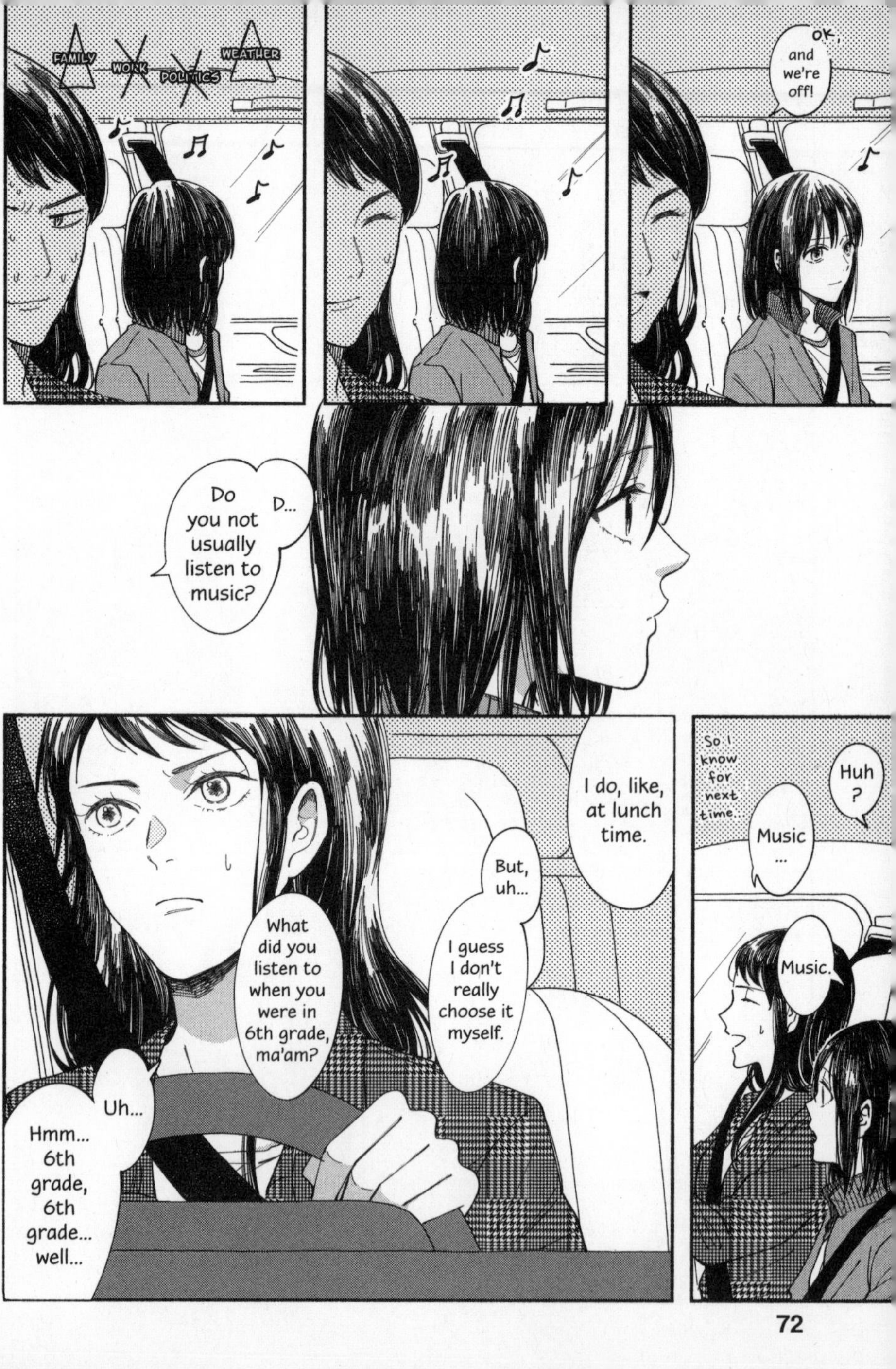
OK, and we're off!
FAMILY
WORK
POLITICS
WEATHER
D...
Do you not usually listen to music?
Huh?
So I know for next time...
Music...
Music.
I do, like, at lunch time.
But, uh...
I guess I don't really choose it myself.
What did you listen to when you were in 6th grade, ma'am?
Uh...
Hmm... 6th grade, 6th grade... well...

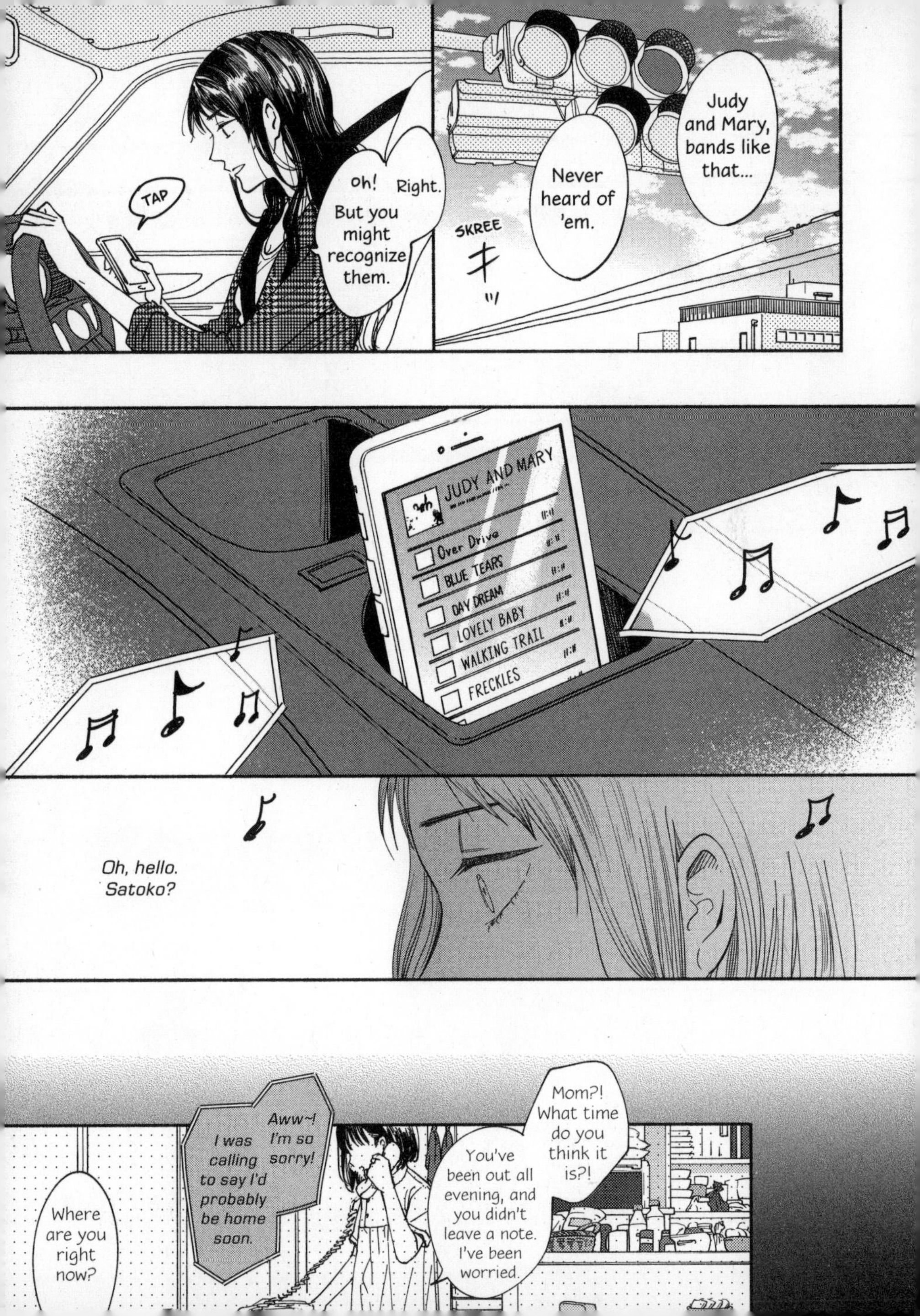
Judy and Mary, bands like that...
Never heard of 'em.
SKREE
Oh! Right.
But you might recognize them.
TAP
JUDY AND MARY
Over Drive
BLUE TEARS
DAY DREAM
LOVELY BABY
WALKING TRAIL
FRECKLES
Oh, hello. Satoko?
Mom?! What time do you think it is?!
You've been out all evening, and you didn't leave a note. I've been worried.
Aww~! I'm so sorry!
I was calling to say I'd probably be home soon.
Where are you right now?

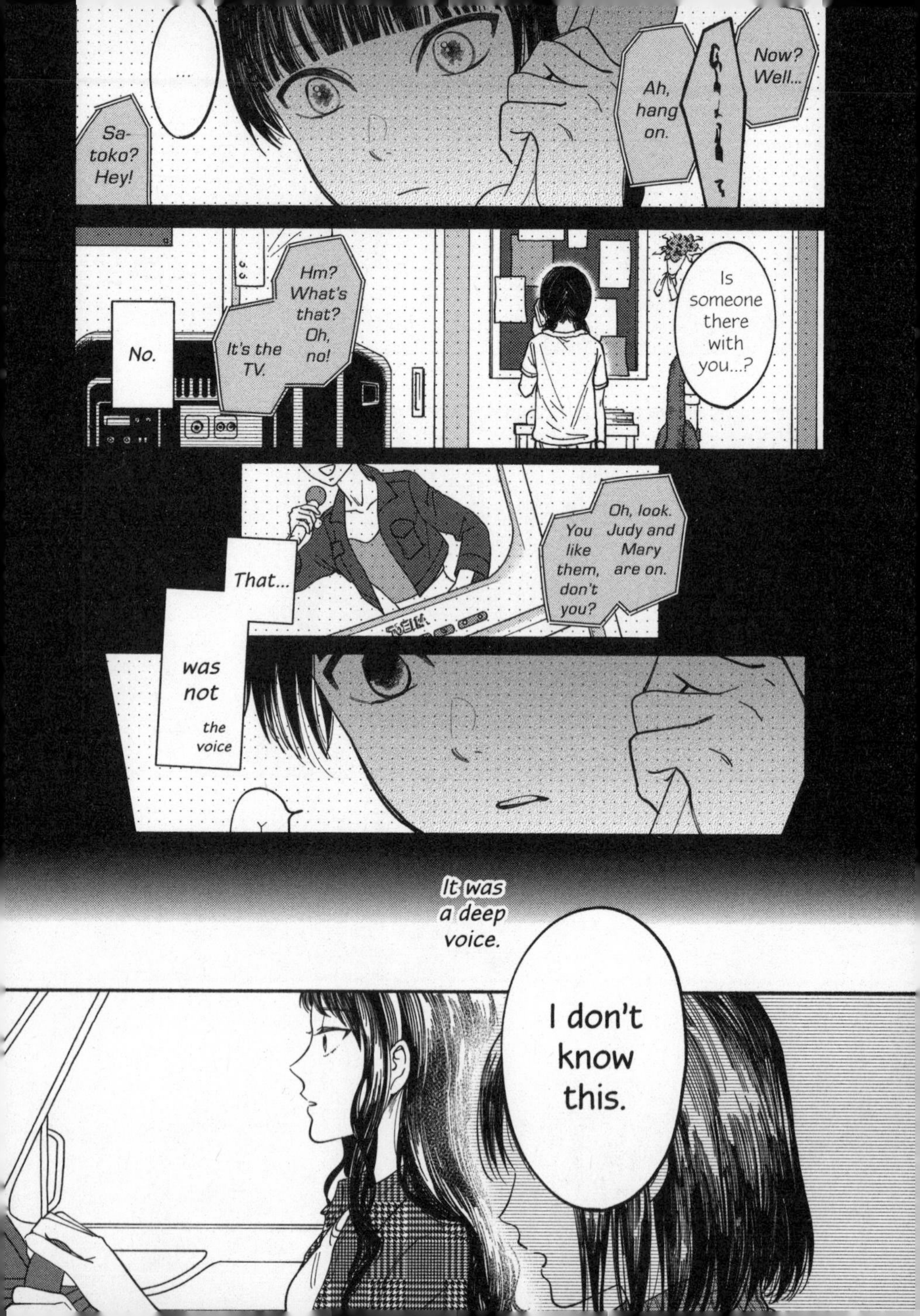
Now? Well...
Ah, hang on.
...
Sa-toko? Hey!
Is someone there with you...?
Hm? What's that? Oh, no!
It's the TV.
No.
Oh, look. Judy and Mary are on.
You like them, don't you?
That...
was not the voice
It was a deep voice.
I don't know this.

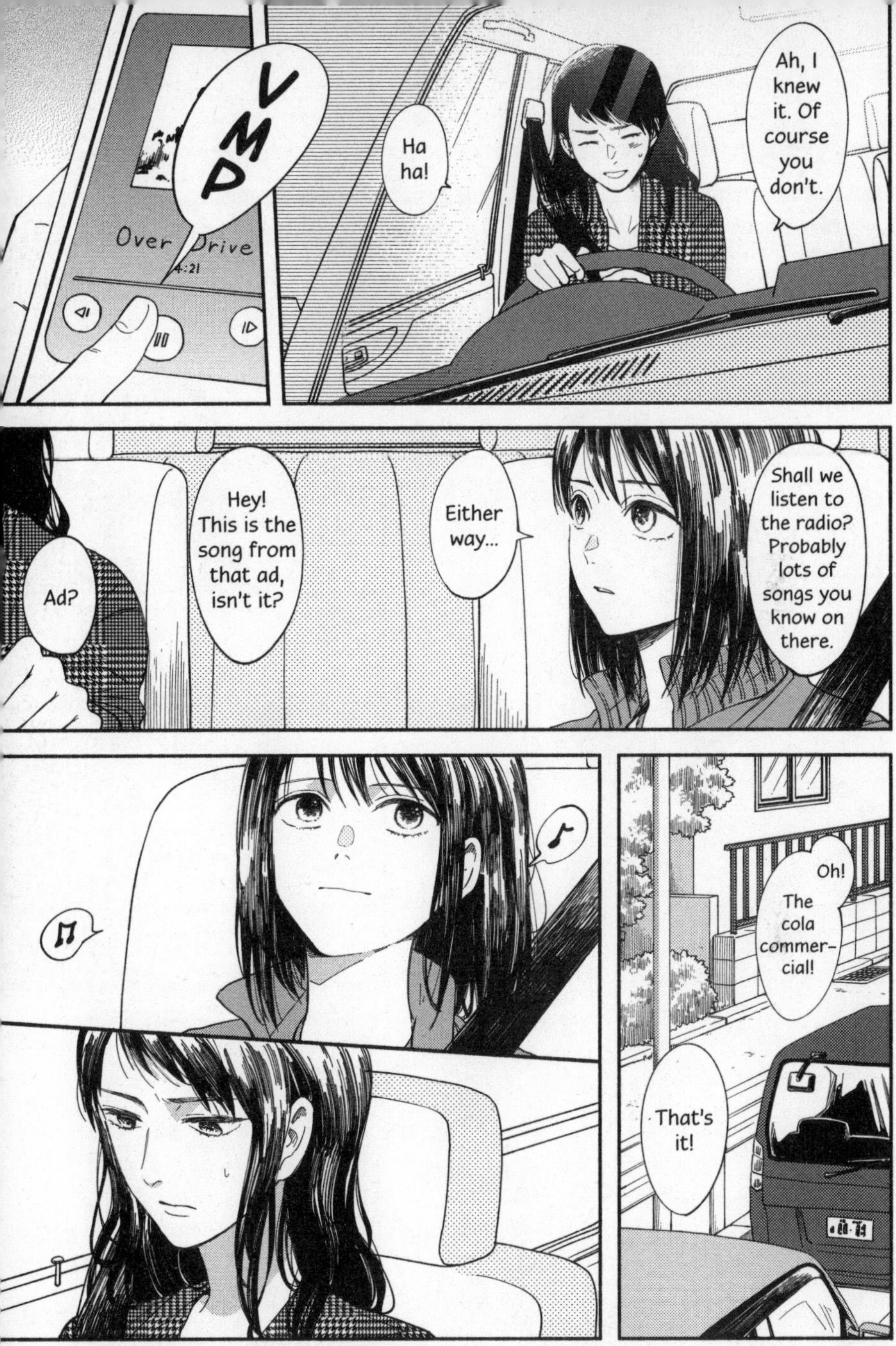
Ah, I knew it. Of course you don't.
Ha ha!
VMP
Over Drive
4:21
Shall we listen to the radio? Probably lots of songs you know on there.
Either way...
Hey! This is the song from that ad, isn't it?
Ad?
Oh! The cola commercial!
That's it!

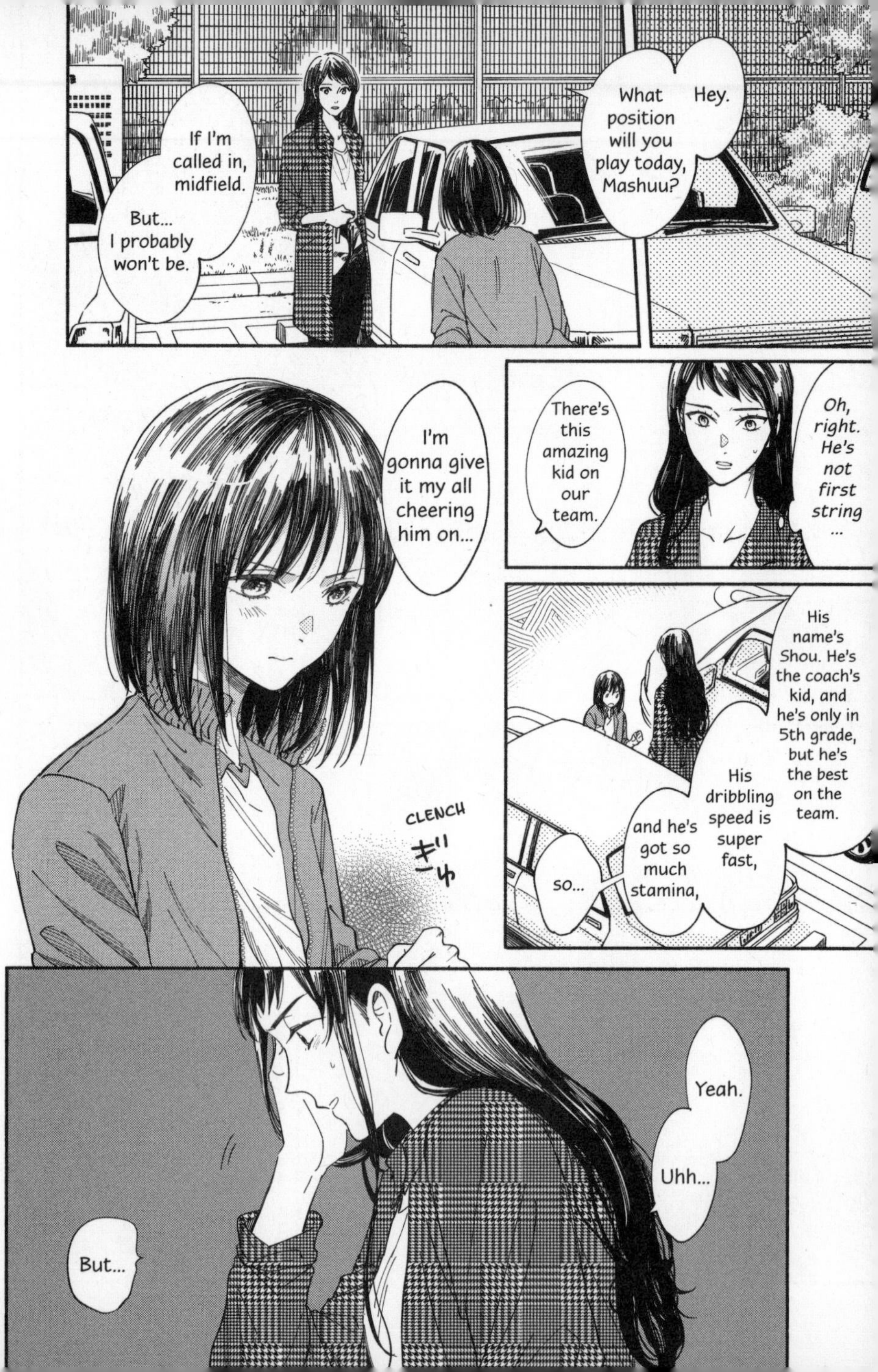
Hey.
What position will you play today, Mashuu?
If I'm called in, midfield.
But... I probably won't be.
Oh, right. He's not first string ...
There's this amazing kid on our team.
His name's Shou. He's the coach's kid, and he's only in 5th grade, but he's the best on the team.
His dribbling speed is super fast,
and he's got so much stamina,
so...
I'm gonna give it my all cheering him on...
CLENCH
ぎゅ
Yeah.
Uhh...
But...

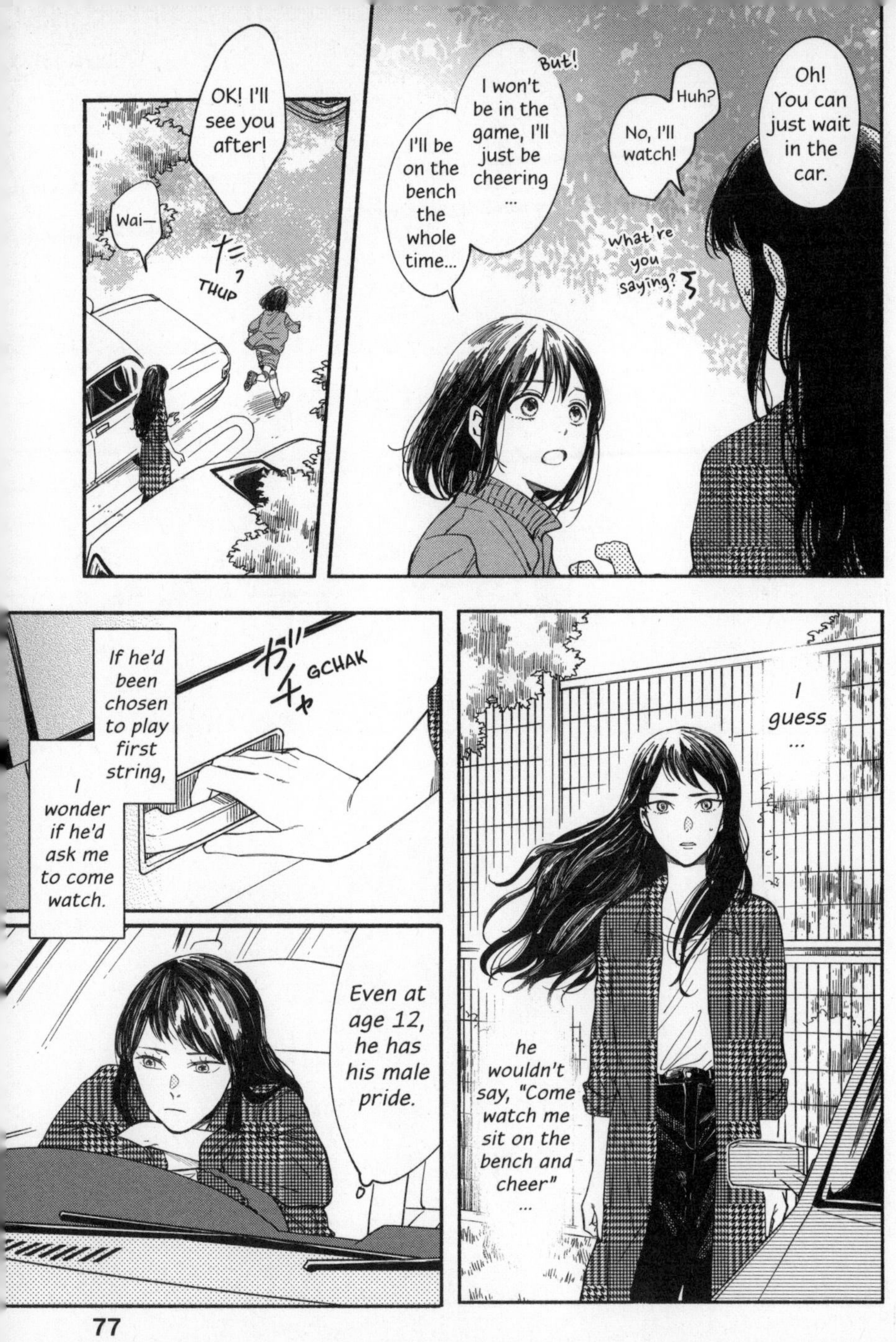
Oh! You can just wait in the car.
Huh?
No, I'll watch!
what're you saying?
But!
I won't be in the game, I'll just be cheering ...
I'll be on the bench the whole time...
OK! I'll see you after!
Wai—
THUP
I guess ...
he wouldn't say, "Come watch me sit on the bench and cheer" ...
GCHAK
If he'd been chosen to play first string,
I wonder if he'd ask me to come watch.
Even at age 12, he has his male pride.

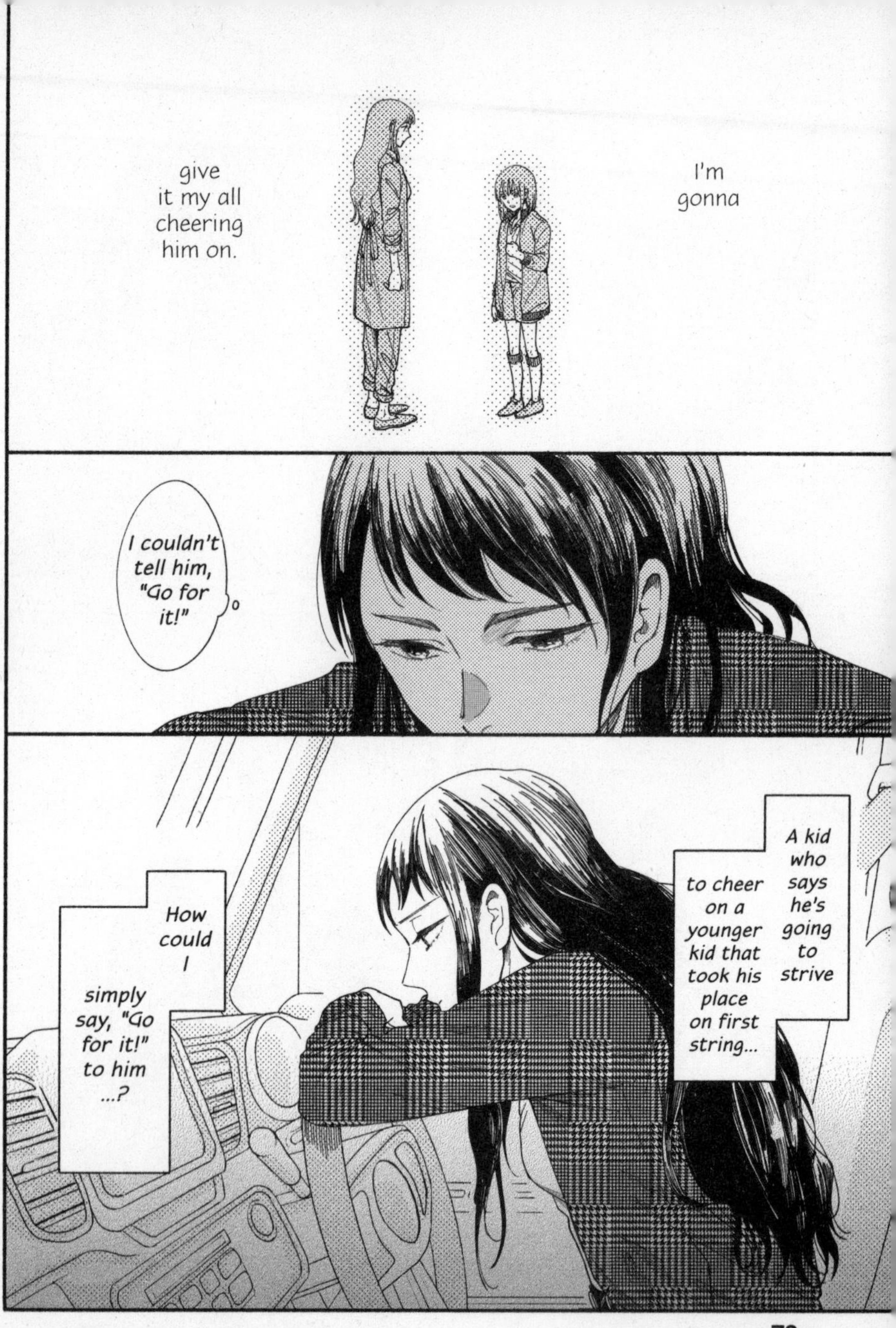
I'm gonna
give it my all cheering him on.
I couldn't tell him, "Go for it!"
A kid who says he's going to strive
to cheer on a younger kid that took his place on first string...
How could I
simply say, "Go for it!" to him ...?

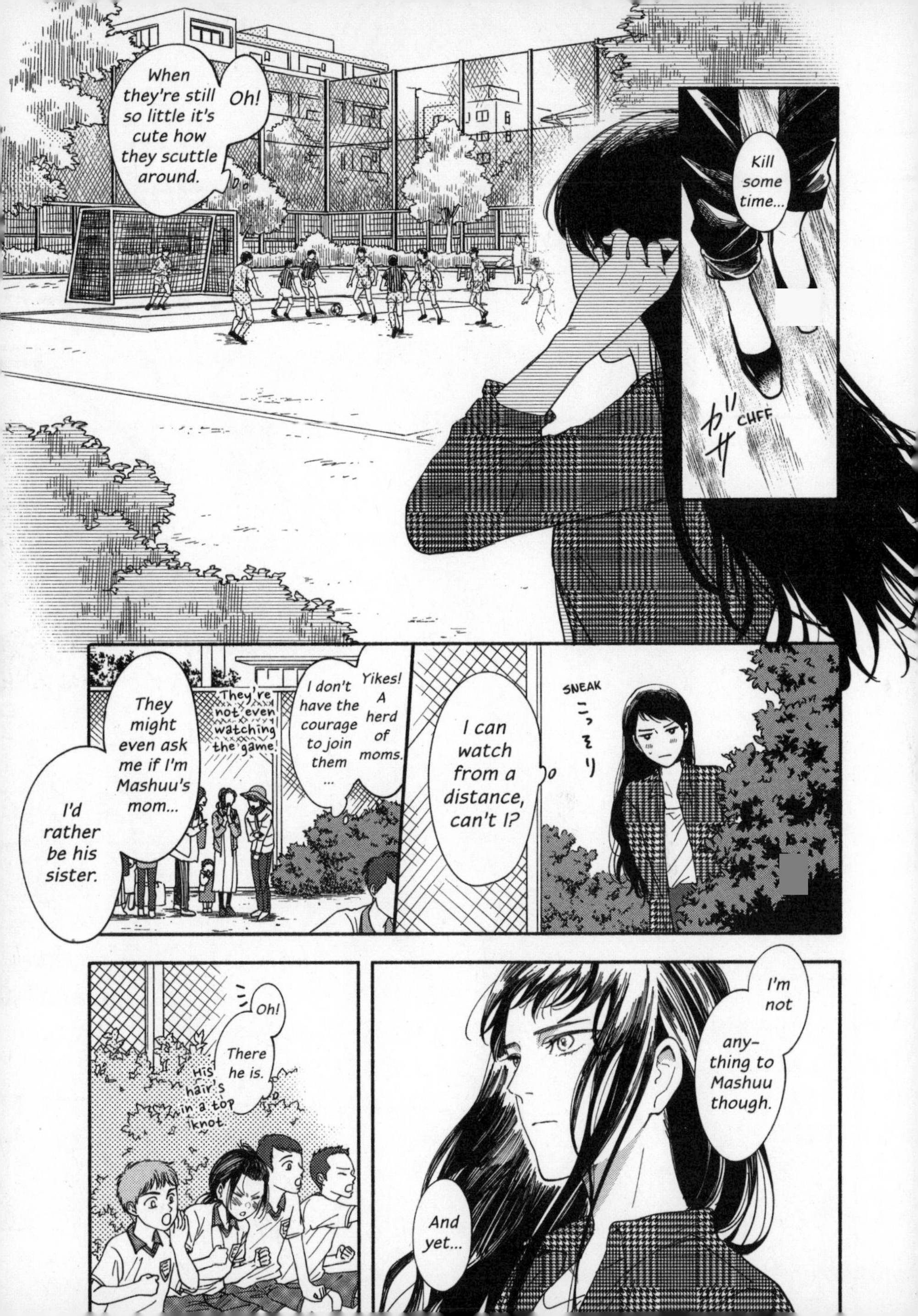
Kill some time...
ガサ
CHFF
Oh!
When they're still so little it's cute how they scuttle around.
SNEAK
こっそり
I can watch from a distance, can't I?
Yikes! A herd of moms.
I don't have the courage to join them...
They're not even watching the game!
They might even ask me if I'm Mashuu's mom...
I'd rather be his sister.
I'm not anything to Mashuu though.
And yet...
Oh!
There he is.
His hair's in a top knot.

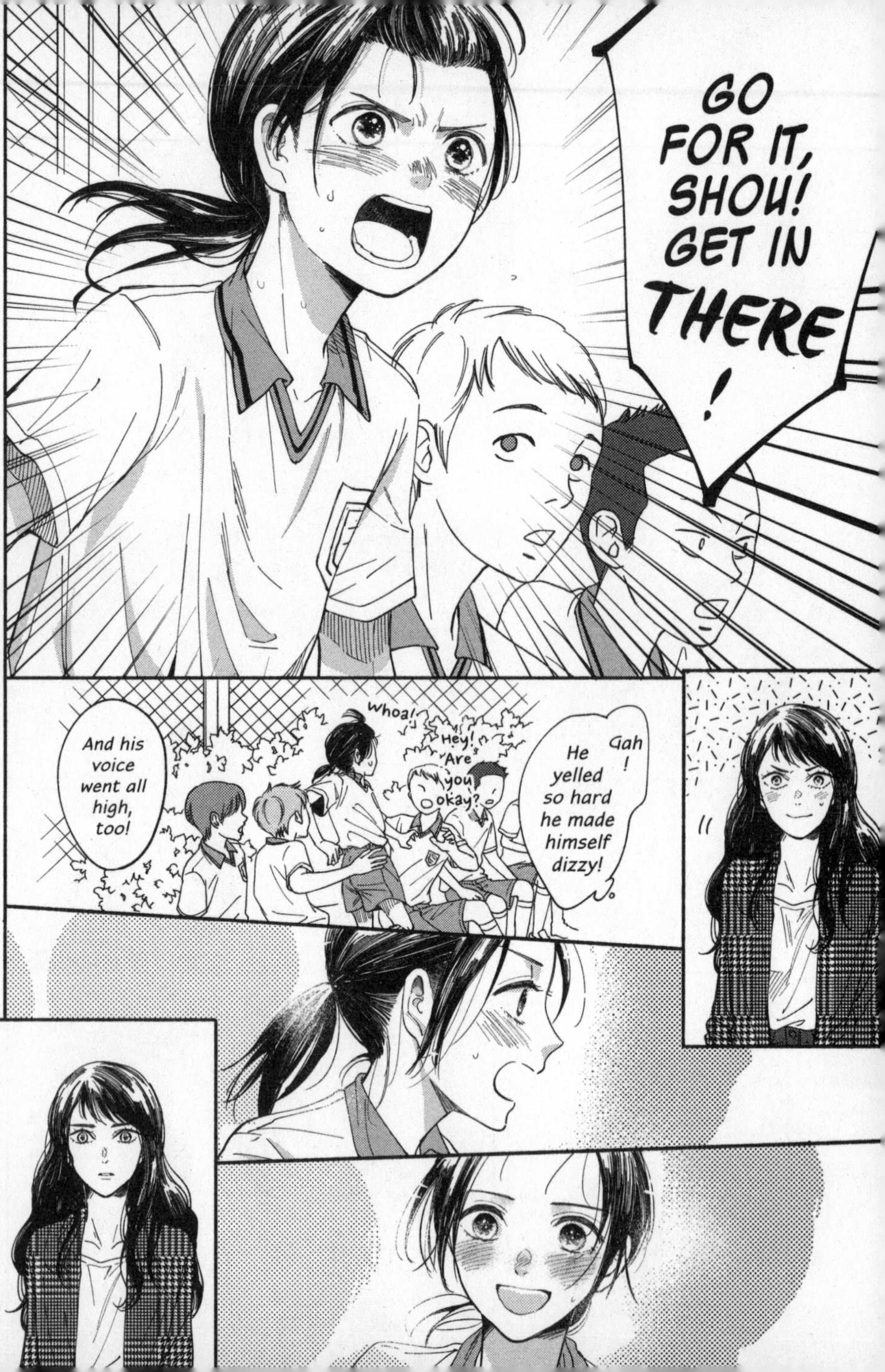
GO FOR IT, SHOU! GET IN THERE!
Gah!
He yelled so hard he made himself dizzy!
Hey! Are you okay?
Whoa!
And his voice went all high, too!

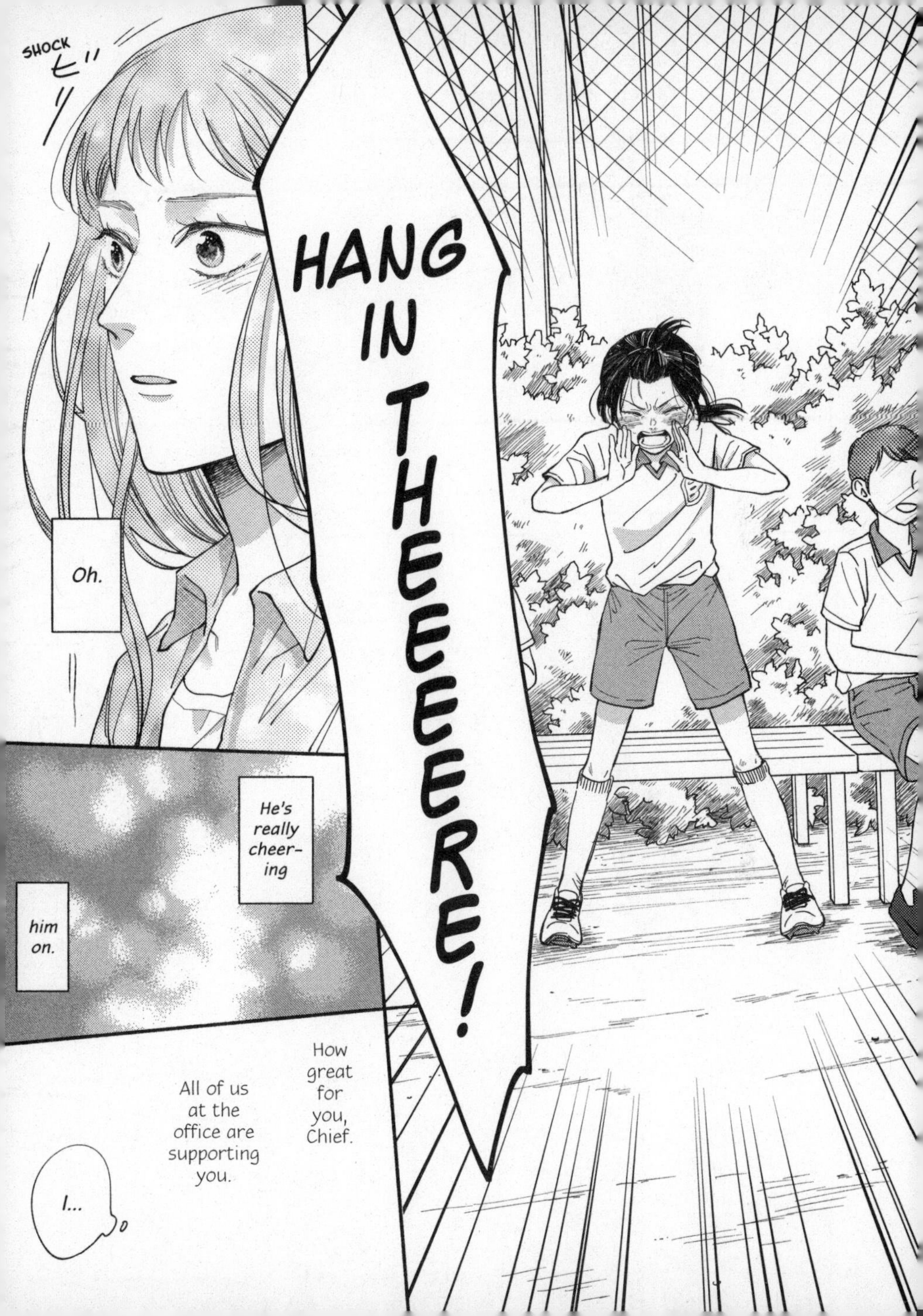
HANG IN THEEEERE!
SHOCK
Oh.
He's really cheering him on.
How great for you, Chief.
All of us at the office are supporting you.
I...

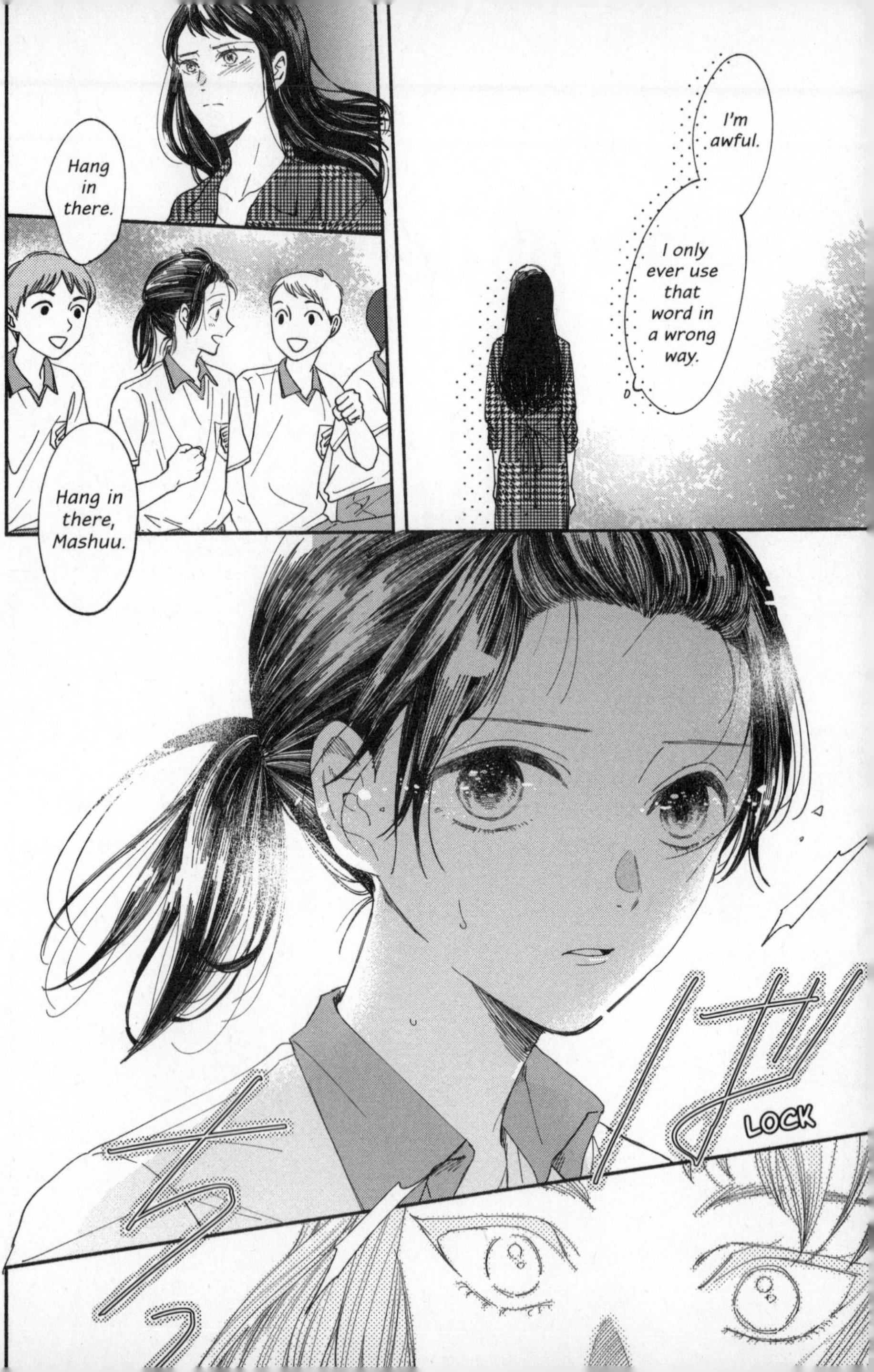
I'm awful.
I only ever use that word in a wrong way.
Hang in there.
Hang in there, Mashuu.
LOCK

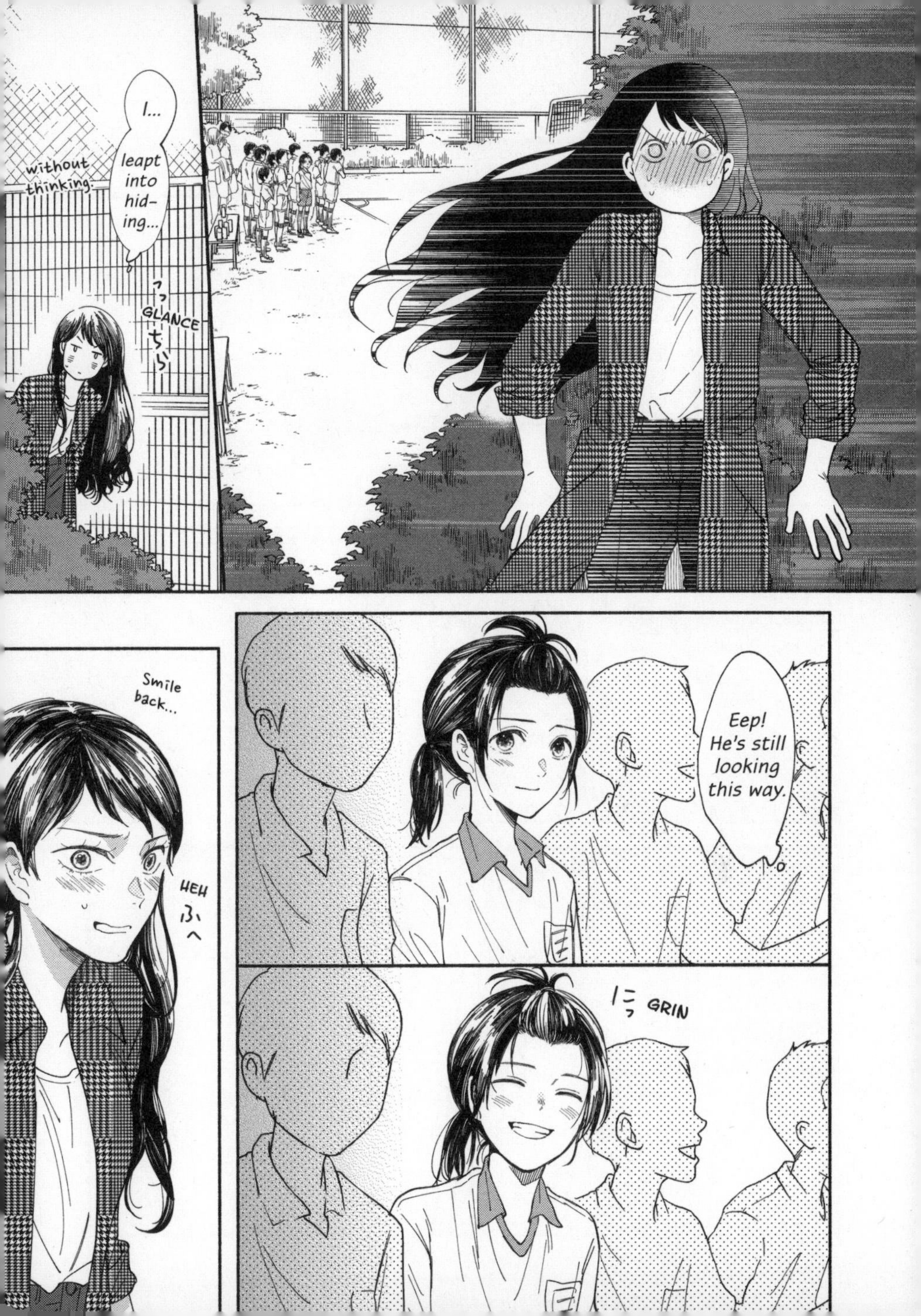
I... leapt into hiding...
without thinking.
GLANCE
ちらっ
Eep! He's still looking this way.
にっ
GRIN
Smile back...
HEH
ふへ

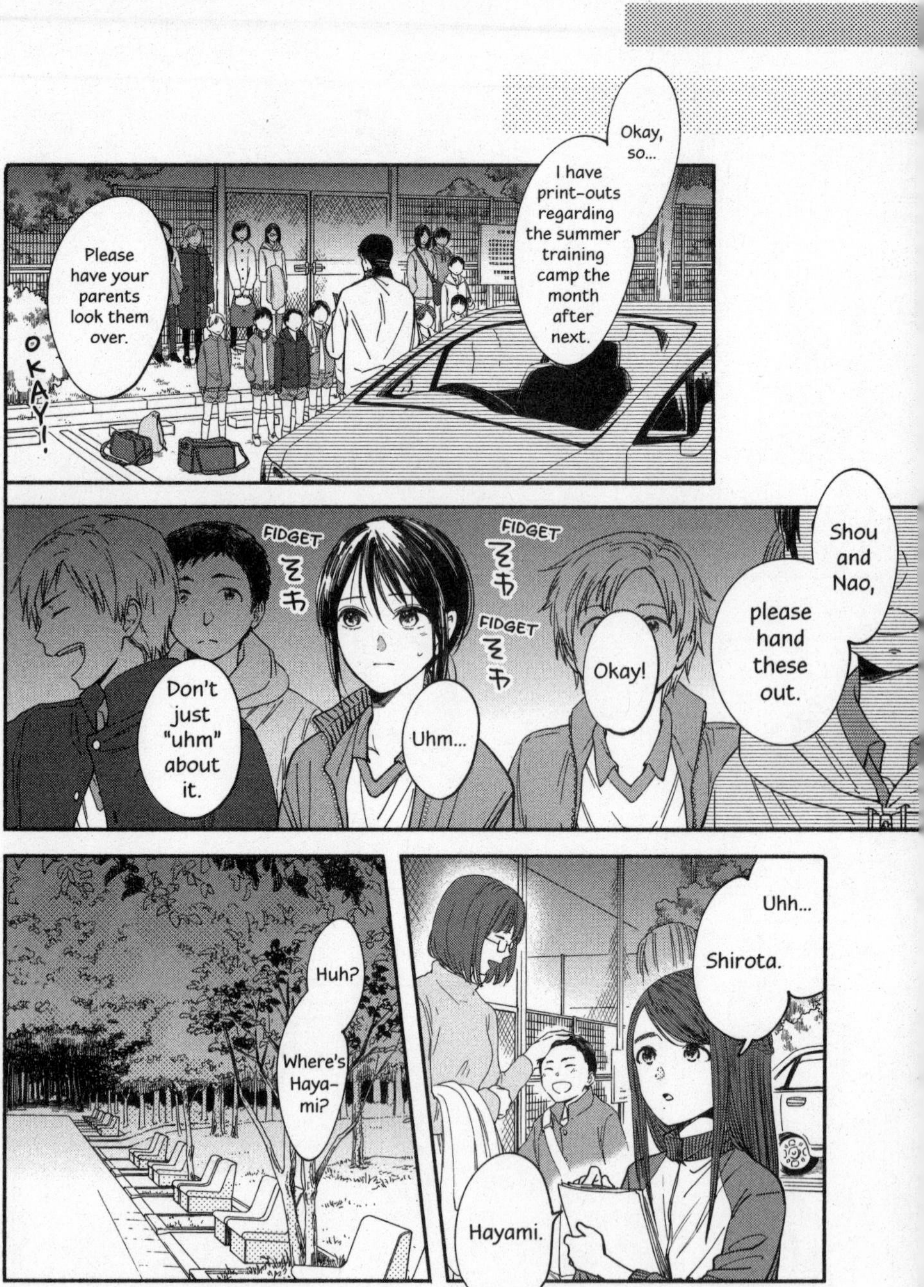
Okay, so... I have print-outs regarding the summer training camp the month after next.
Please have your parents look them over.
OKAY!
Shou and Nao, please hand these out.
Okay!
FIDGET
FIDGET
FIDGET
Uhm...
Don't just "uhm" about it.
Uhh... Shirota.
Hayami.
Huh?
Where's Haya-mi?

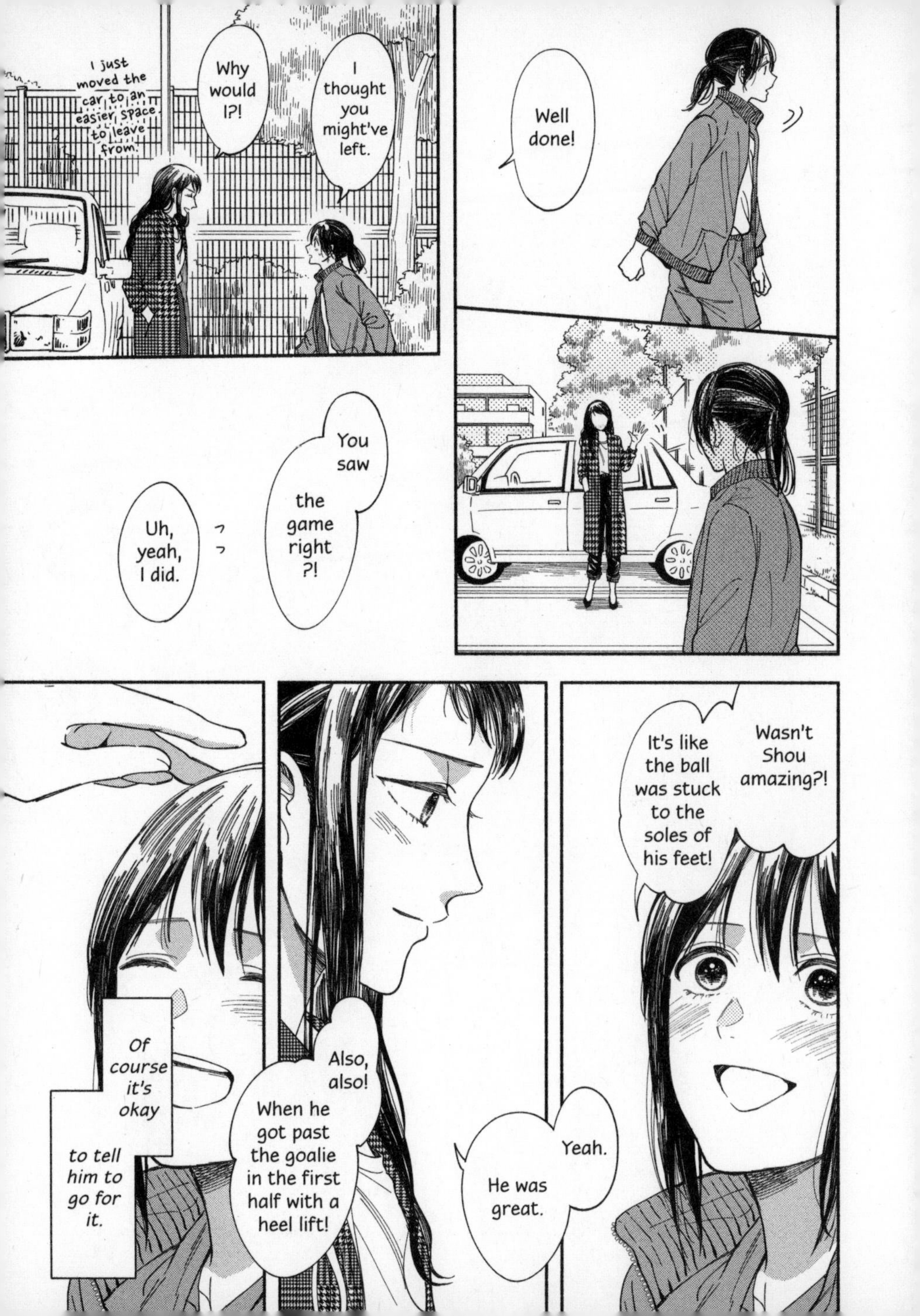
Well done!
I thought you might've left.
Why would I?!
I just moved the car to an easier space to leave from.
You saw the game right?!
Uh, yeah, I did.
Wasn't Shou amazing?!
It's like the ball was stuck to the soles of his feet!
Yeah. He was great.
Also, also! When he got past the goalie in the first half with a heel lift!
Of course it's okay to tell him to go for it.

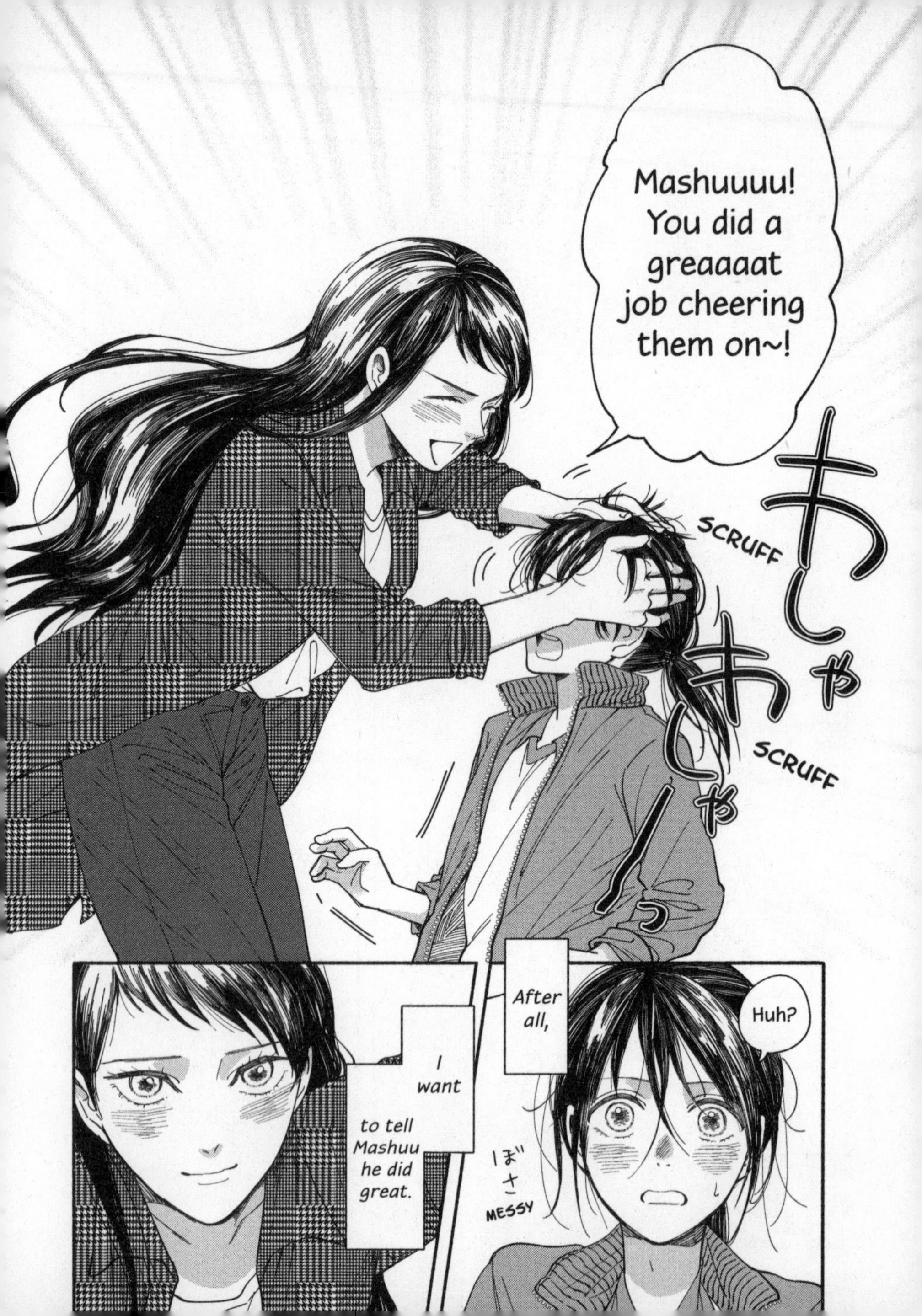
Mashuuuu! You did a greaaaat job cheering them on~!
わしゃわしゃーっ
SCRUFF
SCRUFF
Huh?
ぼさ
MESSY
After all,
I want
to tell Mashuu he did great.

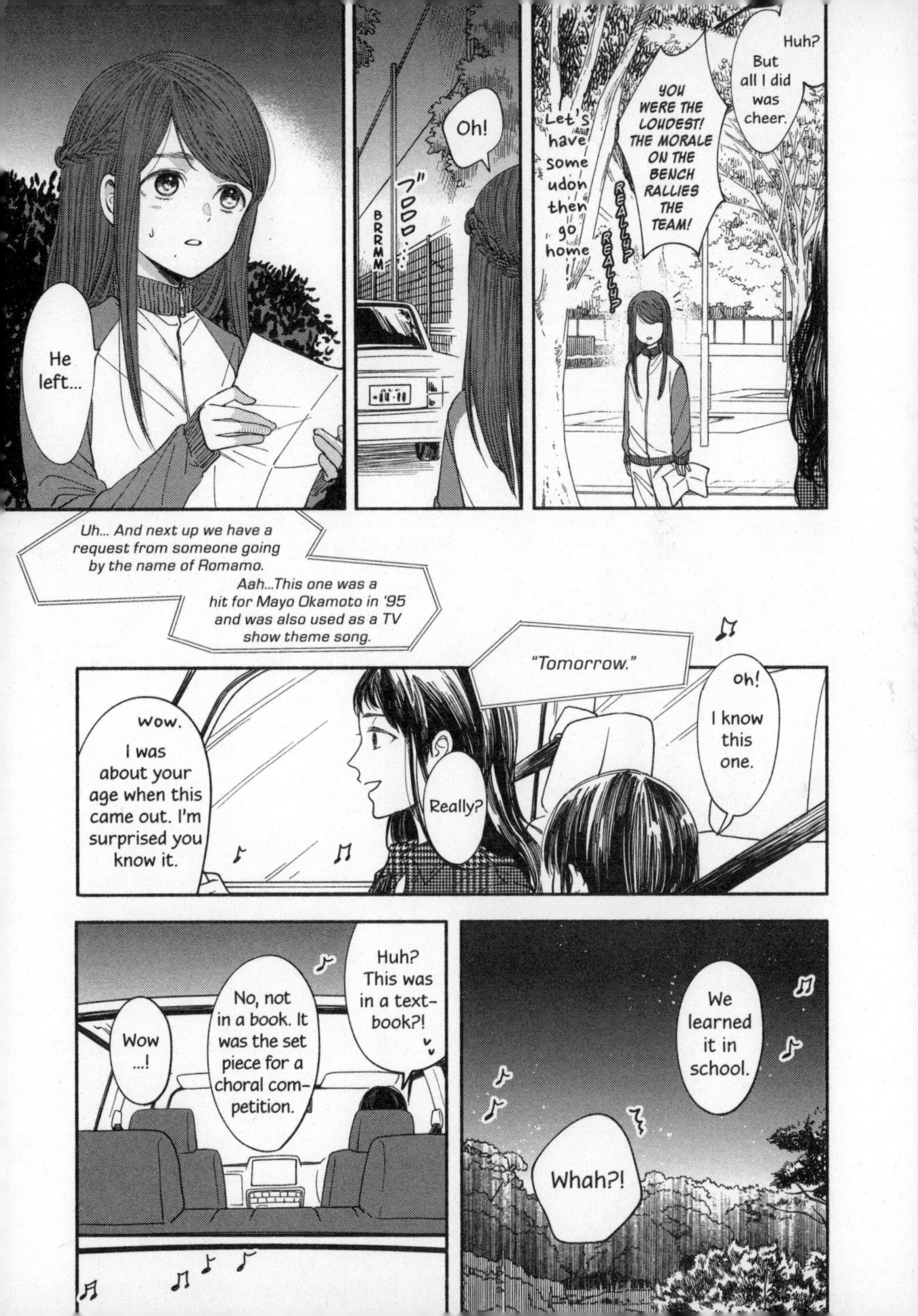
Huh? But all I did was cheer.
YOU WERE THE LOUDEST! THE MORALE ON THE BENCH RALLIES THE TEAM!
REALLY
REALLY
REALLY
Let's have some udon then go home!
Oh!
ブロロロ…
BRRRMM
He left...
Uh... And next up we have a request from someone going by the name of Romamo.
Aah...This one was a hit for Mayo Okamoto in '95 and was also used as a TV show theme song.
"Tomorrow."
Oh! I know this one.
Really?
Wow. I was about your age when this came out. I'm surprised you know it.
We learned it in school.
Whah?!
Huh? This was in a text-book?!
No, not in a book. It was the set piece for a choral com-petition.
Wow ...!

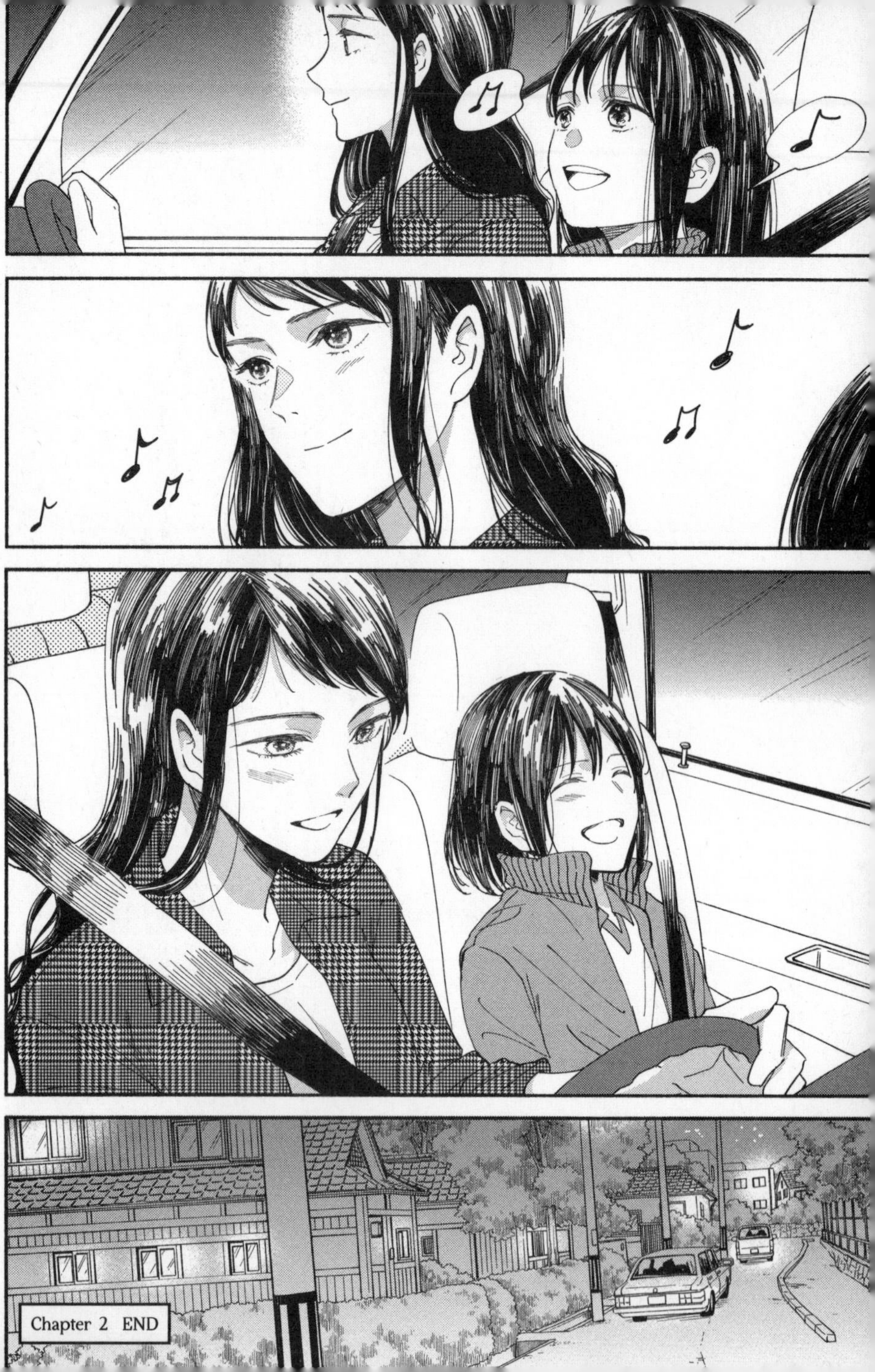
Chapter 2 END

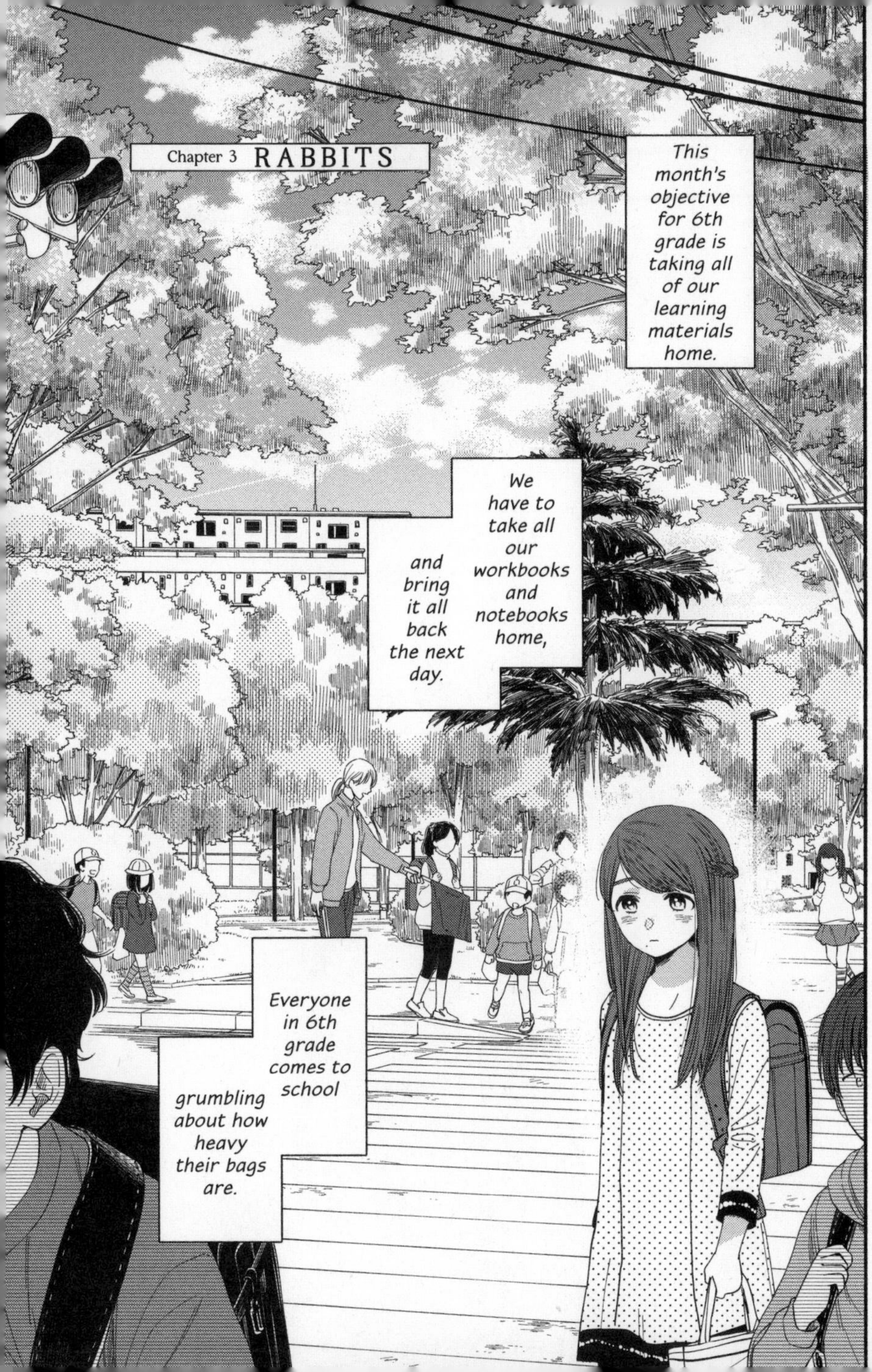
Chapter 3 RABBITS
This month's objective for 6th grade is taking all of our learning materials home.
We have to take all our workbooks and notebooks home,
and bring it all back the next day.
Everyone in 6th grade comes to school
grumbling about how heavy their bags are.

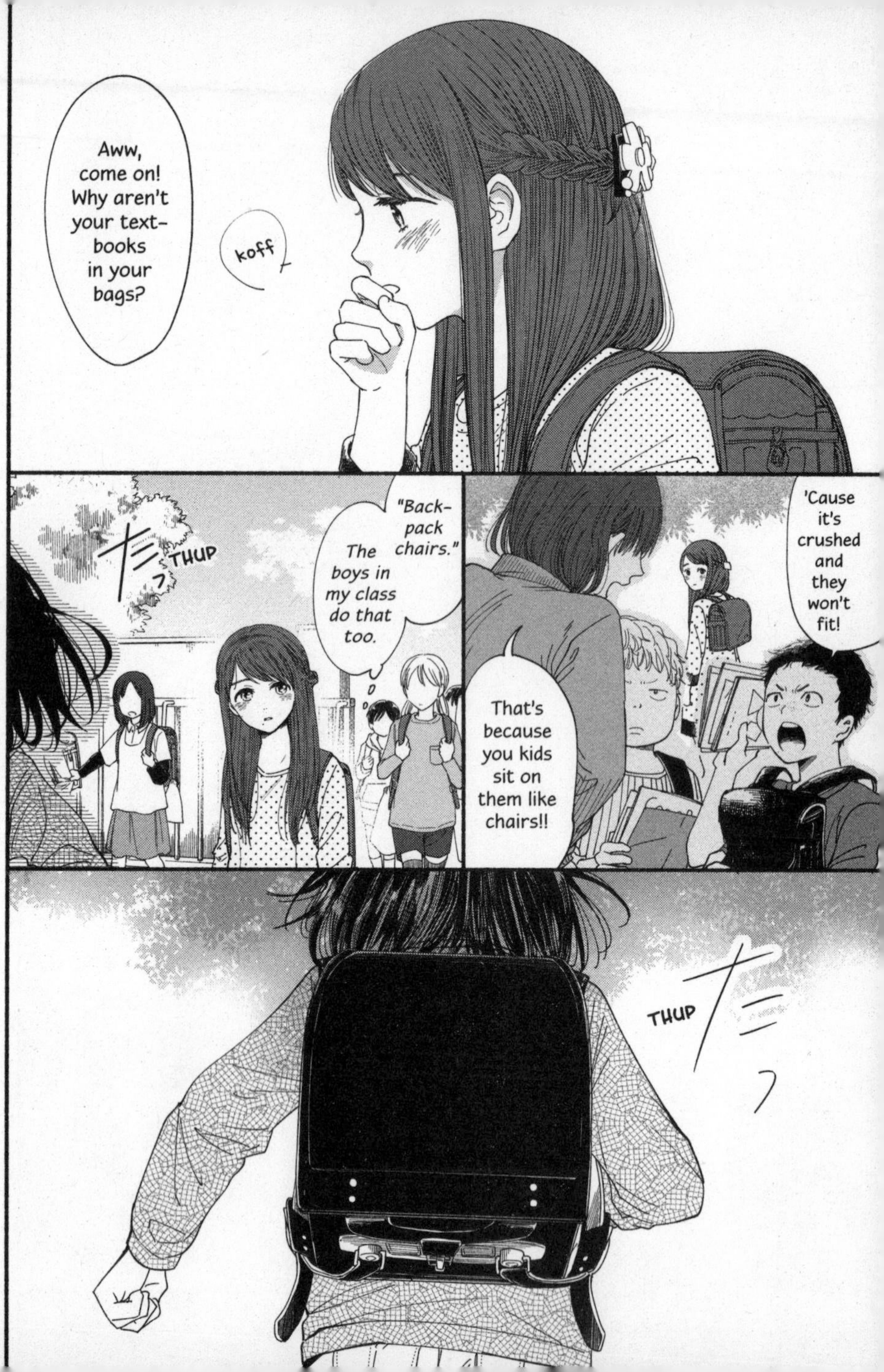
Aww, come on! Why aren't your text-books in your bags?
koff
'Cause it's crushed and they won't fit!
That's because you kids sit on them like chairs!!
"Back-pack chairs." The boys in my class do that too.
THUP
THUP

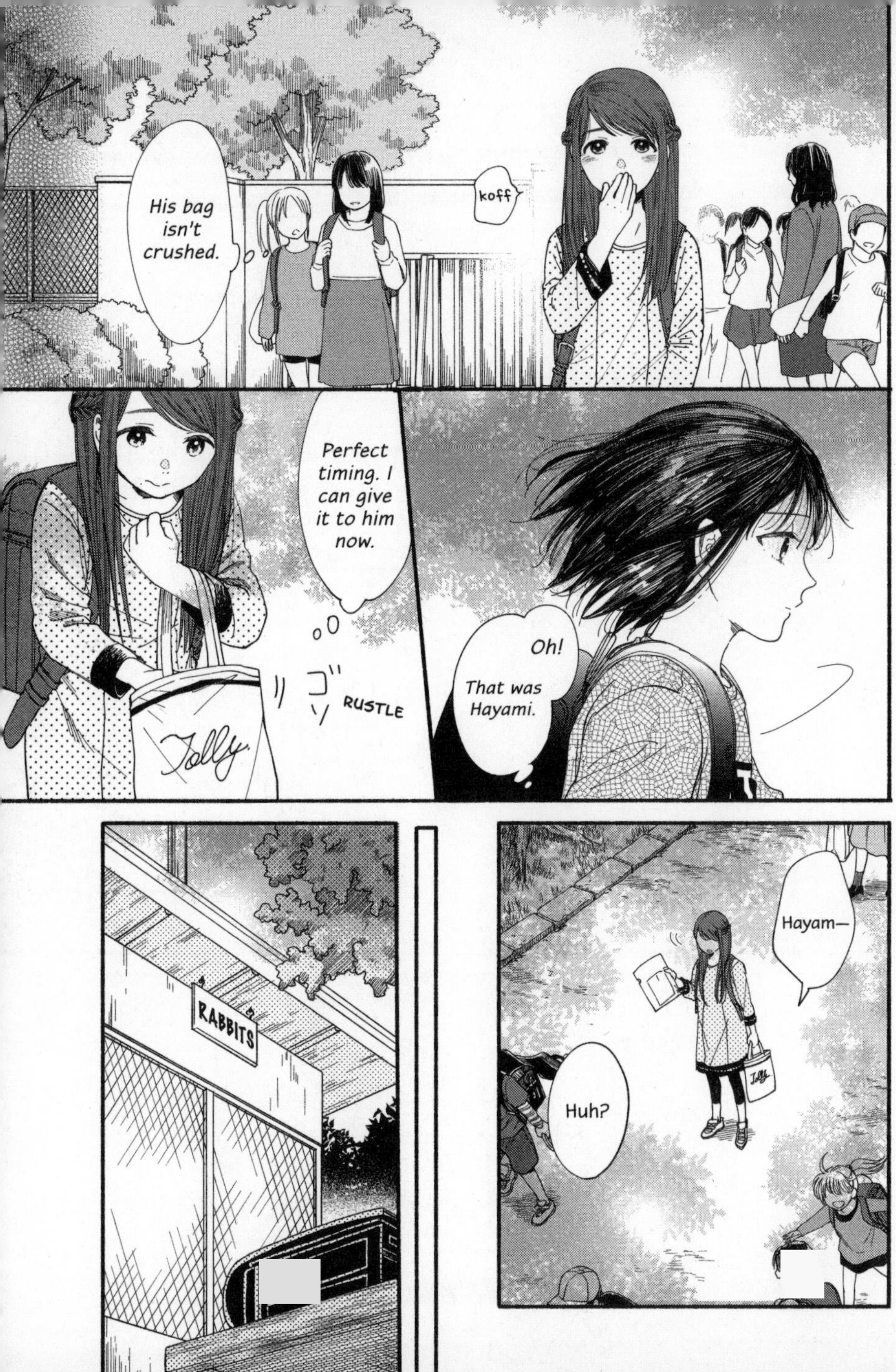
koff
His bag isn't crushed.
Oh!
That was Hayami.
Perfect timing. I can give it to him now.
RUSTLE
Hayam—
Huh?
RABBITS

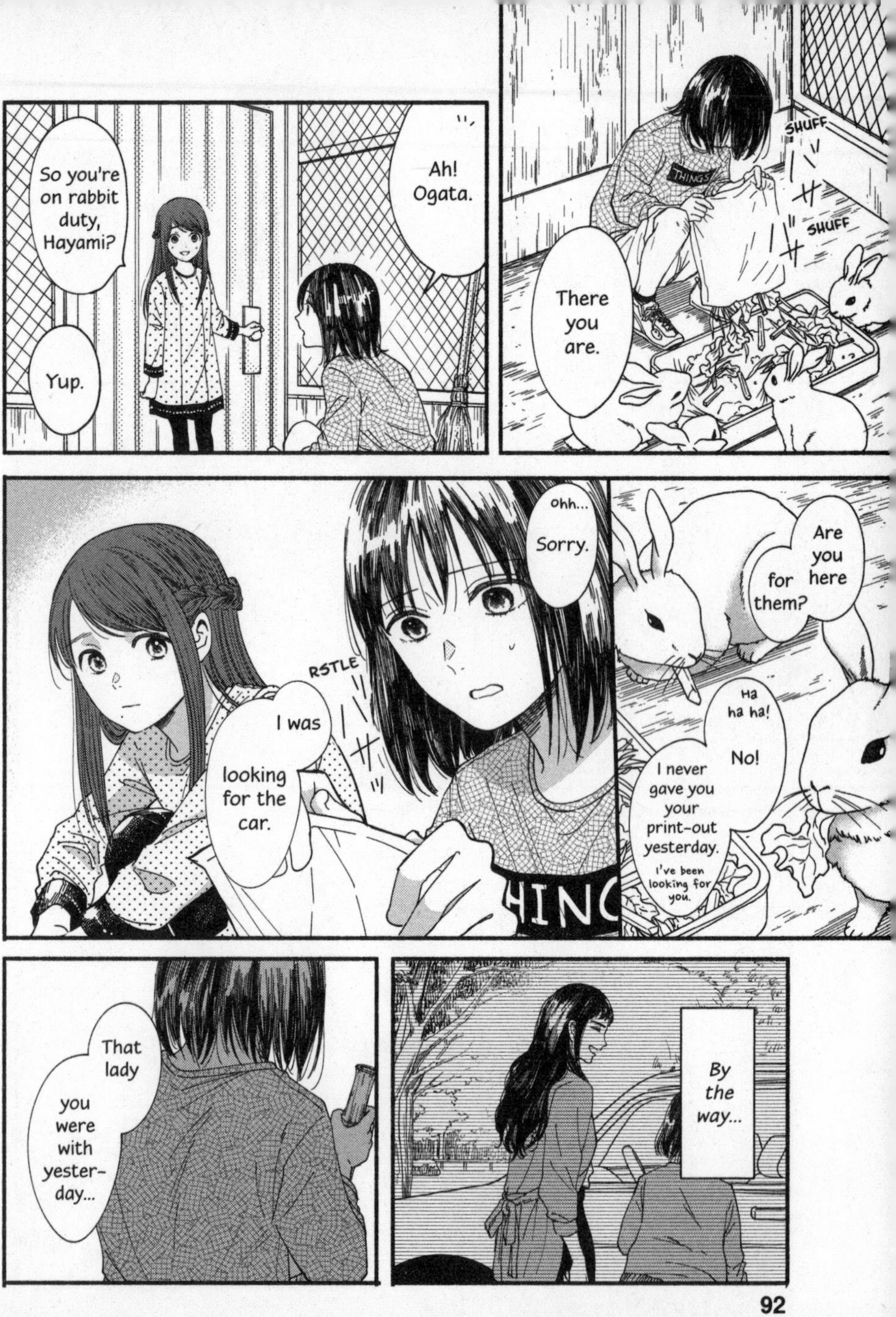
SHUFF
THINGS
SHUFF
There you are.
Ah! Ogata.
So you're on rabbit duty, Hayami?
Yup.
Are you here for them?
Ha ha ha!
No!
I never gave you your print-out yesterday.
I've been looking for you.
ohh...
Sorry.
RSTLE
I was looking for the car.
THING
By the way...
That lady you were with yester-day...

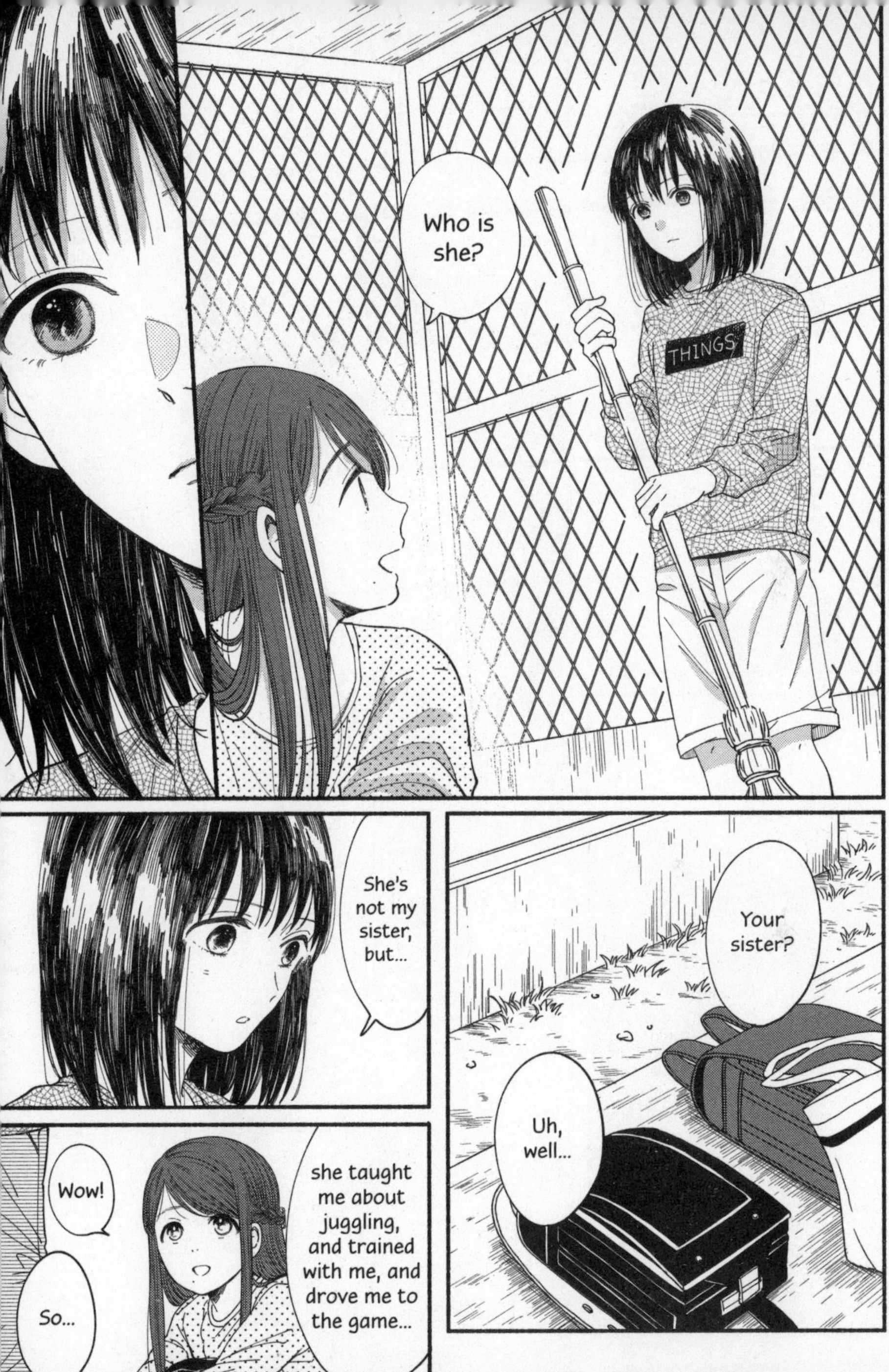
Who is she?
THINGS
Your sister?
Uh, well...
She's not my sister, but...
she taught me about juggling, and trained with me, and drove me to the game...
Wow!
So...

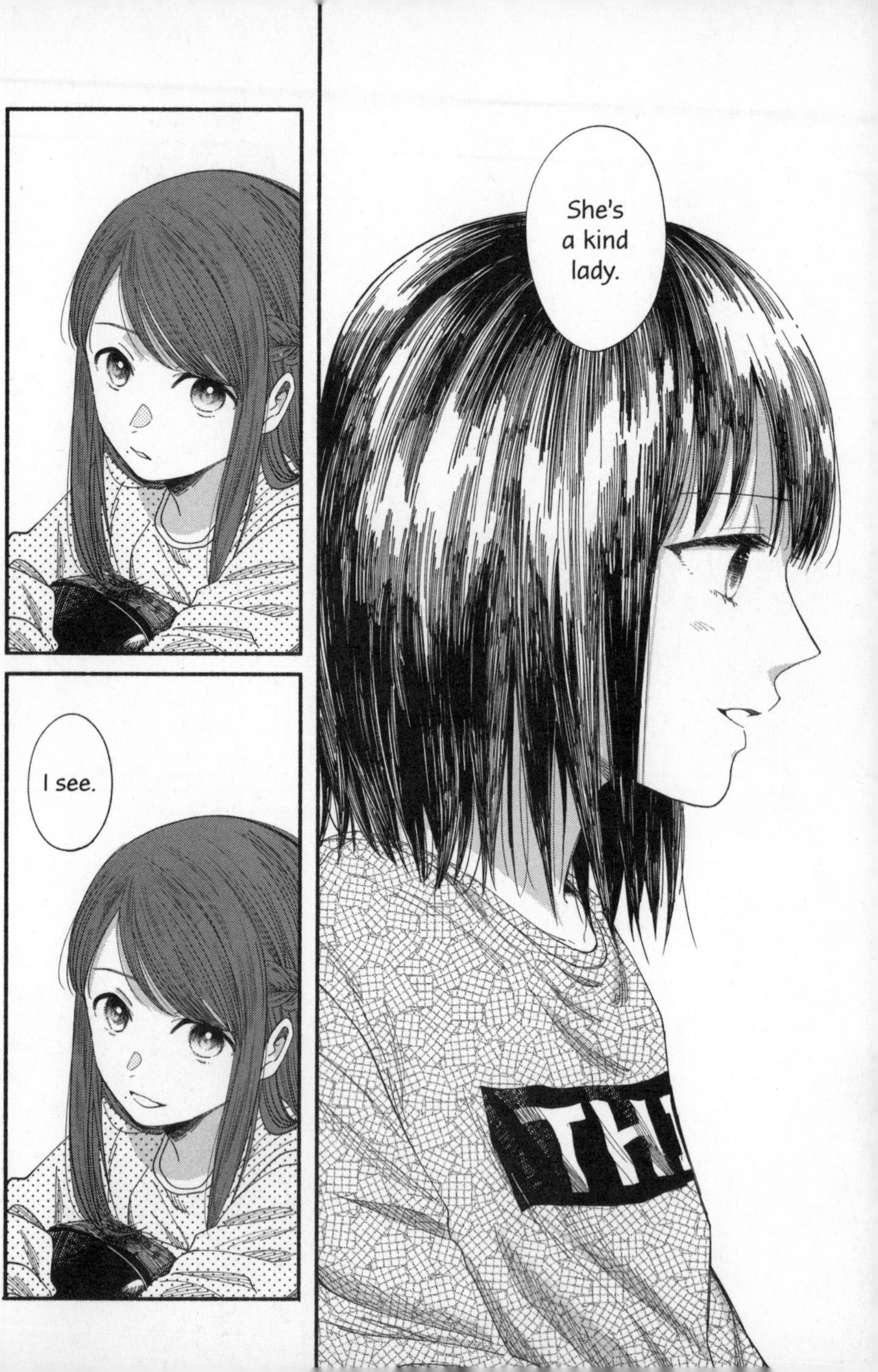
She's a kind lady.
I see.

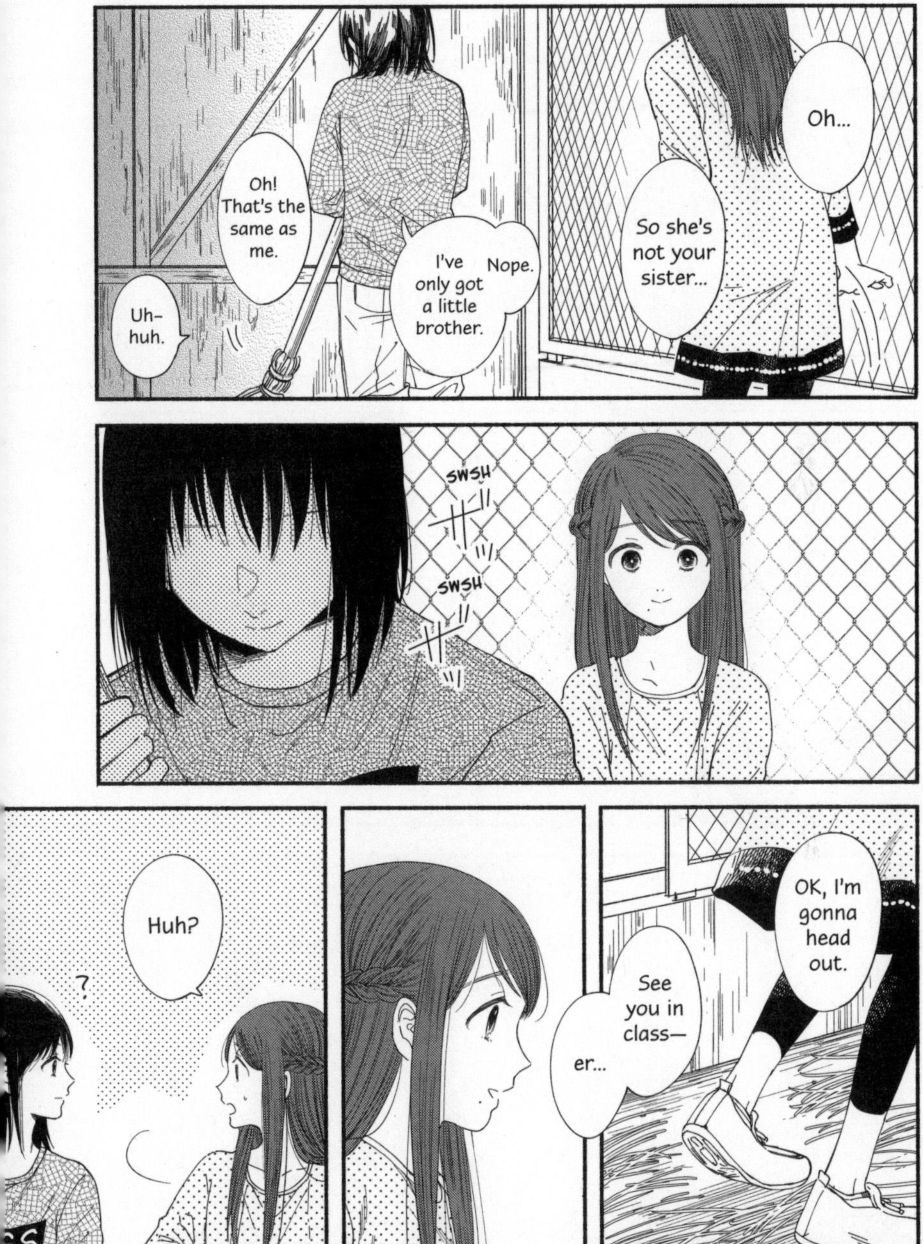
Oh...
So she's not your sister...
Nope.
I've only got a little brother.
Oh! That's the same as me.
Uh-huh.
SWSH
SWSH
OK, I'm gonna head out.
See you in class— er...
Huh?
?

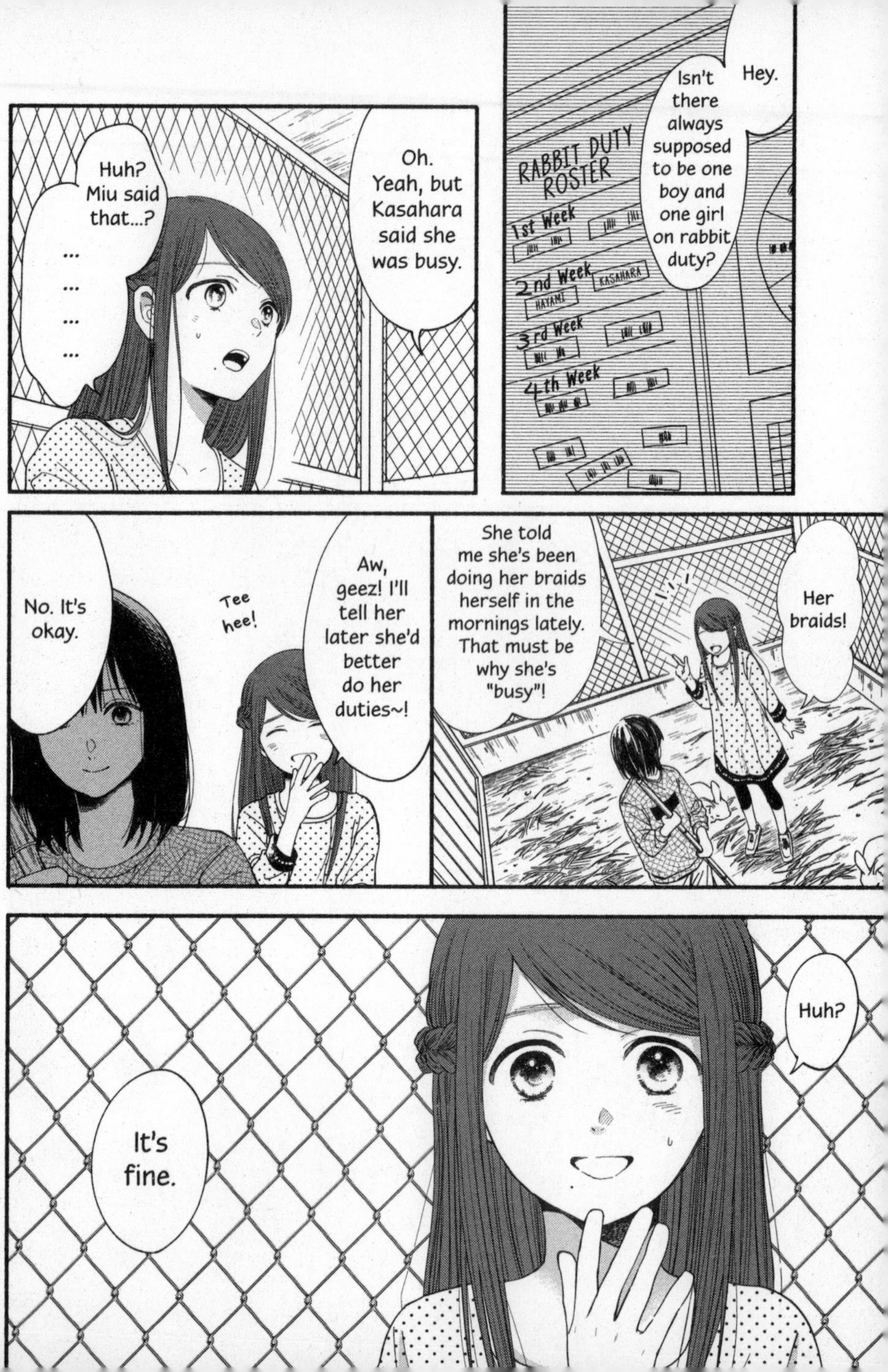
Hey.
Isn't there always supposed to be one boy and one girl on rabbit duty?
RABBIT DUTY ROSTER
1st Week
2nd Week
KASAHARA
HAYAMI
3rd Week
4th Week
...
Oh. Yeah, but Kasahara said she was busy.
Huh? Miu said that...?
...
...
...
...
Her braids!
She told me she's been doing her braids herself in the mornings lately. That must be why she's "busy"!
Aw, geez! I'll tell her later she'd better do her duties~!
Tee hee!
No. It's okay.
Huh?
It's fine.

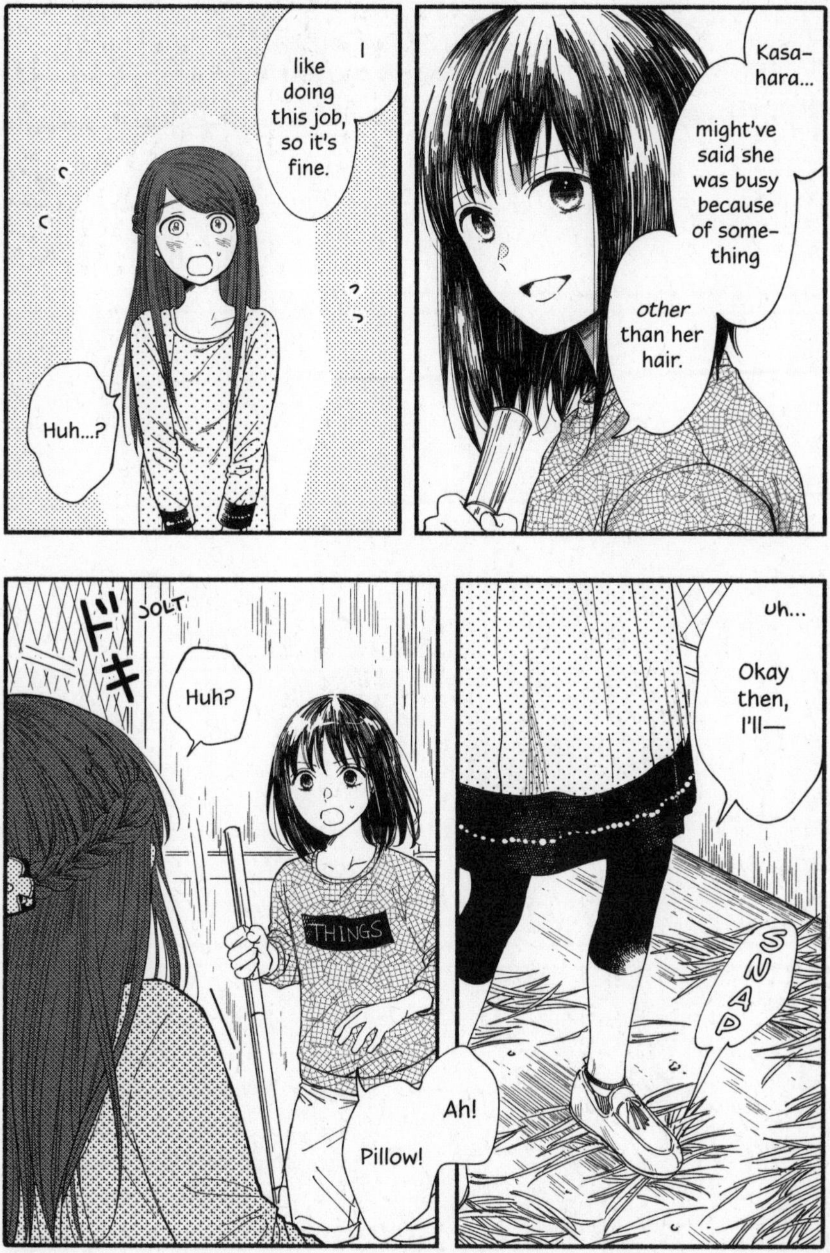
Kasa-hara...
might've said she was busy because of some-thing
other than her hair.
I like doing this job, so it's fine.
Huh...?
Uh...
Okay then, I'll—
SNAP
ドキ
JOLT
Huh?
Ah!
Pillow!

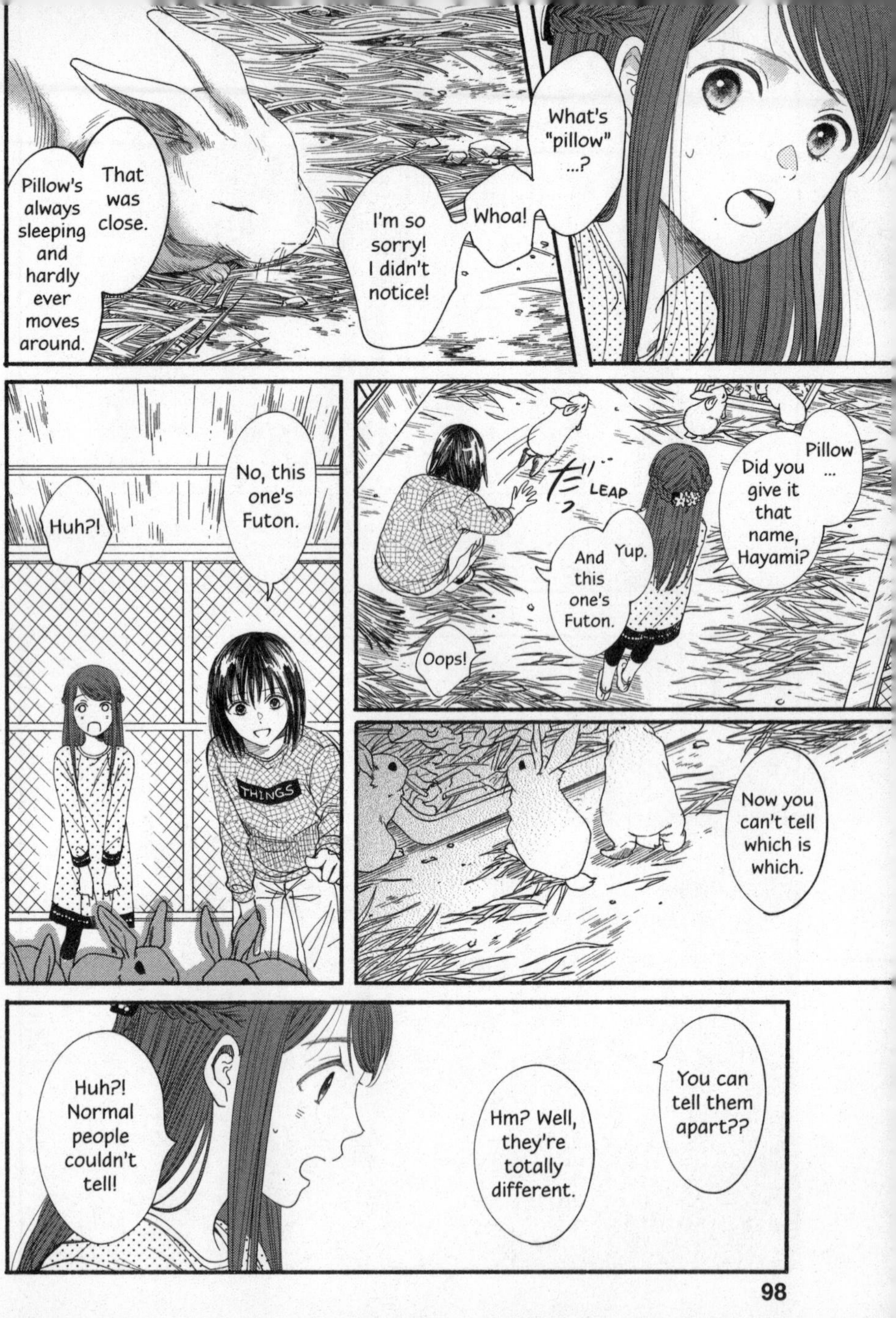

What's "pillow" ...?
Whoa!
I'm so sorry! I didn't notice!
That was close.
Pillow's always sleeping and hardly ever moves around.
Pillow ... Did you give it that name, Hayami?
Yup.
And this one's Futon.
LEAP
Oops!
Now you can't tell which is which.
No, this one's Futon.
Huh?!
THINGS
You can tell them apart??
Hm? Well, they're totally different.
Huh?! Normal people couldn't tell!

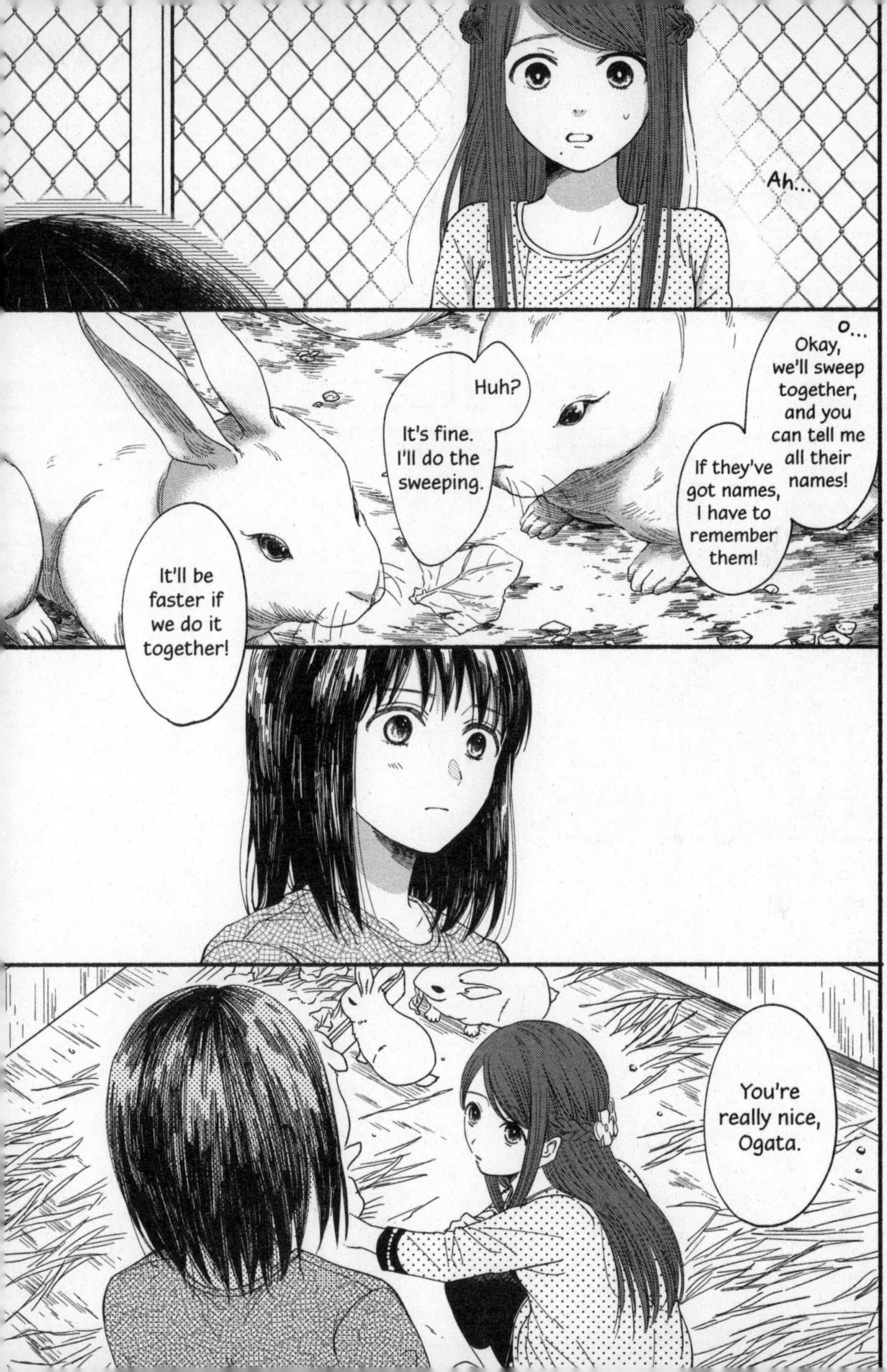

Ah...
O... Okay, we'll sweep together, and you can tell me all their names!
If they've got names, I have to remember them!
Huh?
It's fine. I'll do the sweeping.
It'll be faster if we do it together!
You're really nice, Ogata.

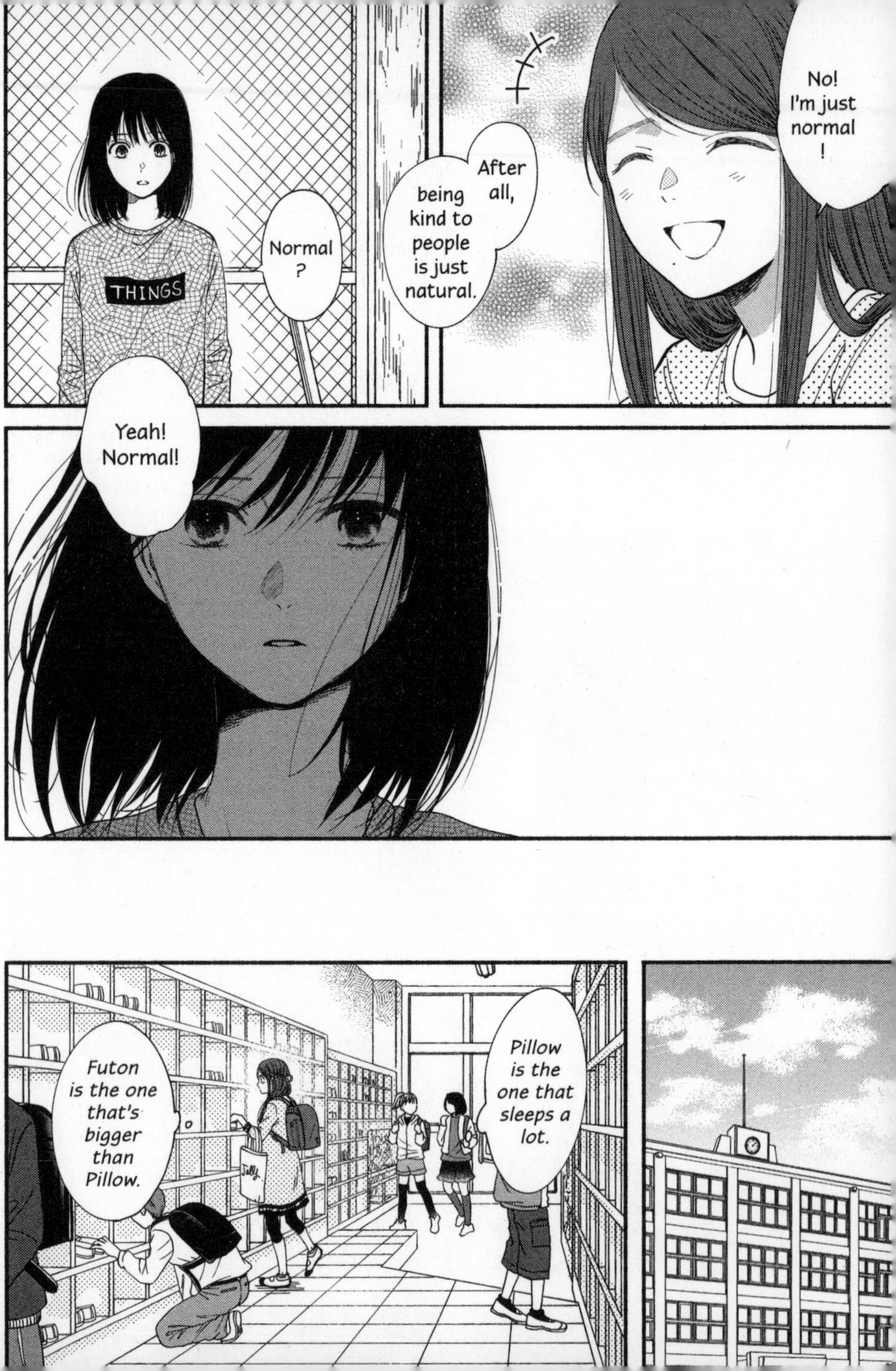
No! I'm just normal!
After all, being kind to people is just natural.
Normal?
THINGS
Yeah! Normal!
Pillow is the one that sleeps a lot.
Futon is the one that's bigger than Pillow.

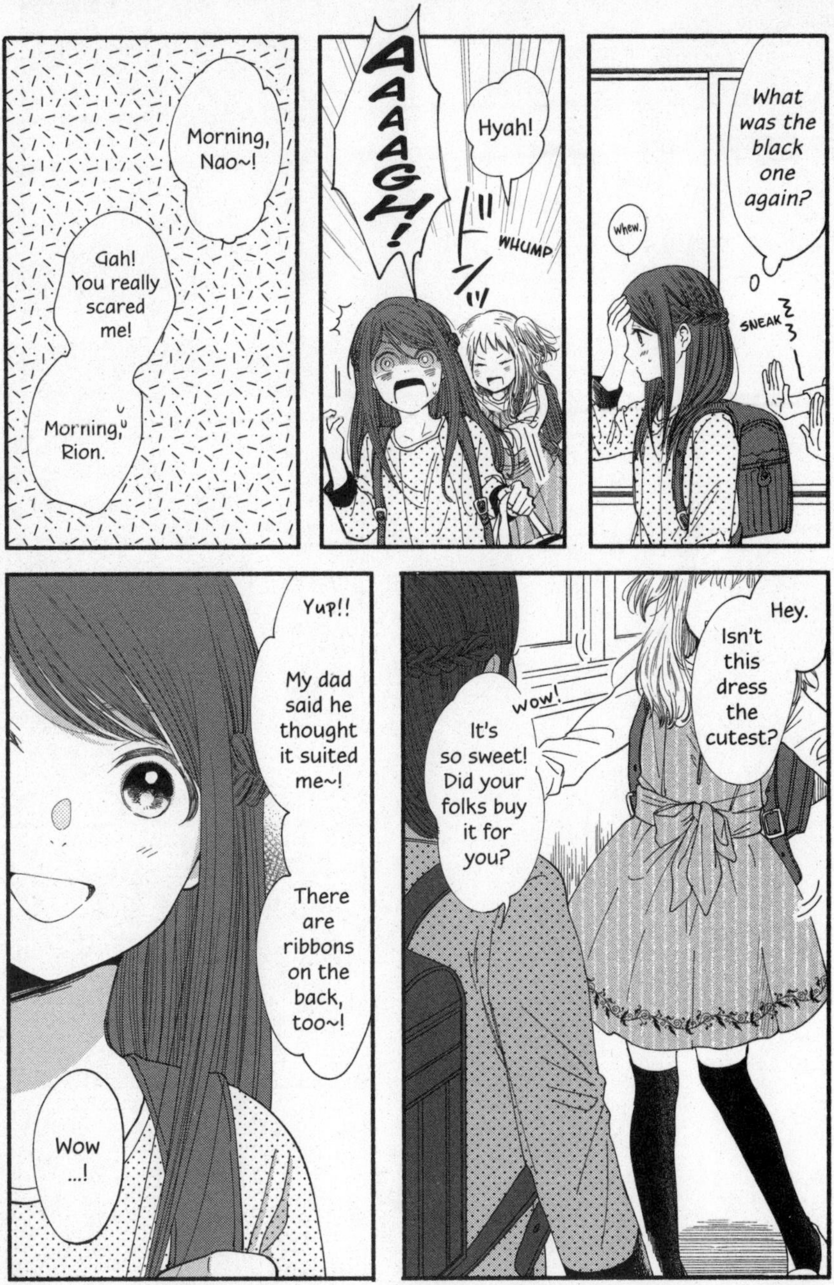
What was the black one again?
Whew.
SNEAK
AAAAGH!
Hyah!
WHUMP
Morning, Nao~!
Gah! You really scared me!
Morning, Rion.
Hey. Isn't this dress the cutest?
WOW!
It's so sweet! Did your folks buy it for you?
Yup!!
My dad said he thought it suited me~!
There are ribbons on the back, too~!
Wow ...!

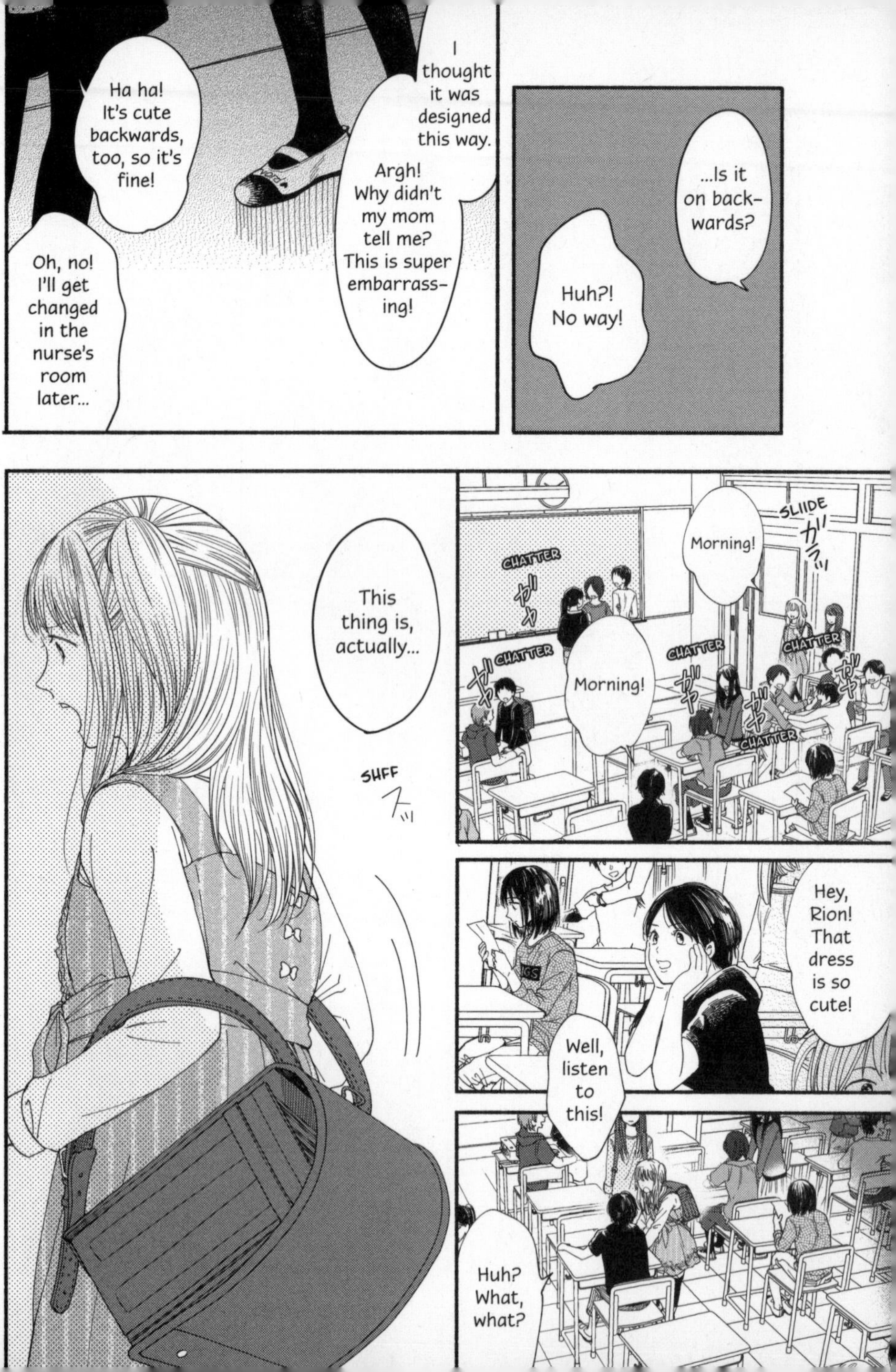
...Is it on backwards?
Huh?! No way!
I thought it was designed this way.
Argh! Why didn't my mom tell me? This is super embarrassing!
Ha ha! It's cute backwards, too, so it's fine!
Oh, no! I'll get changed in the nurse's room later...
SLIIDE
Morning!
CHATTER
Morning!
CHATTER
CHATTER
CHATTER
CHATTER
Hey, Rion! That dress is so cute!
Well, listen to this!
Huh? What, what?
This thing is, actually...
SHFF

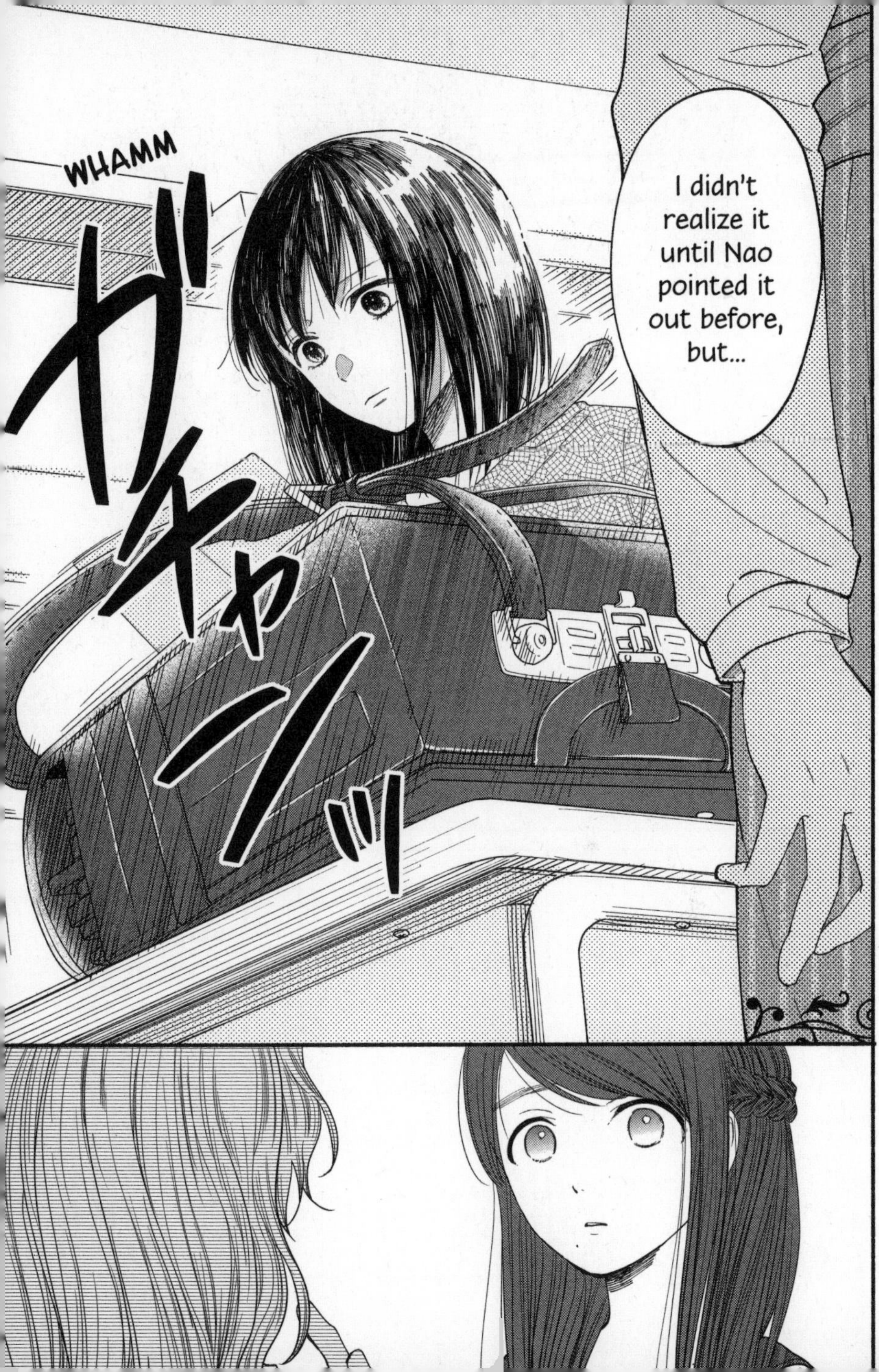
I didn't realize it until Nao pointed it out before, but...
WHAMM
ガチャンッ

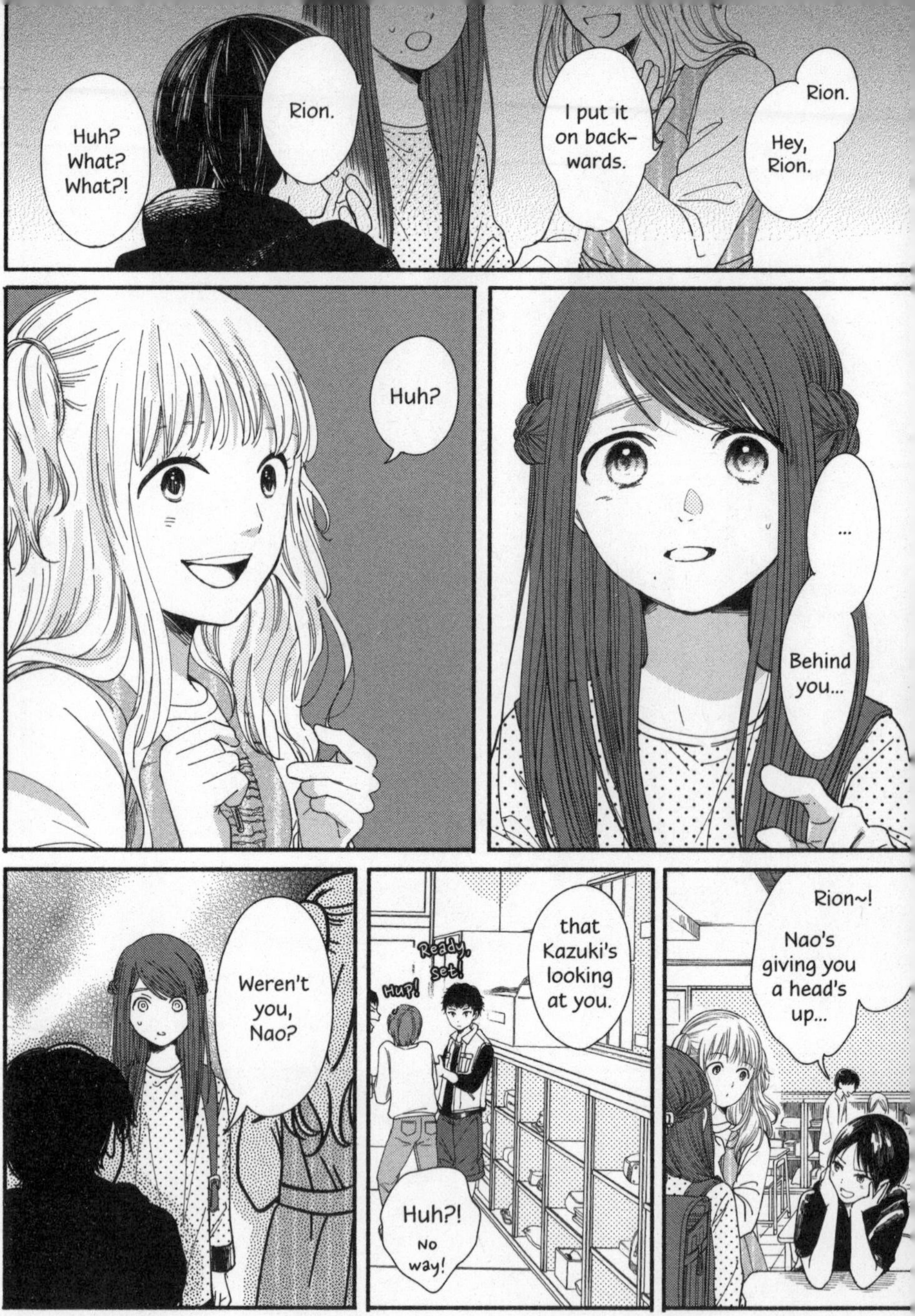
Rion.
Hey, Rion.
I put it on back-wards.
Rion.
Huh? What? What?!
...
Behind you...
Huh?
Rion~!
Nao's giving you a head's up...
that Kazuki's looking at you.
Ready, set!
Hup!
Huh?!
No way!
Weren't you, Nao?

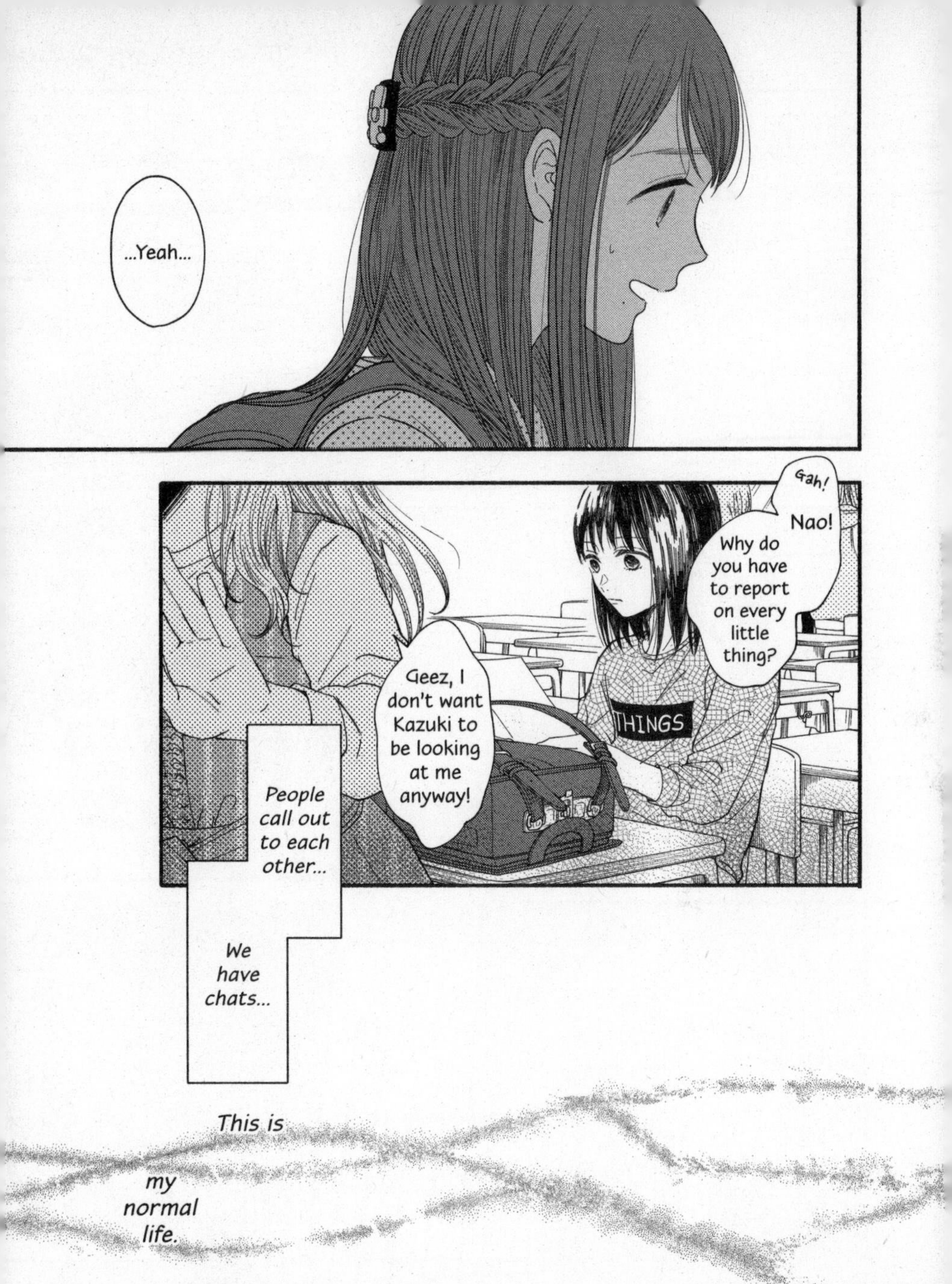
...Yeah...
Gah!
Nao! Why do you have to report on every little thing?
THINGS
Geez, I don't want Kazuki to be looking at me anyway!
People call out to each other...
We have chats...
This is my normal life.

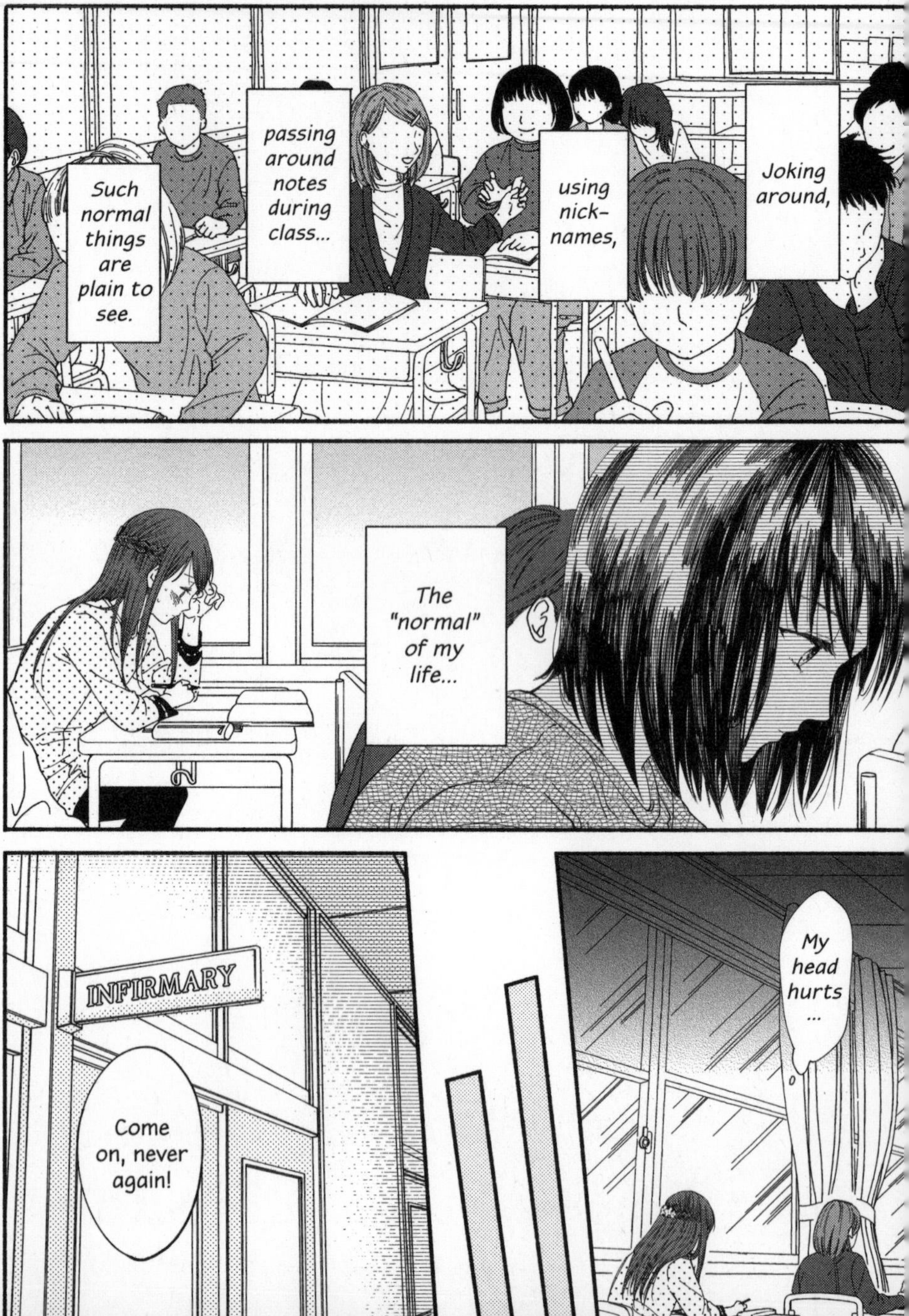
Joking around,
using nick-names,
passing around notes during class...
Such normal things are plain to see.
The "normal" of my life...
My head hurts ...
INFIRMARY
Come on, never again!

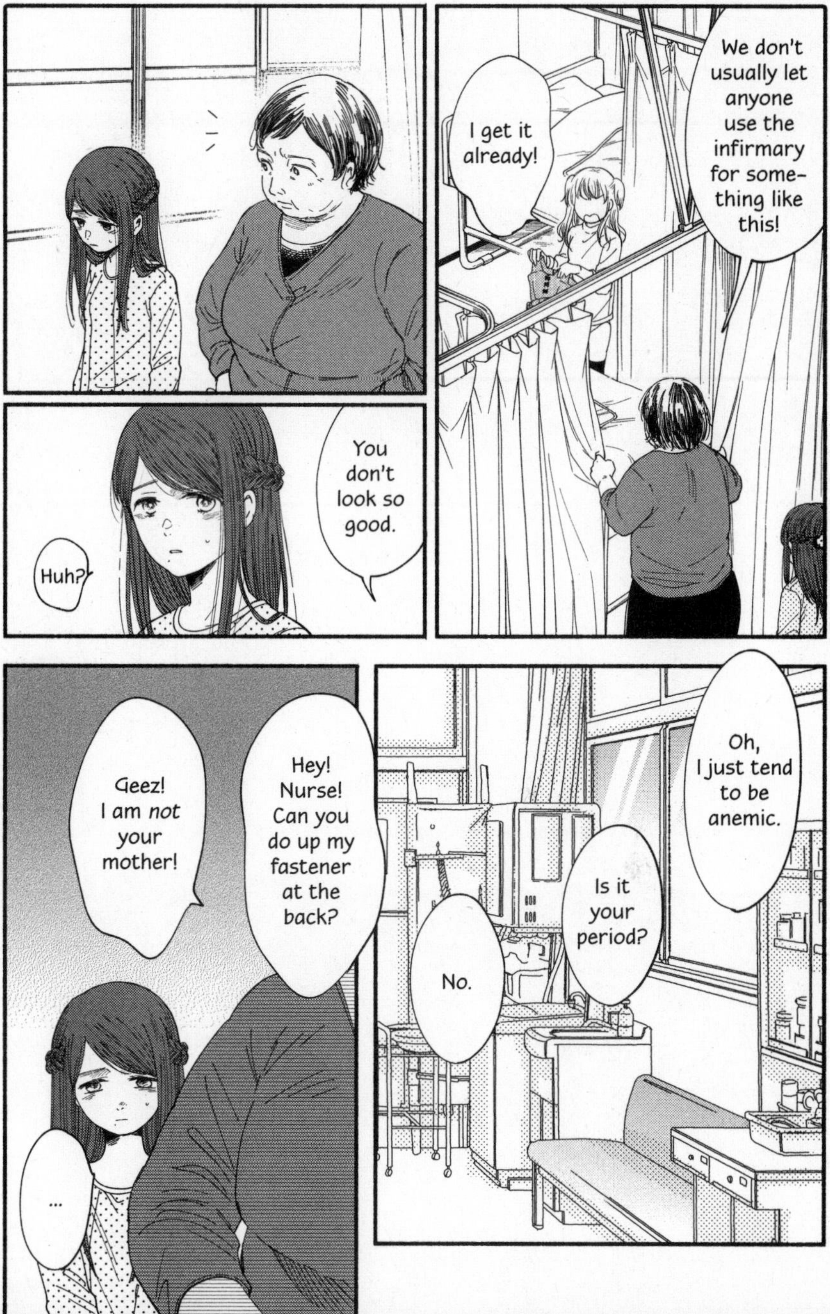
We don't usually let anyone use the infirmary for some-thing like this!
I get it already!
You don't look so good.
Huh?
Oh, I just tend to be anemic.
Is it your period?
No.
Hey! Nurse! Can you do up my fastener at the back?
Geez! I am *not* your mother!
...

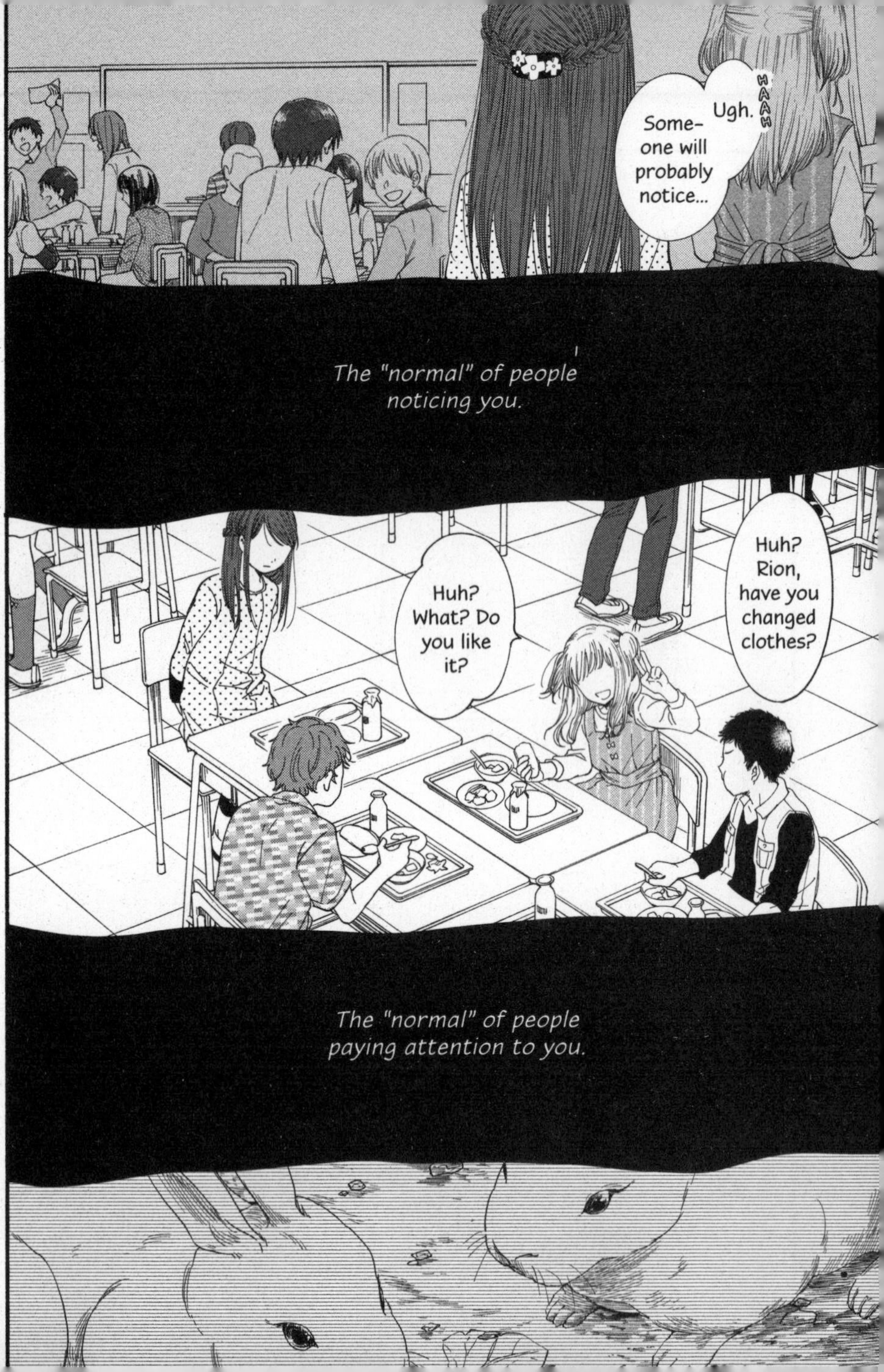
Ugh.
HAAAH
Someone will probably notice...
The "normal" of people noticing you.
Huh? Rion, have you changed clothes?
Huh? What? Do you like it?
The "normal" of people paying attention to you.

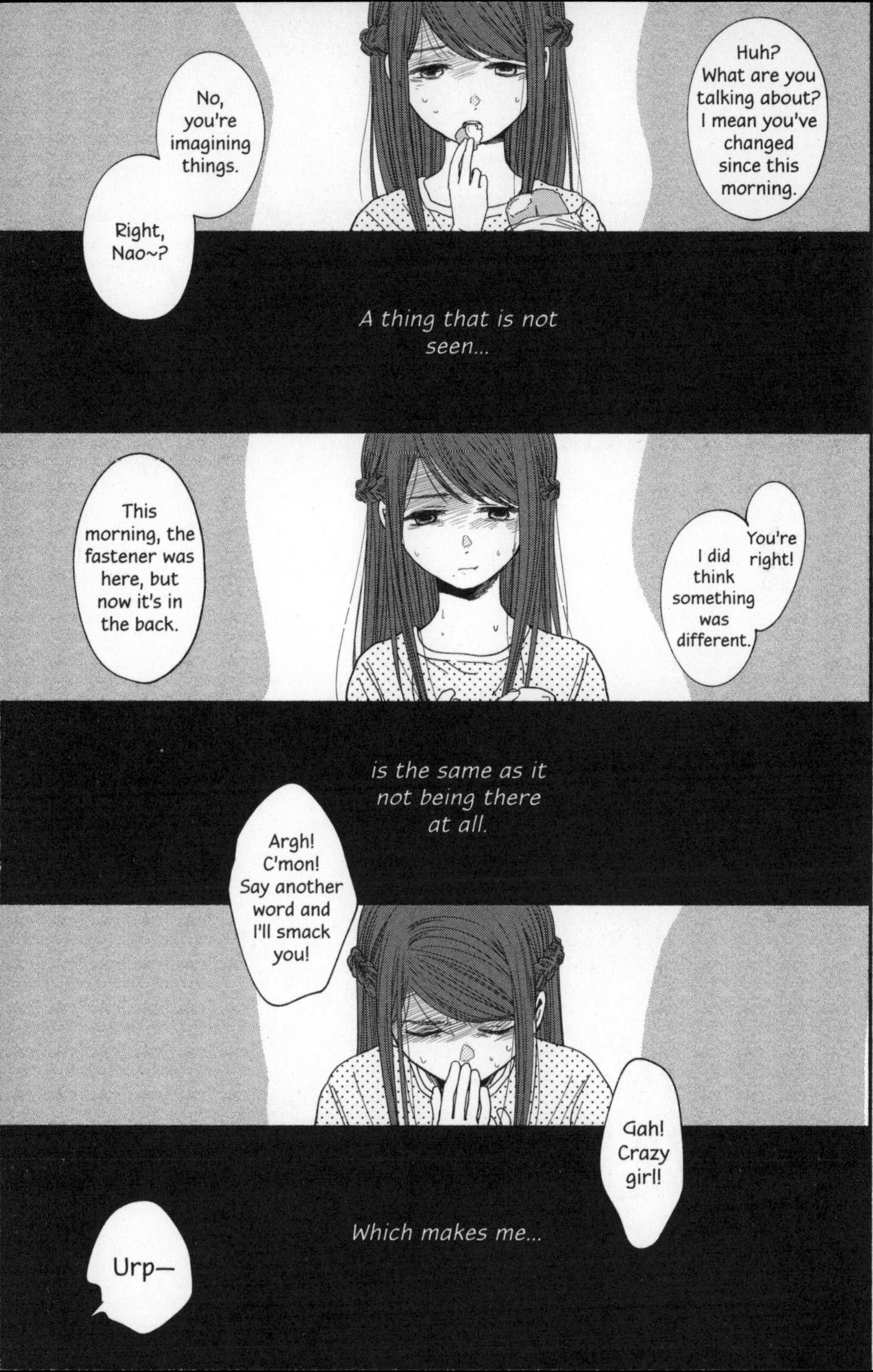
Huh? What are you talking about? I mean you've changed since this morning.
No, you're imagining things.
Right, Nao~?
A thing that is not seen...
You're right! I did think something was different.
This morning, the fastener was here, but now it's in the back.
is the same as it not being there at all.
Argh! C'mon! Say another word and I'll smack you!
Gah! Crazy girl!
Which makes me...
Urp—

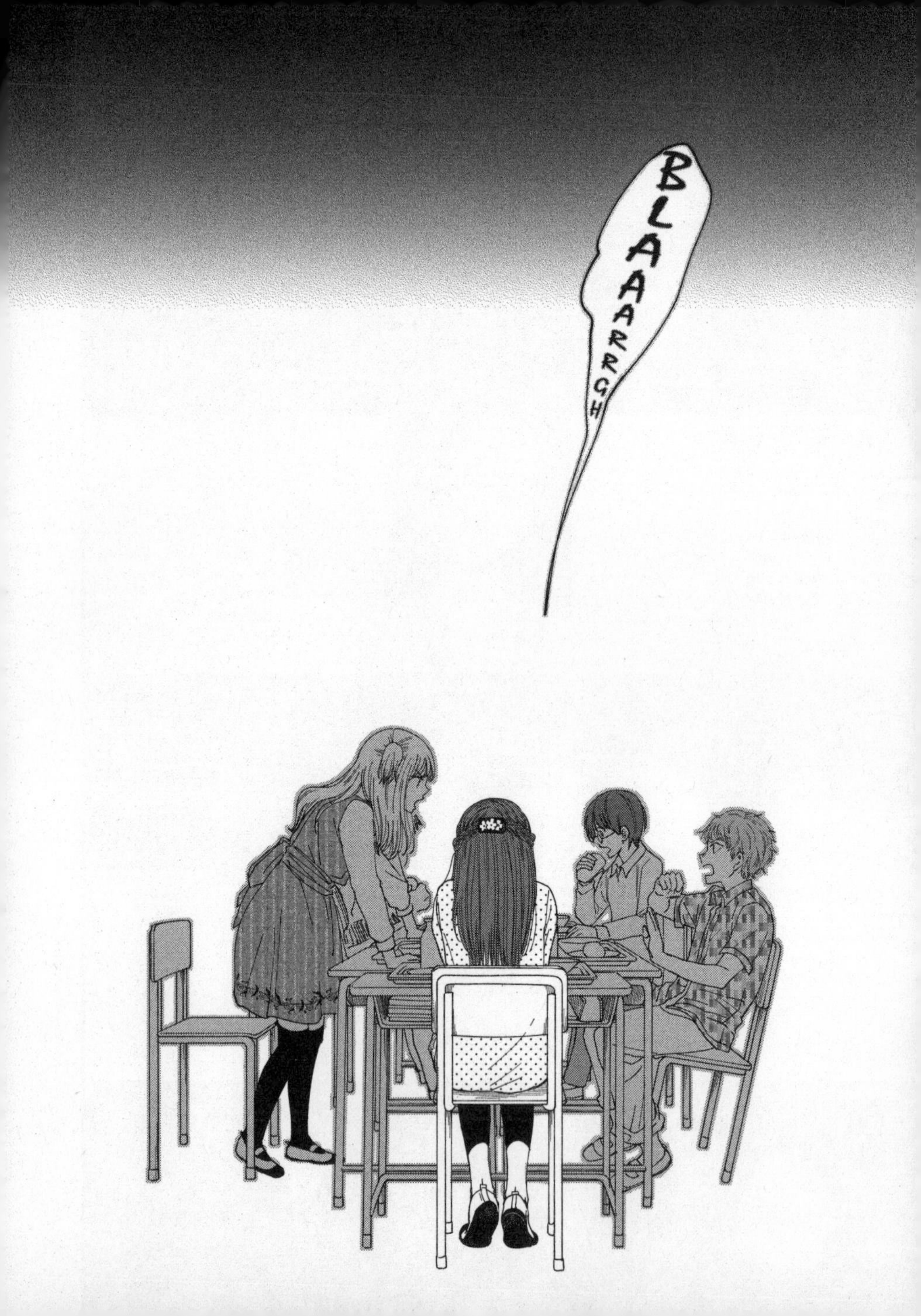
BLAAARRGH

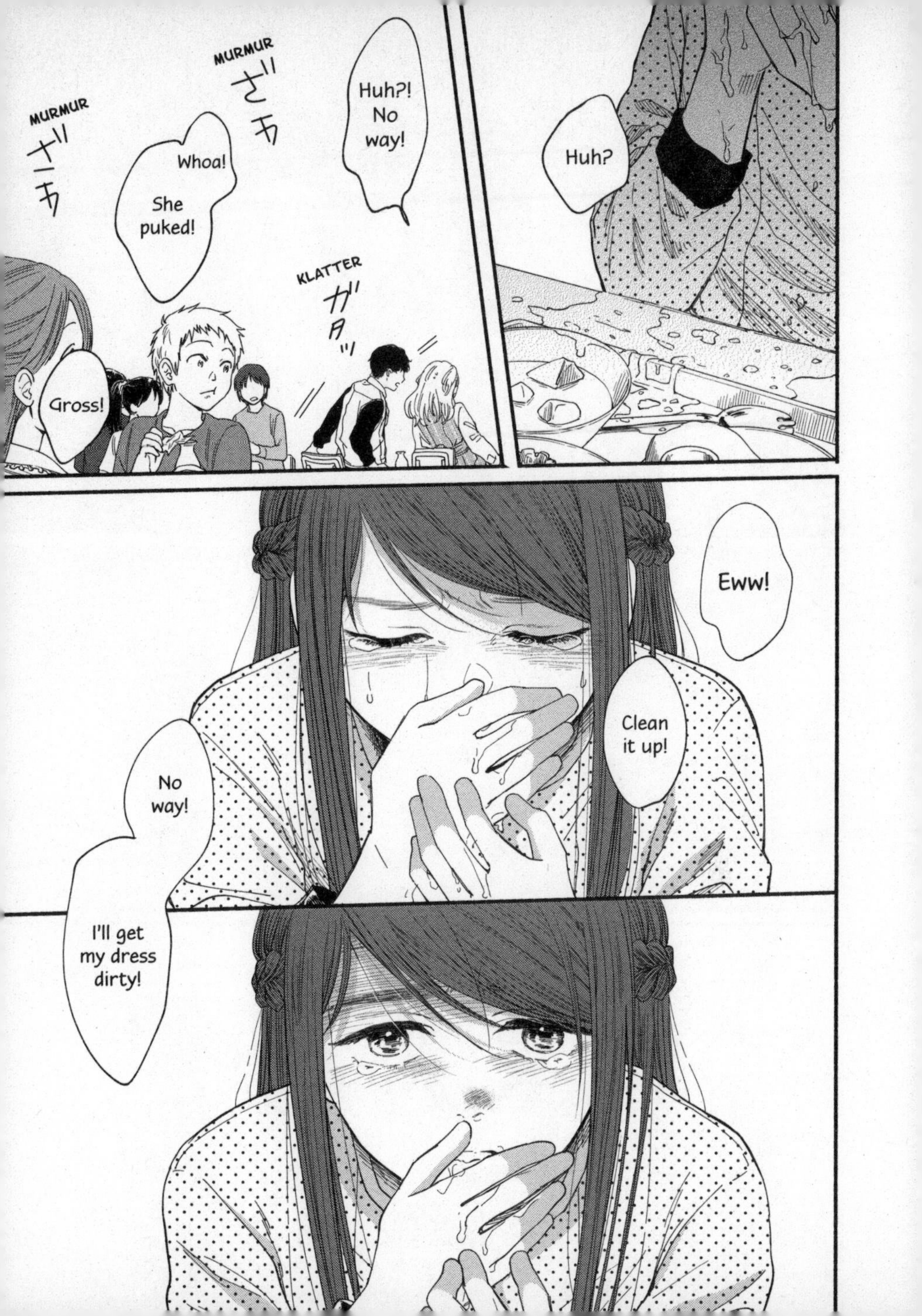
Huh?
Huh?! No way!
MURMUR
Whoa! She puked!
KLATTER
MURMUR
Gross!
Eww!
Clean it up!
No way!
I'll get my dress dirty!

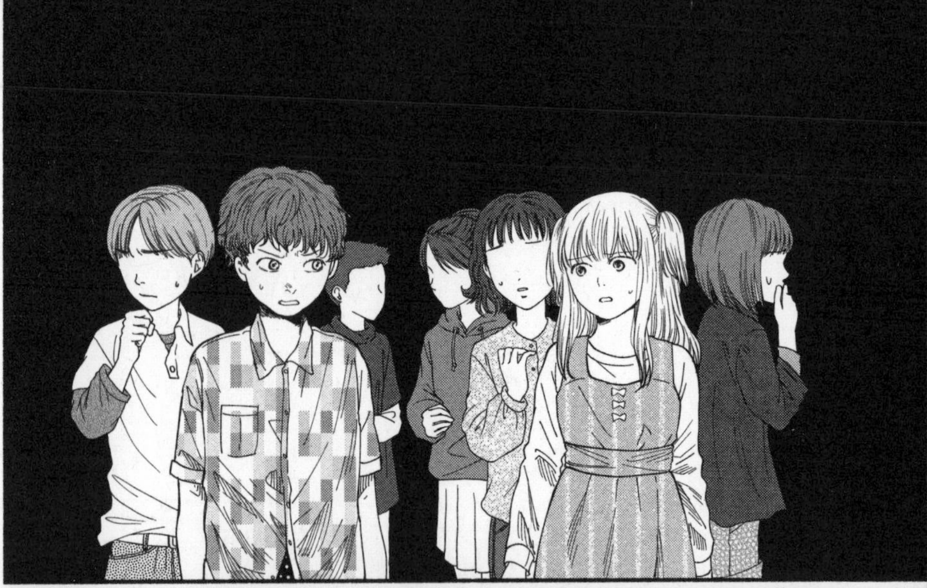
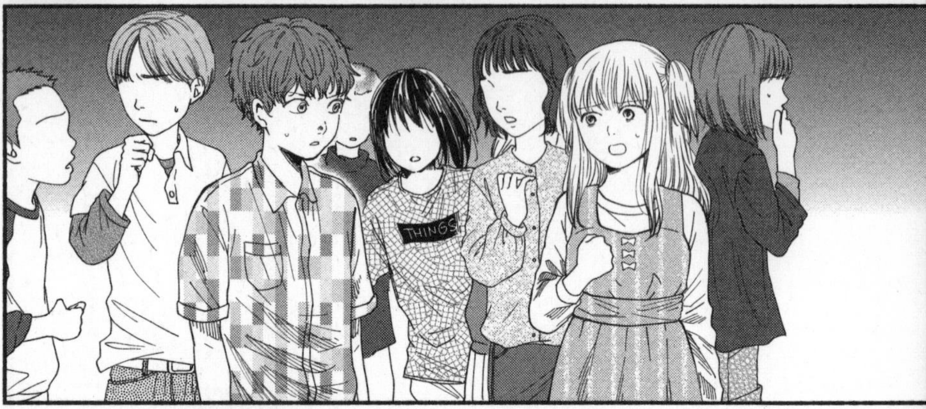
THINGS
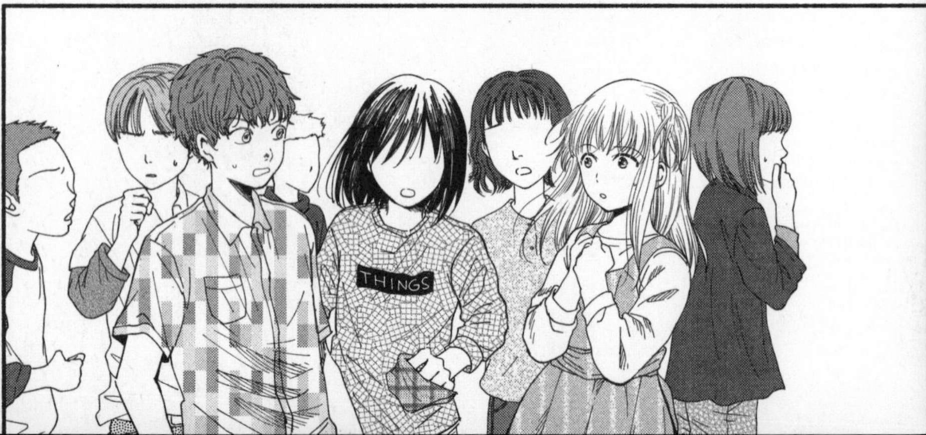
THINGS

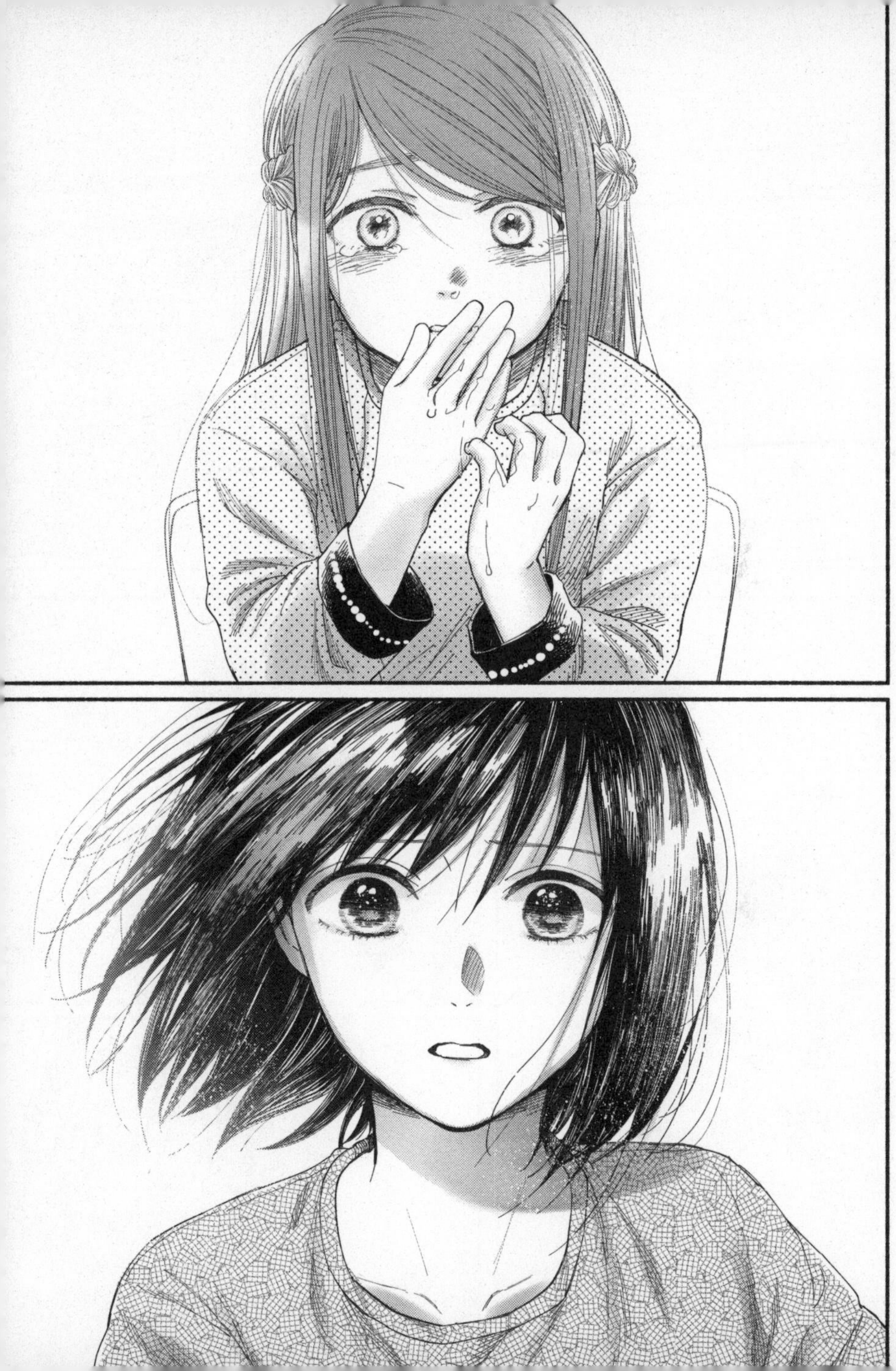

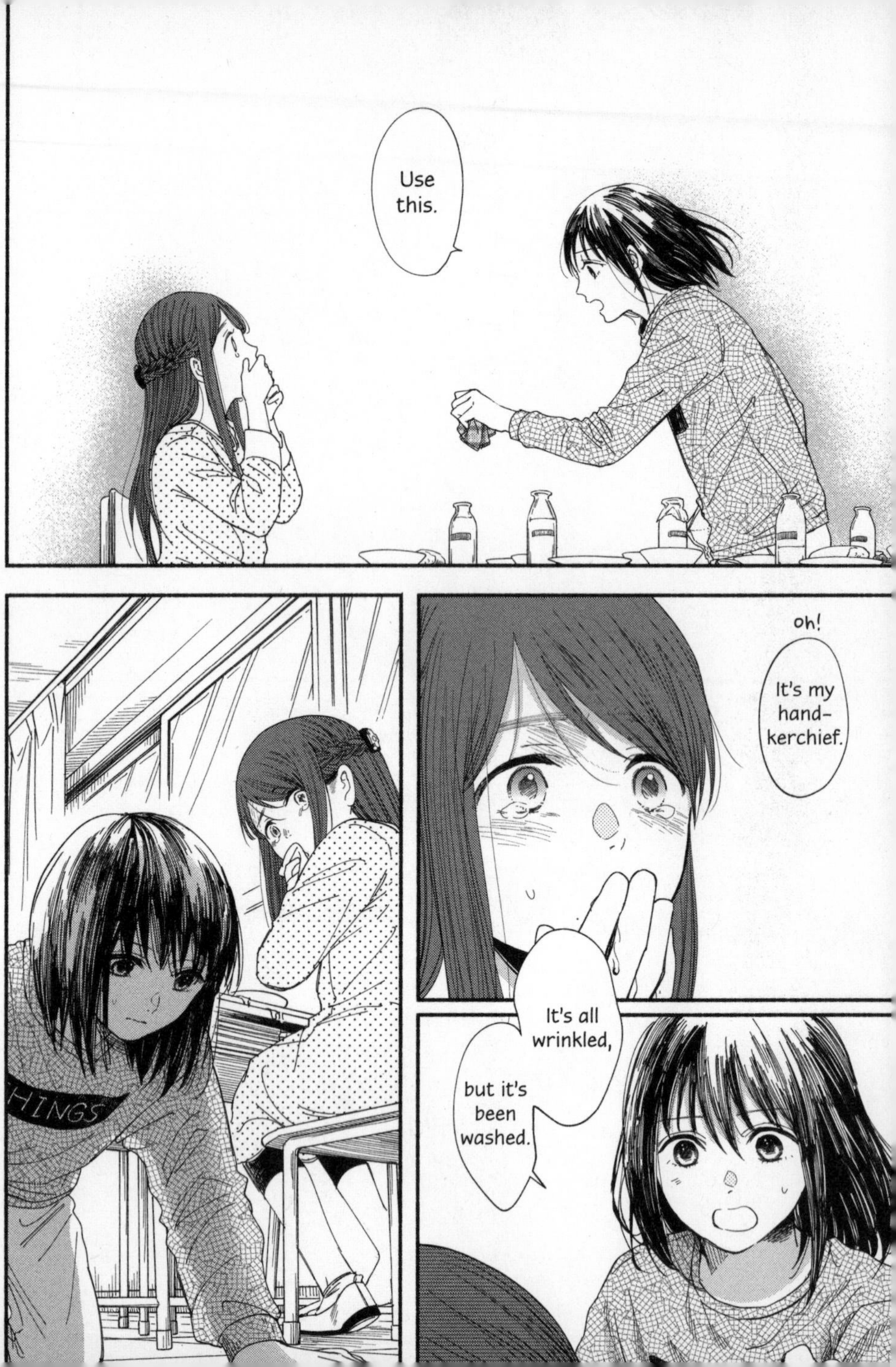
Use this.
oh!
It's my handkerchief.
It's all wrinkled,
but it's been washed.
HINGS

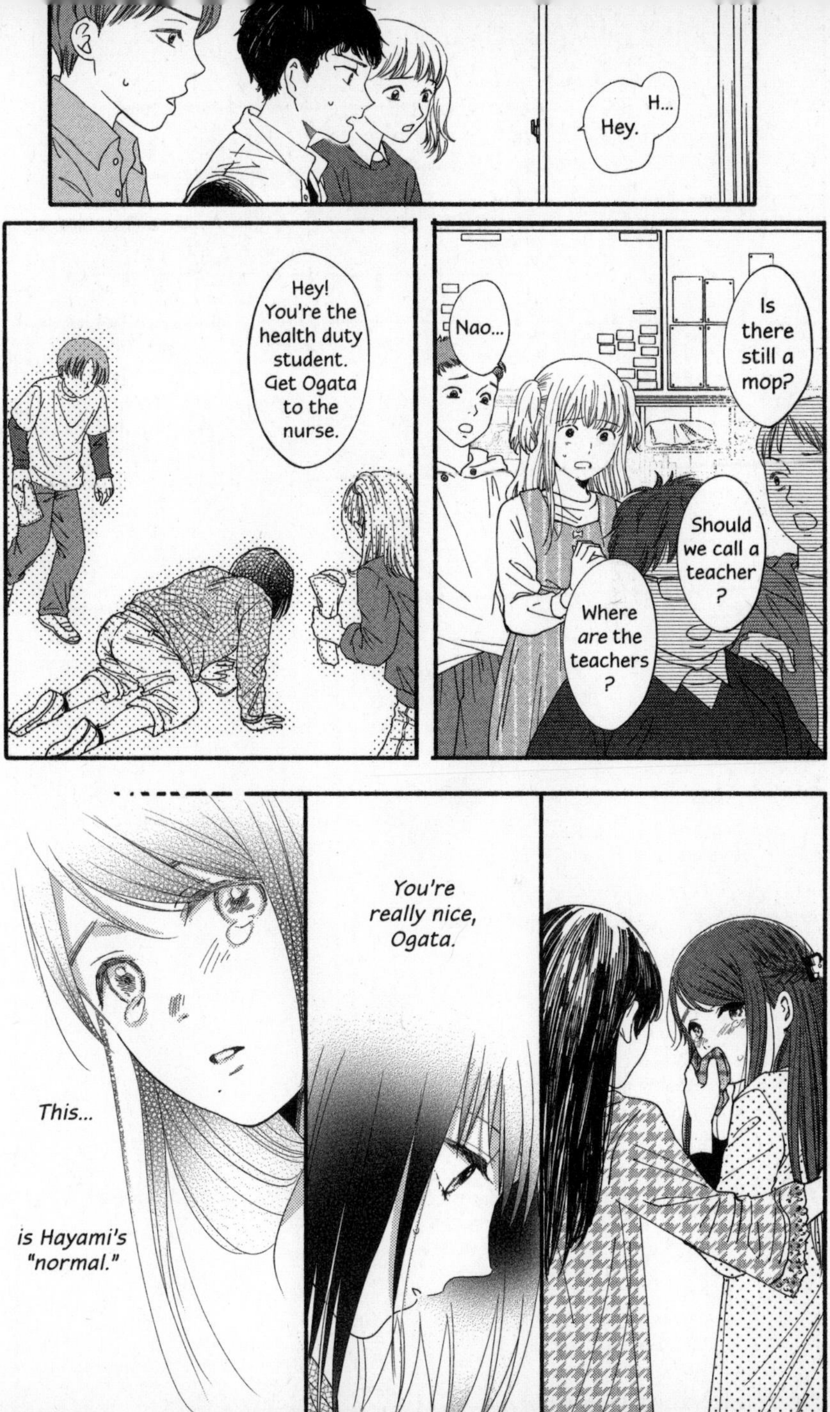
H... Hey.
Is there still a mop?
Nao...
Should we call a teacher?
Where are the teachers?
Hey! You're the health duty student. Get Ogata to the nurse.
You're really nice, Ogata.
This...
is Hayami's "normal."

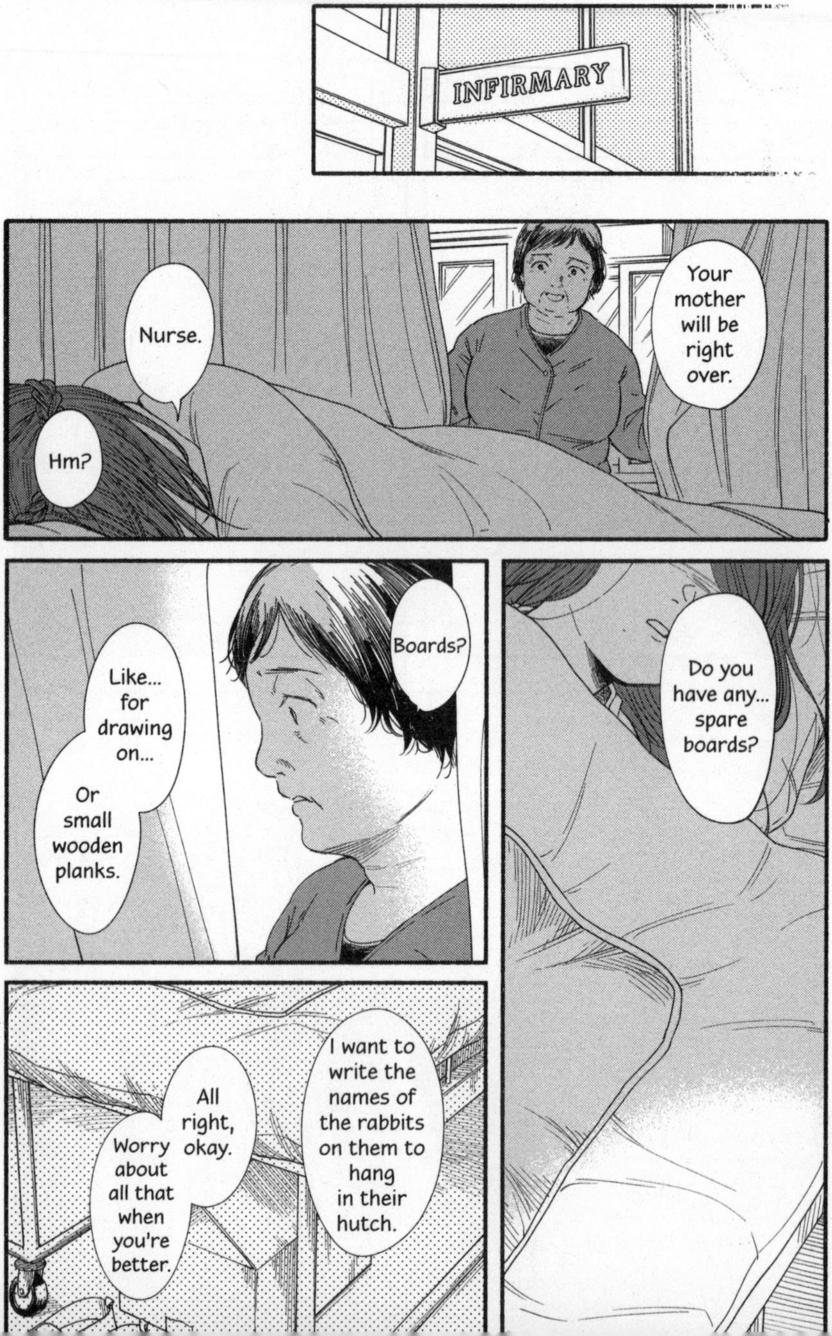
INFIRMARY
Your mother will be right over.
Nurse.
Hm?
Do you have any... spare boards?
Boards?
Like... for drawing on...
Or small wooden planks.
I want to write the names of the rabbits on them to hang in their hutch.
All right, okay.
Worry about all that when you're better.

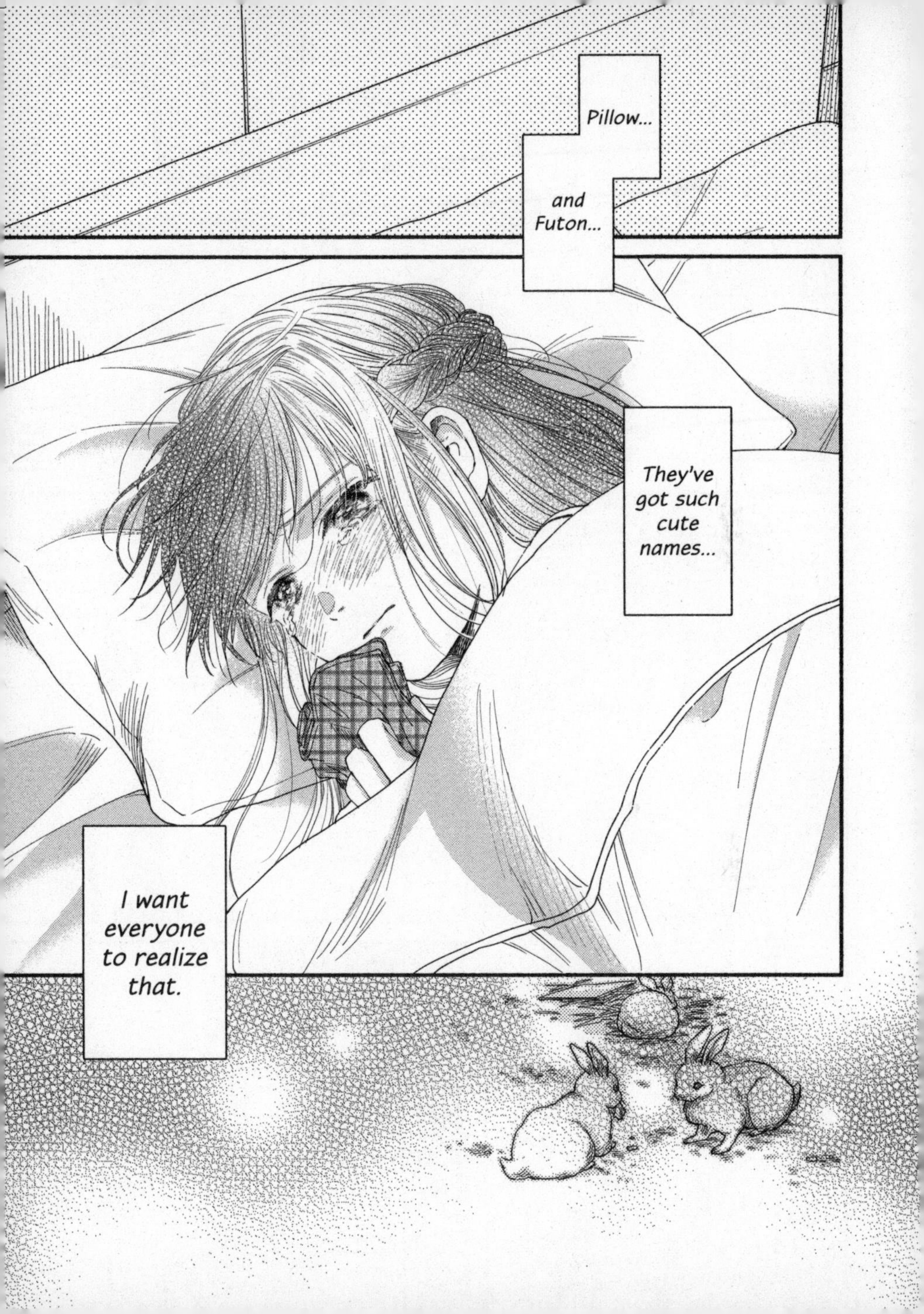
Pillow...
and Futon...
They've got such cute names...
I want everyone to realize that.

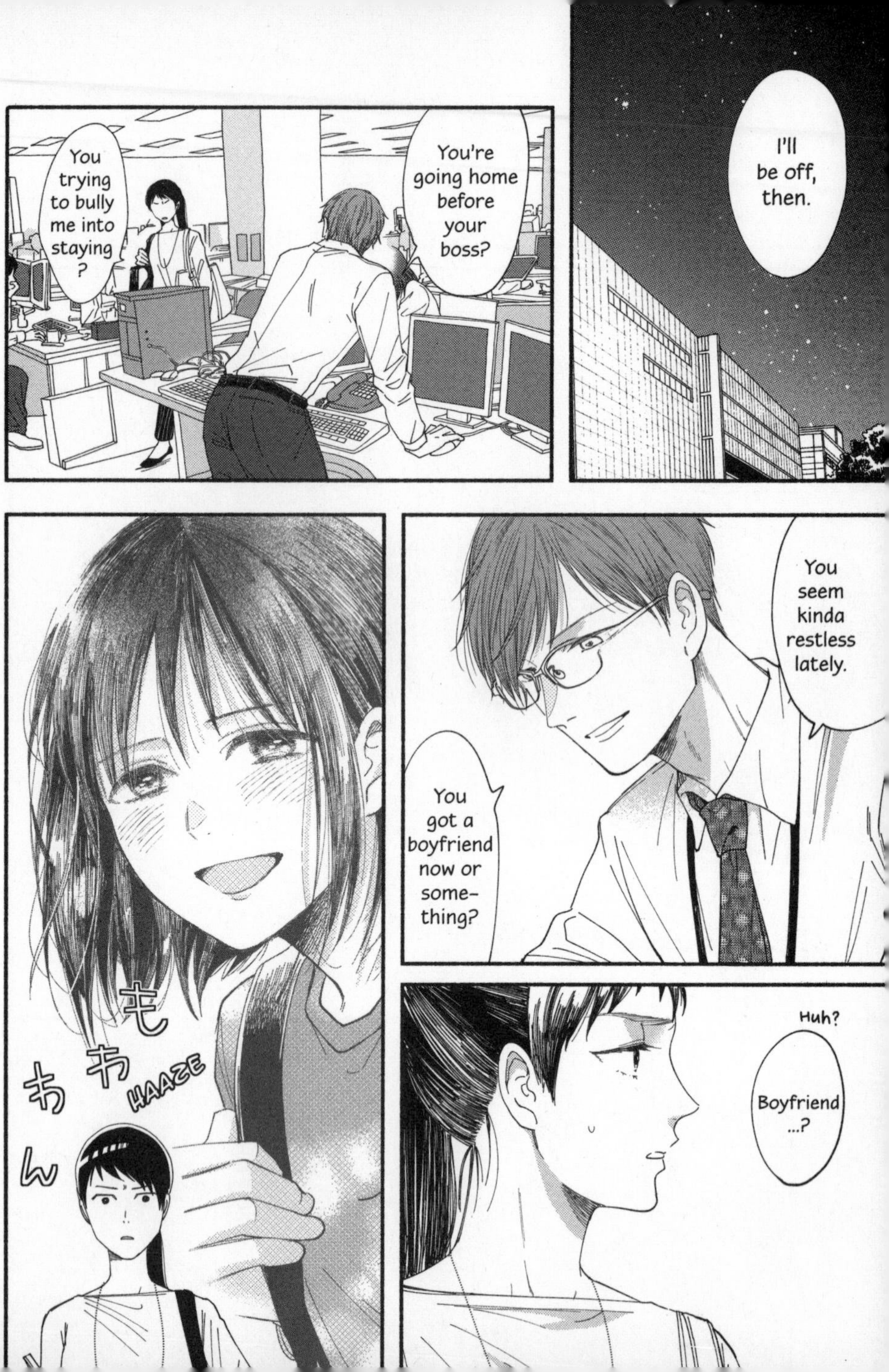
I'll be off, then.
You're going home before your boss?
You trying to bully me into staying?
You seem kinda restless lately.
You got a boyfriend now or something?
Huh?
Boyfriend ...?
HAAZE

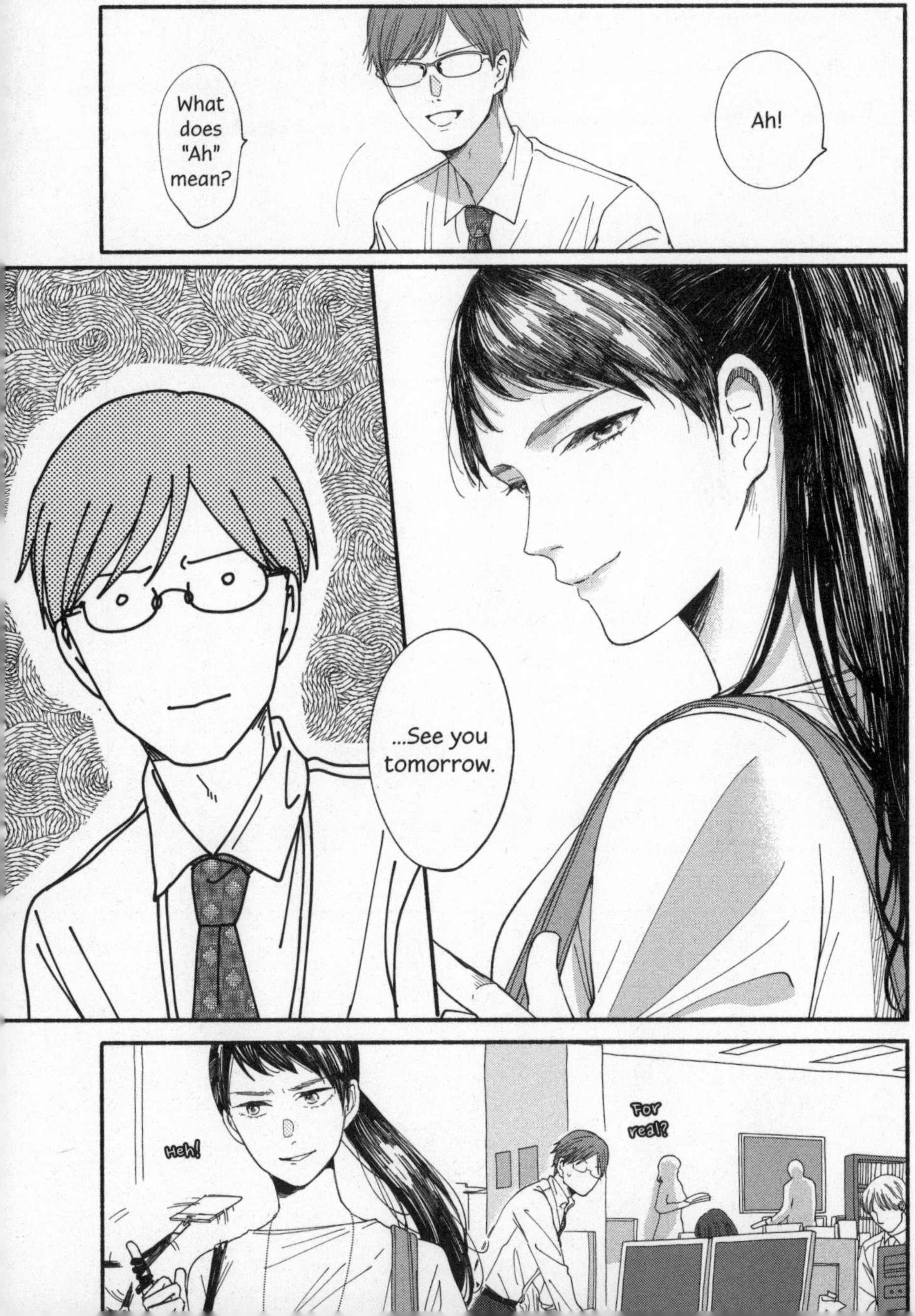
Ah!
What does "Ah" mean?
...See you tomorrow.
For real?
Heh!

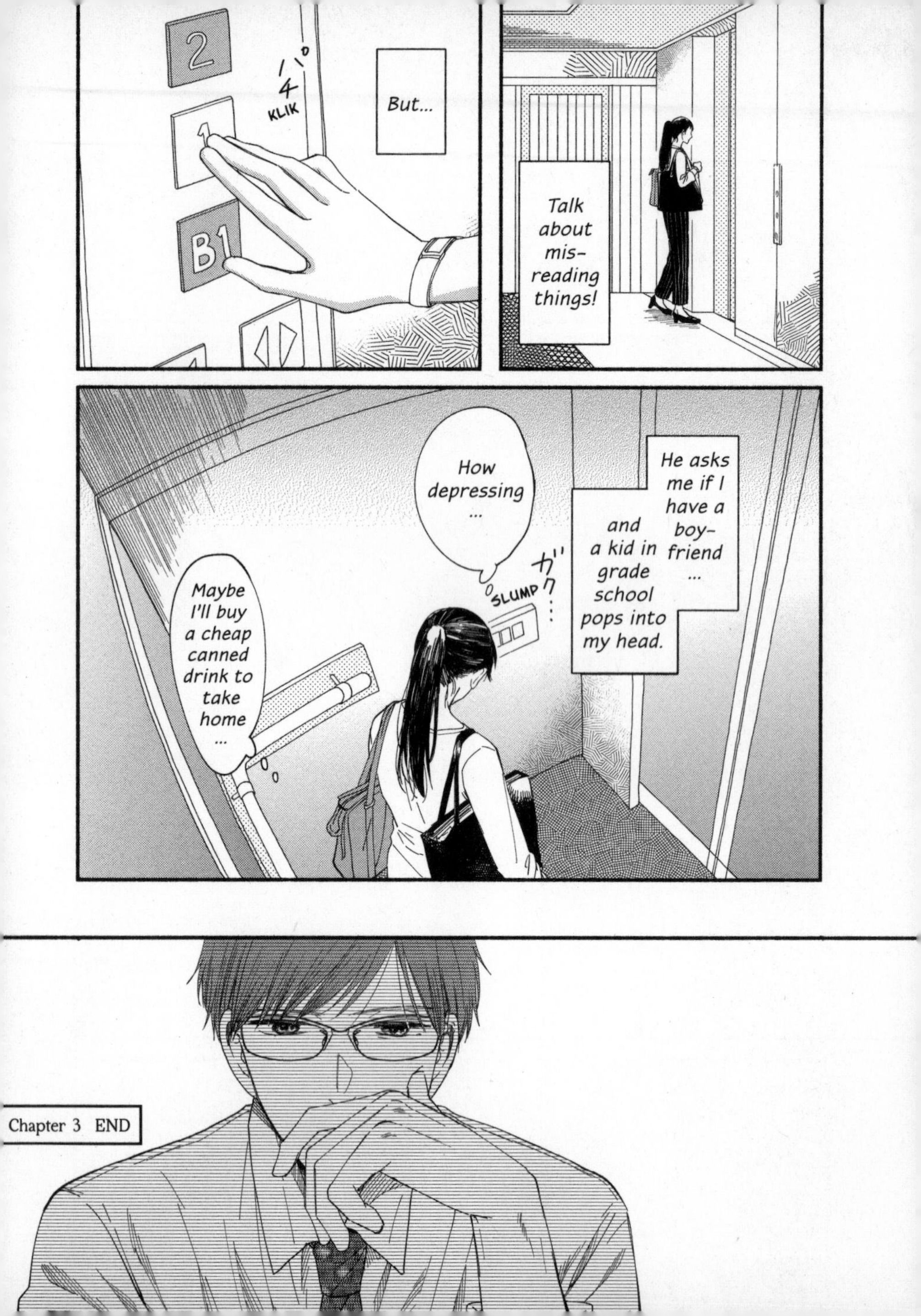
Talk about mis-reading things!
But...
KLIK
He asks me if I have a boy-friend...
and a kid in grade school pops into my head.
How depressing...
SLUMP
Maybe I'll buy a cheap canned drink to take home...
Chapter 3 END

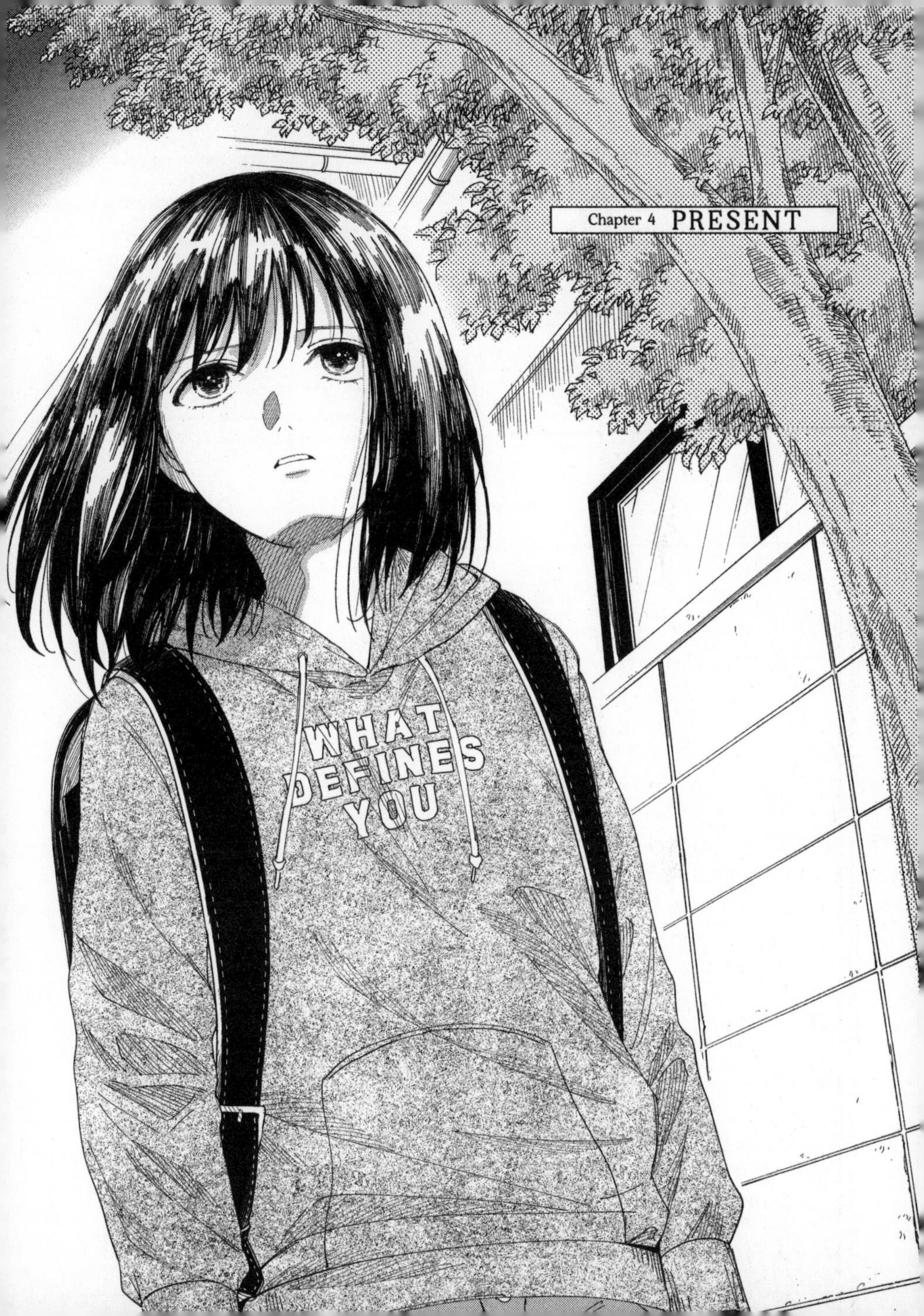
Chapter 4 PRESENT
WHAT DEFINES YOU

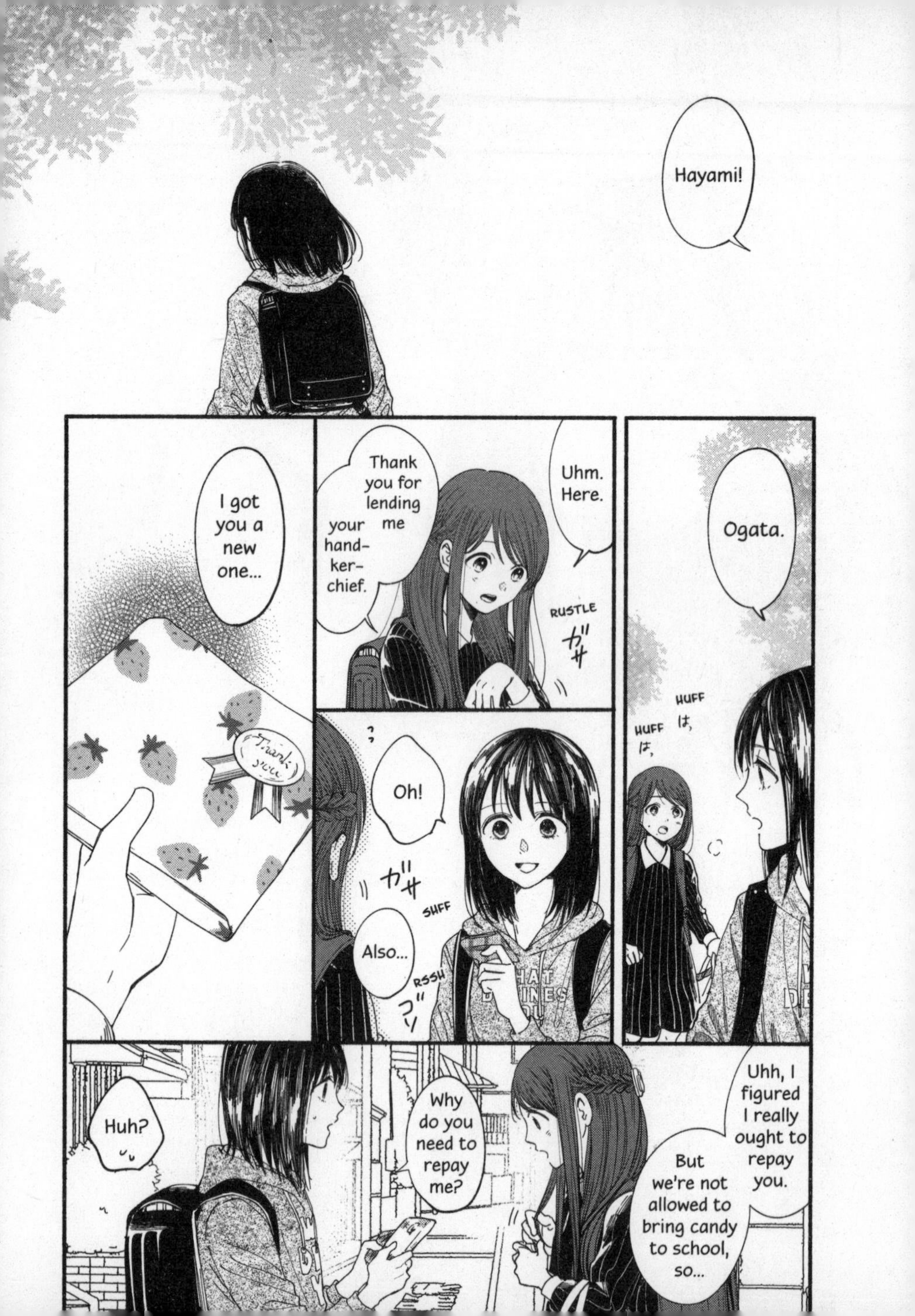
Hayami!
Ogata.
HUFF
は,
HUFF
は,
Uhm. Here.
Thank you for lending me your handkerchief.
RUSTLE
ガサ
Oh!
ガサ
SHFF
Also...
RSSH
ゴソ
I got you a new one...
Thank you
Uhh, I figured I really ought to repay you.
But we're not allowed to bring candy to school, so...
Why do you need to repay me?
Huh?

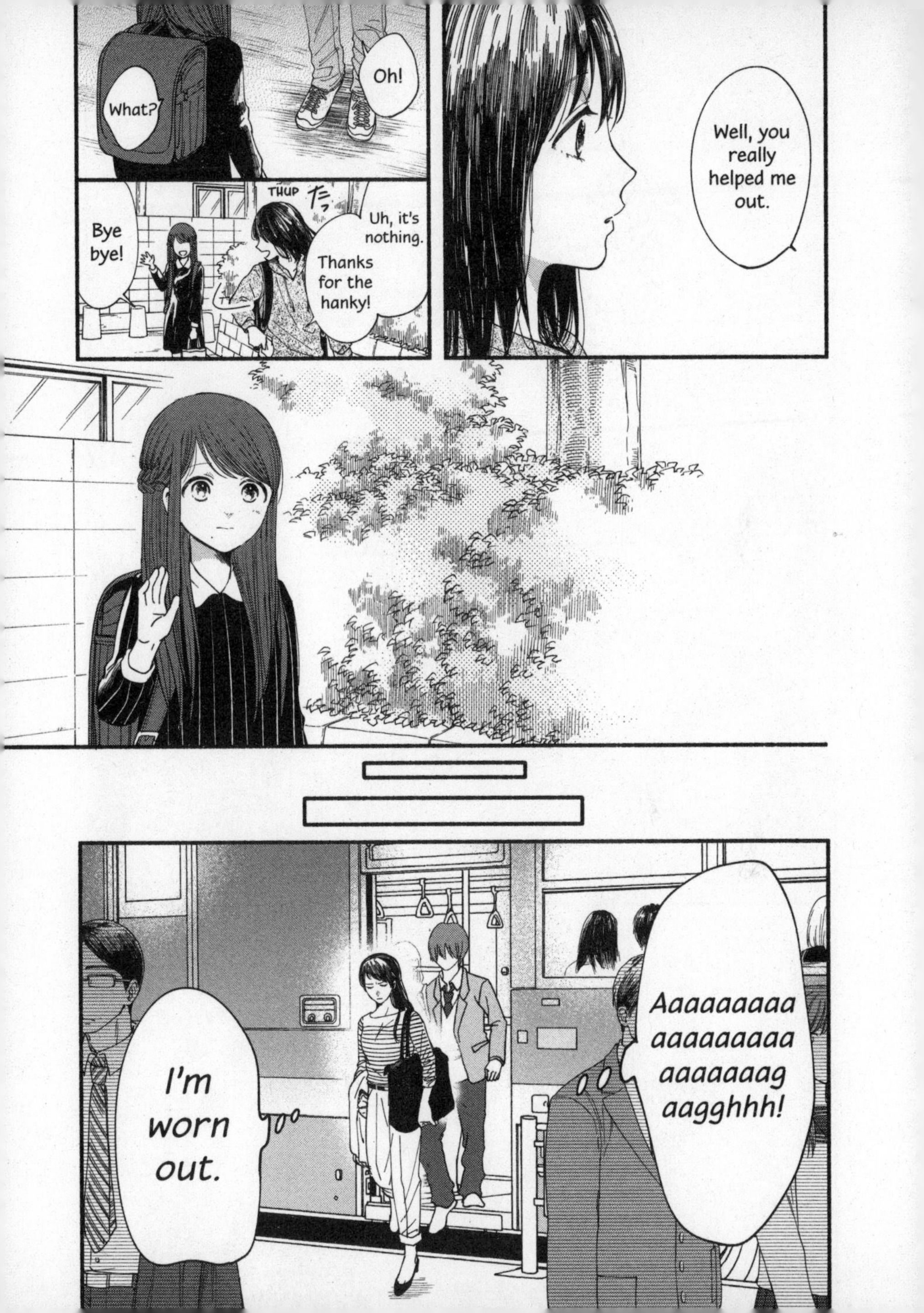
Well, you really helped me out.
Oh!
What?
THUP
Uh, it's nothing.
Thanks for the hanky!
Bye bye!
Aaaaaaaaaaaaaaaaaaaaaaaaaagaagghhh!
I'm worn out.

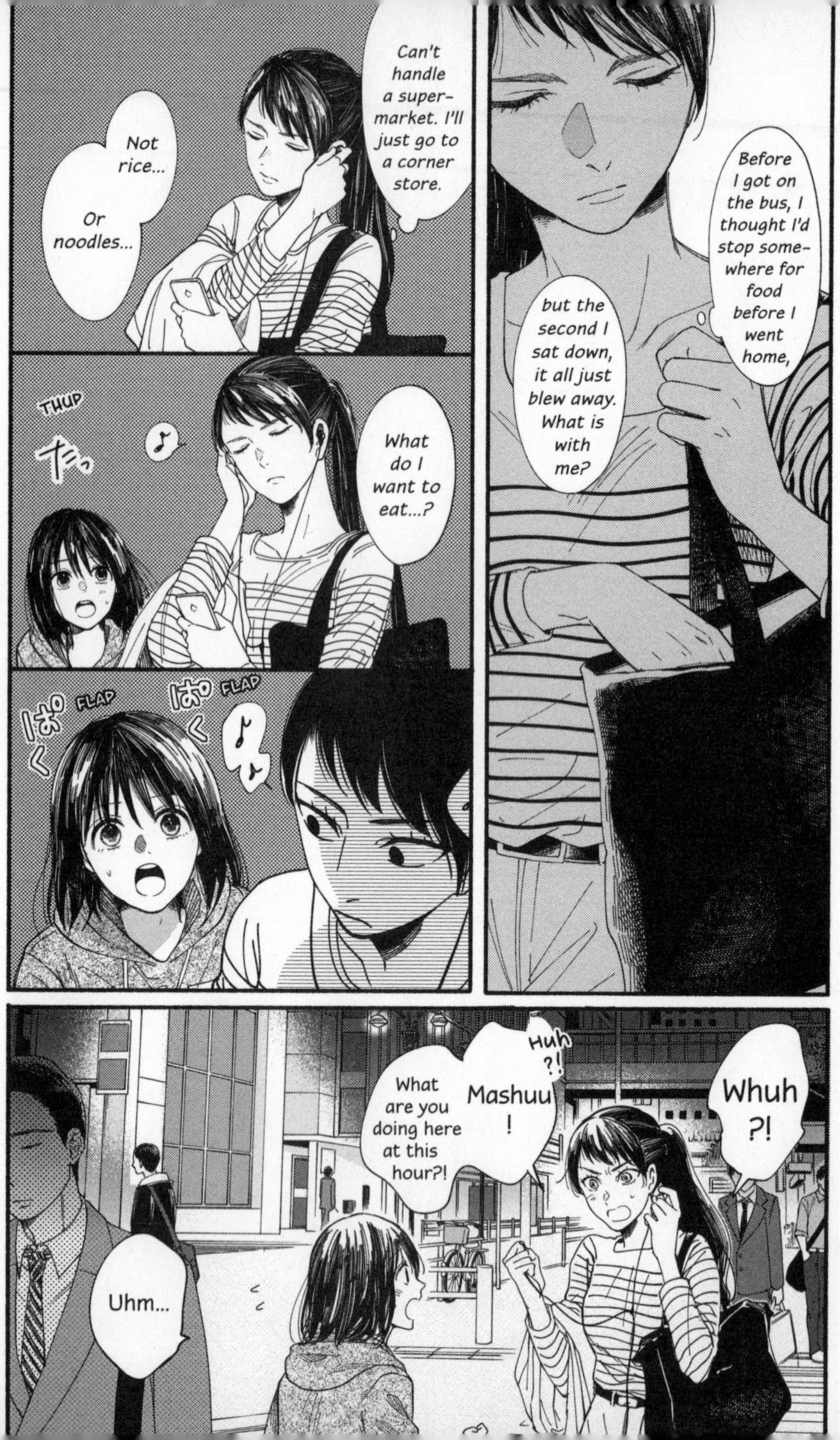
Before I got on the bus, I thought I'd stop somewhere for food before I went home,
but the second I sat down, it all just blew away. What is with me?
Can't handle a supermarket. I'll just go to a corner store.
Not rice...
Or noodles...
What do I want to eat...?
THUP
たっ
FLAP
ぱく
FLAP
ぱく
Whuh ?!
Huh ?!
Mashuu !
What are you doing here at this hour?!
Uhm...

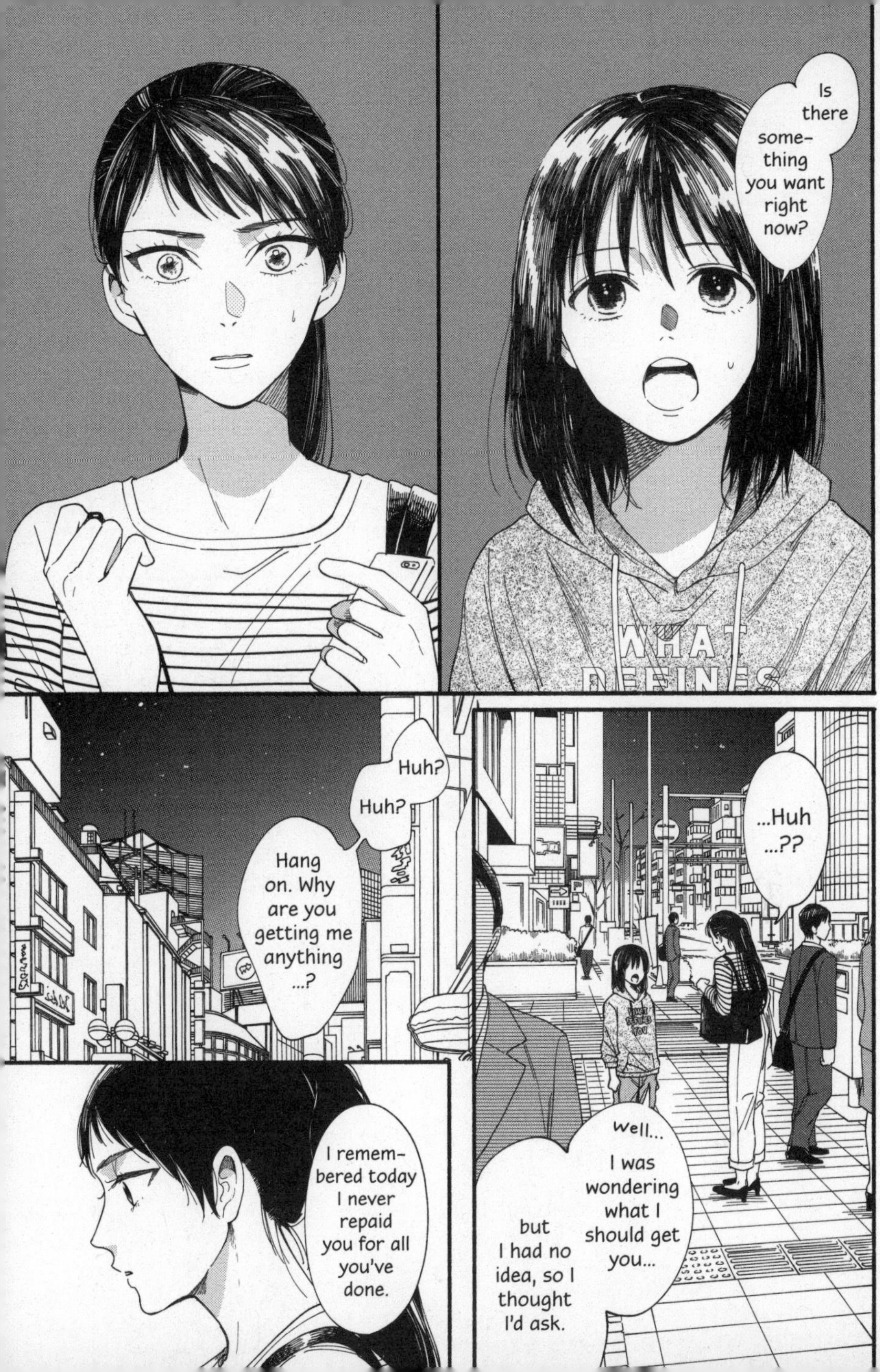
Is there some-thing you want right now?
WHAT DEFINES
...Huh ...??
Well...
I was wondering what I should get you...
but I had no idea, so I thought I'd ask.
Huh?
Huh?
Hang on. Why are you getting me anything ...?
I remem-bered today I never repaid you for all you've done.

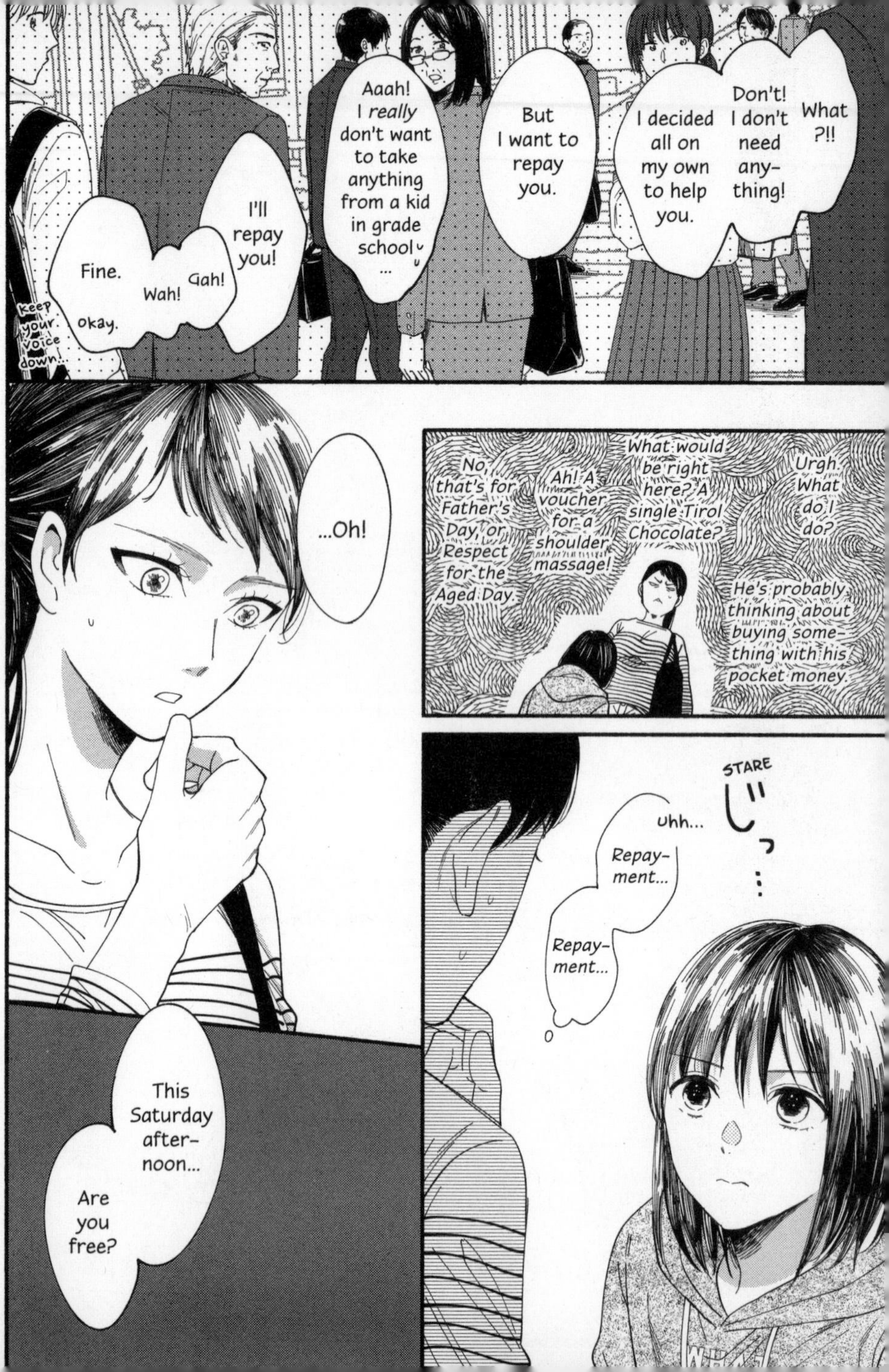
What?!!
Don't! I don't need any-thing!
I decided all on my own to help you.
But I want to repay you.
Aaah! I *really* don't want to take anything from a kid in grade school...
I'll repay you!
Gah!
Wah!
Fine. okay.
keep your voice down...
Urgh. What do I do?
He's probably thinking about buying some-thing with his pocket money.
What would be right here? A single Tirol Chocolate?
Ah! A voucher for a shoulder massage!
No, that's for Father's Day, or Respect for the Aged Day.
STARE
じっ…
uhh...
Repay-ment...
Repay-ment...
...Oh!
This Saturday after-noon...
Are you free?

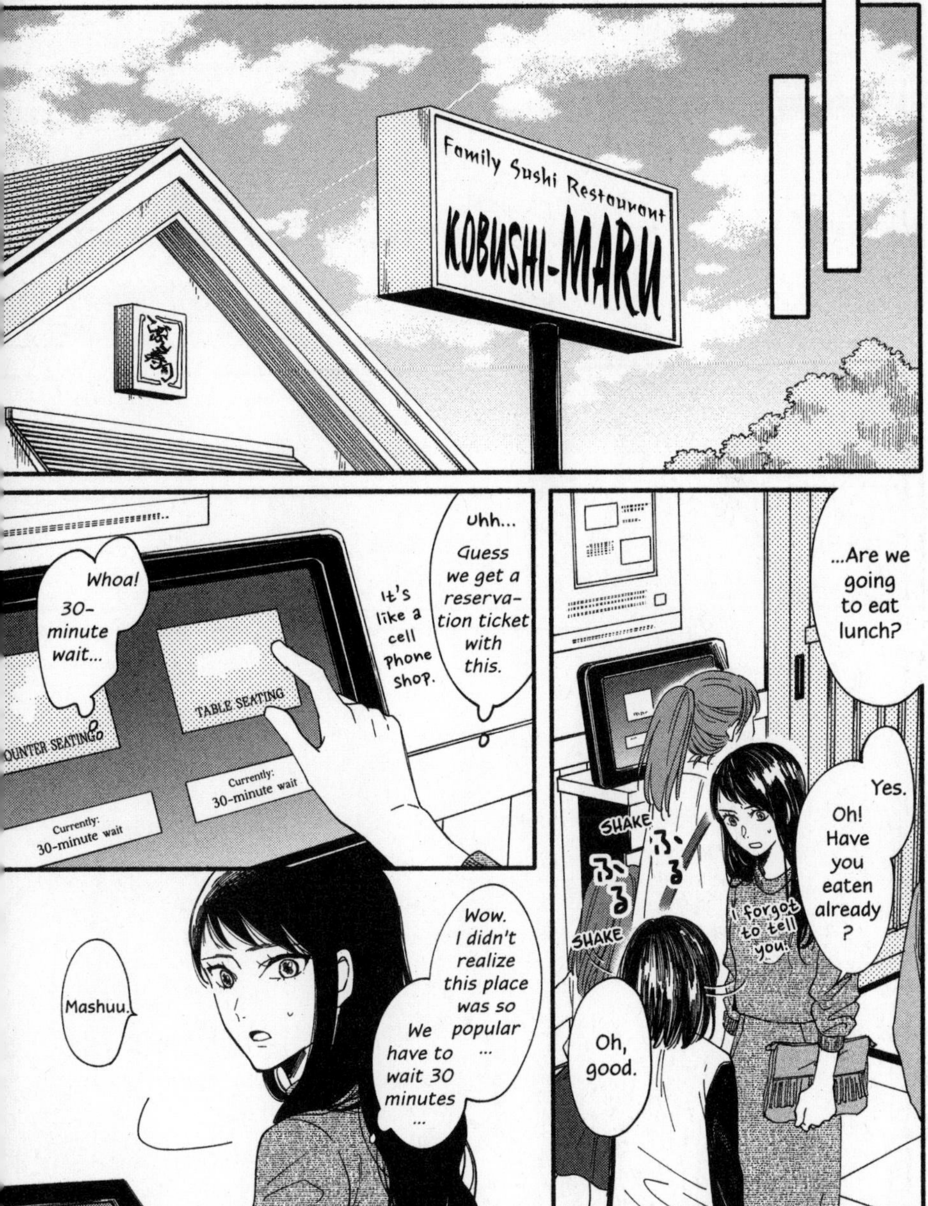
Family Sushi Restaurant
KOBUSHI-MARU
...Are we going to eat lunch?
Yes. Oh! Have you eaten already?
SHAKE
ふる
ふる
SHAKE
I forgot to tell you!
Oh, good.
Uhh... Guess we get a reservation ticket with this.
It's like a cell phone shop.
TABLE SEATING
Currently: 30-minute wait
Whoa! 30-minute wait...
COUNTER SEATING
Currently: 30-minute wait
Wow. I didn't realize this place was so popular...
We have to wait 30 minutes...
Mashuu.

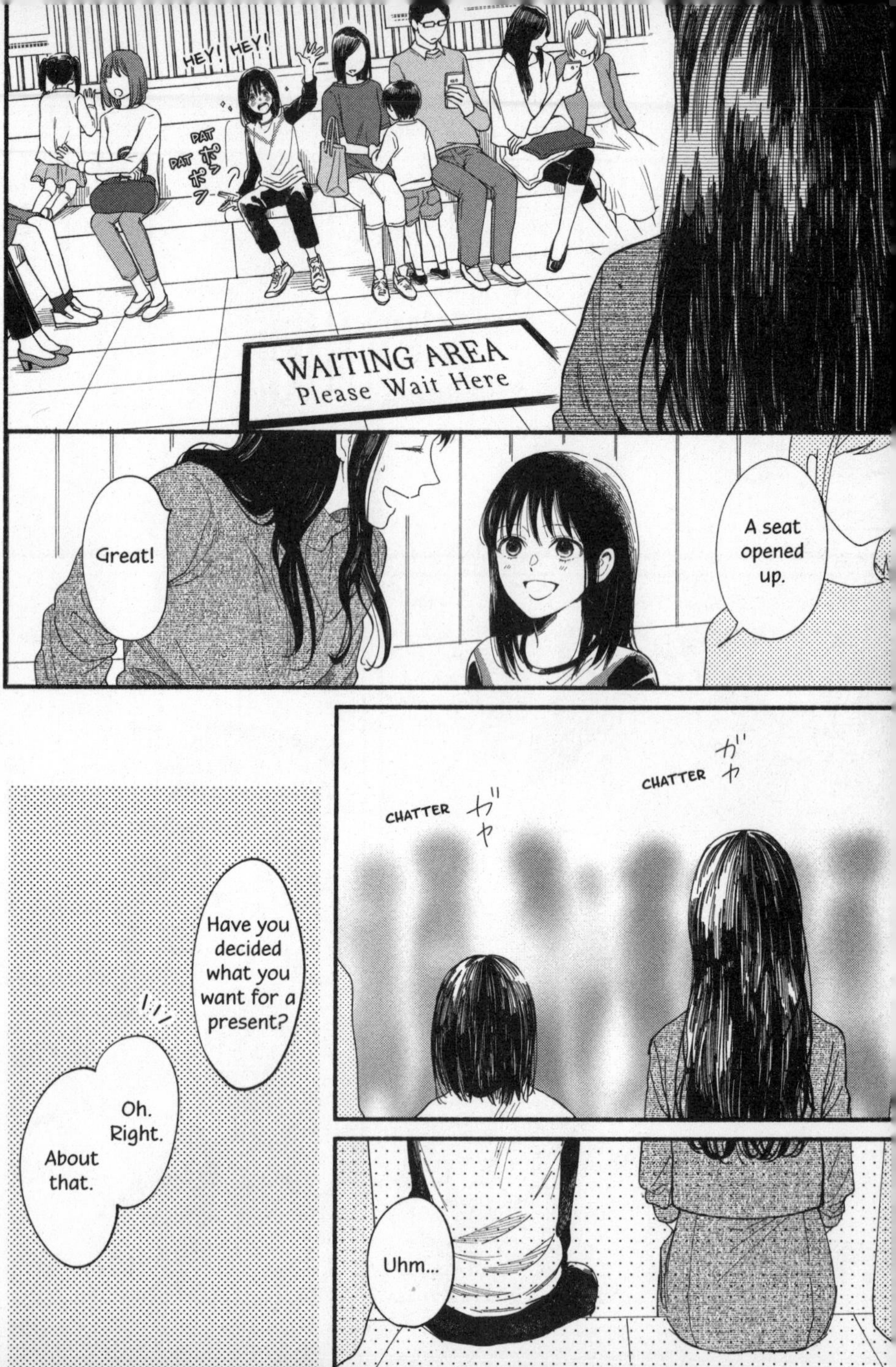
HEY! HEY!
PAT PAT
ポンポン
WAITING AREA
Please Wait Here
A seat opened up.
Great!
CHATTER
ガヤ
CHATTER
ガヤ
Uhm...
Have you decided what you want for a present?
!!!
Oh. Right. About that.

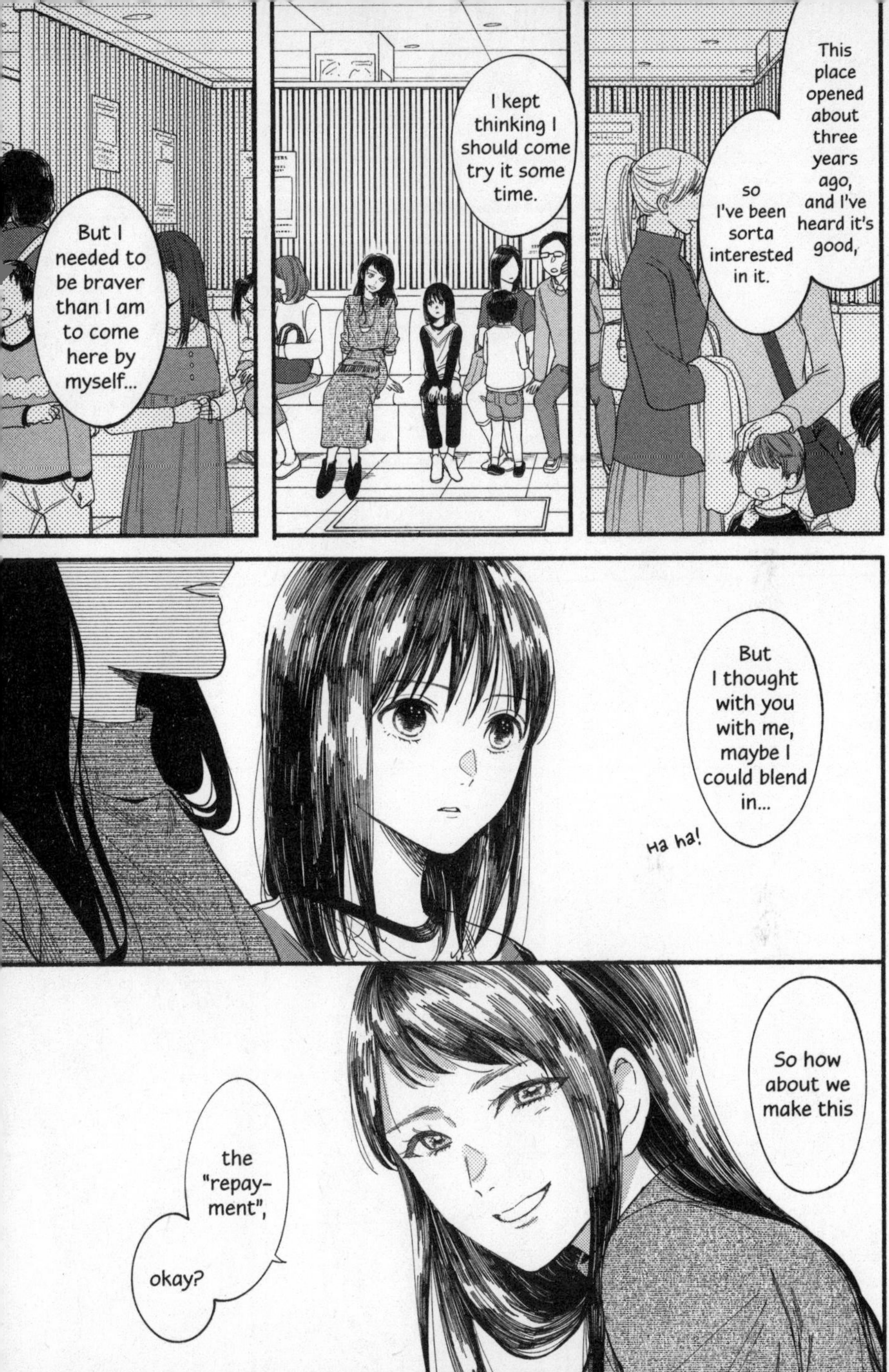
This place opened about three years ago, and I've heard it's good,
so I've been sorta interested in it.
I kept thinking I should come try it some time.
But I needed to be braver than I am to come here by myself...
But I thought with you with me, maybe I could blend in...
Ha ha!
So how about we make this
the "repayment",
okay?

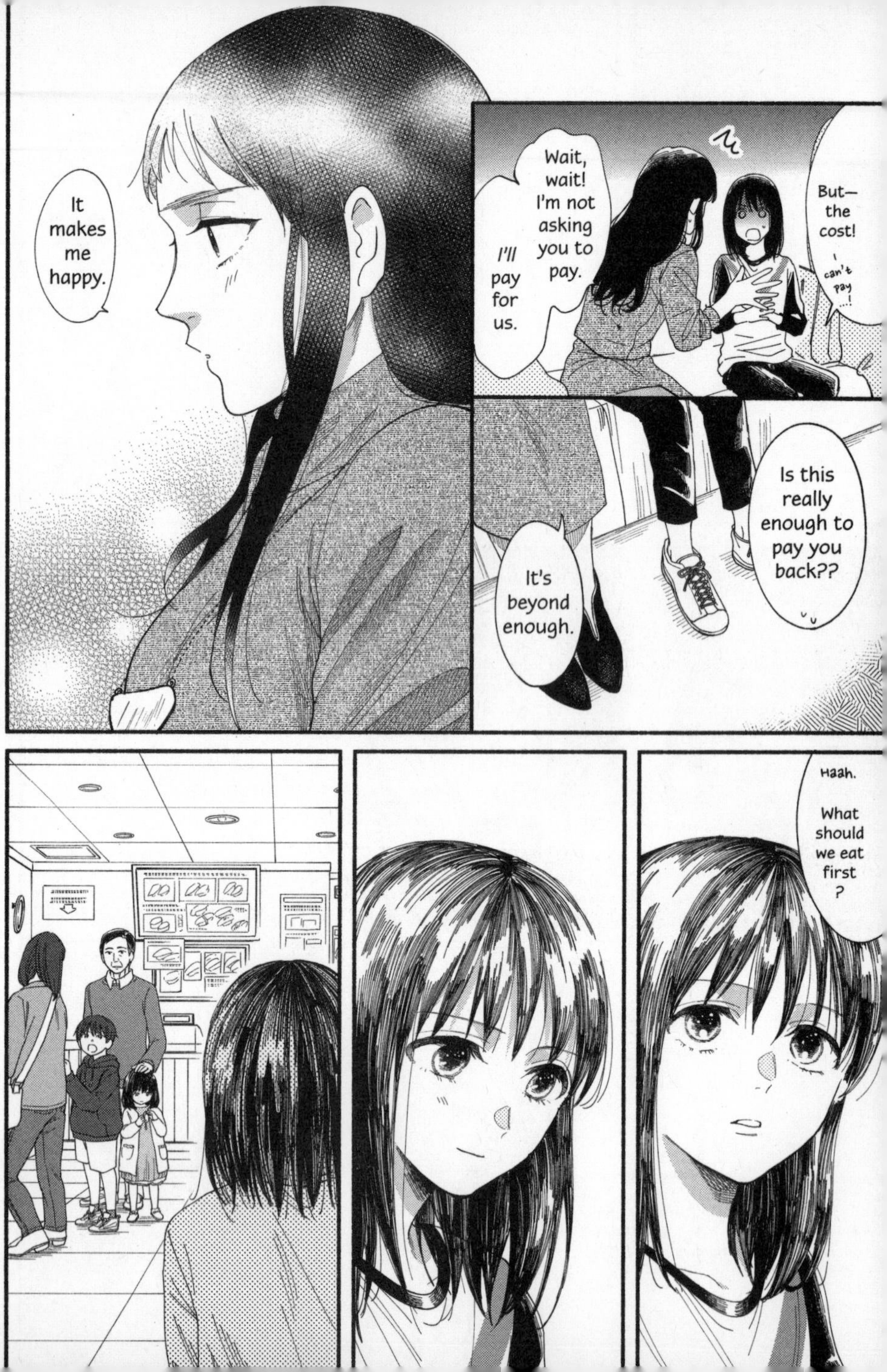
But— the cost!
I can't pay...!
Wait, wait! I'm not asking you to pay.
I'll pay for us.
Is this really enough to pay you back??
It's beyond enough.
It makes me happy.
Haah.
What should we eat first?

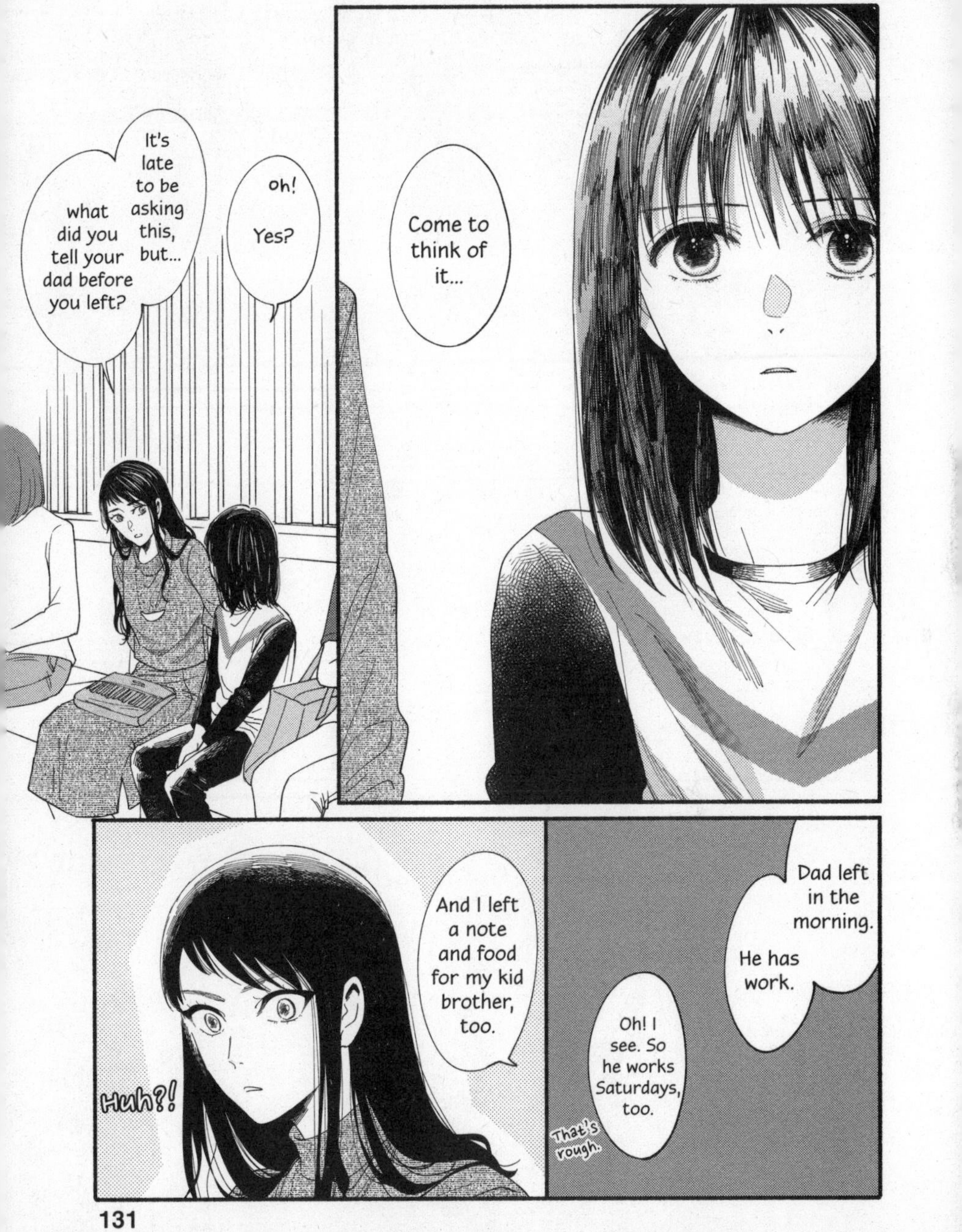
Come to think of it...
oh! Yes?
It's late to be asking this, but... what did you tell your dad before you left?
Dad left in the morning. He has work.
Oh! I see. So he works Saturdays, too.
That's rough.
And I left a note and food for my kid brother, too.
Huh?!

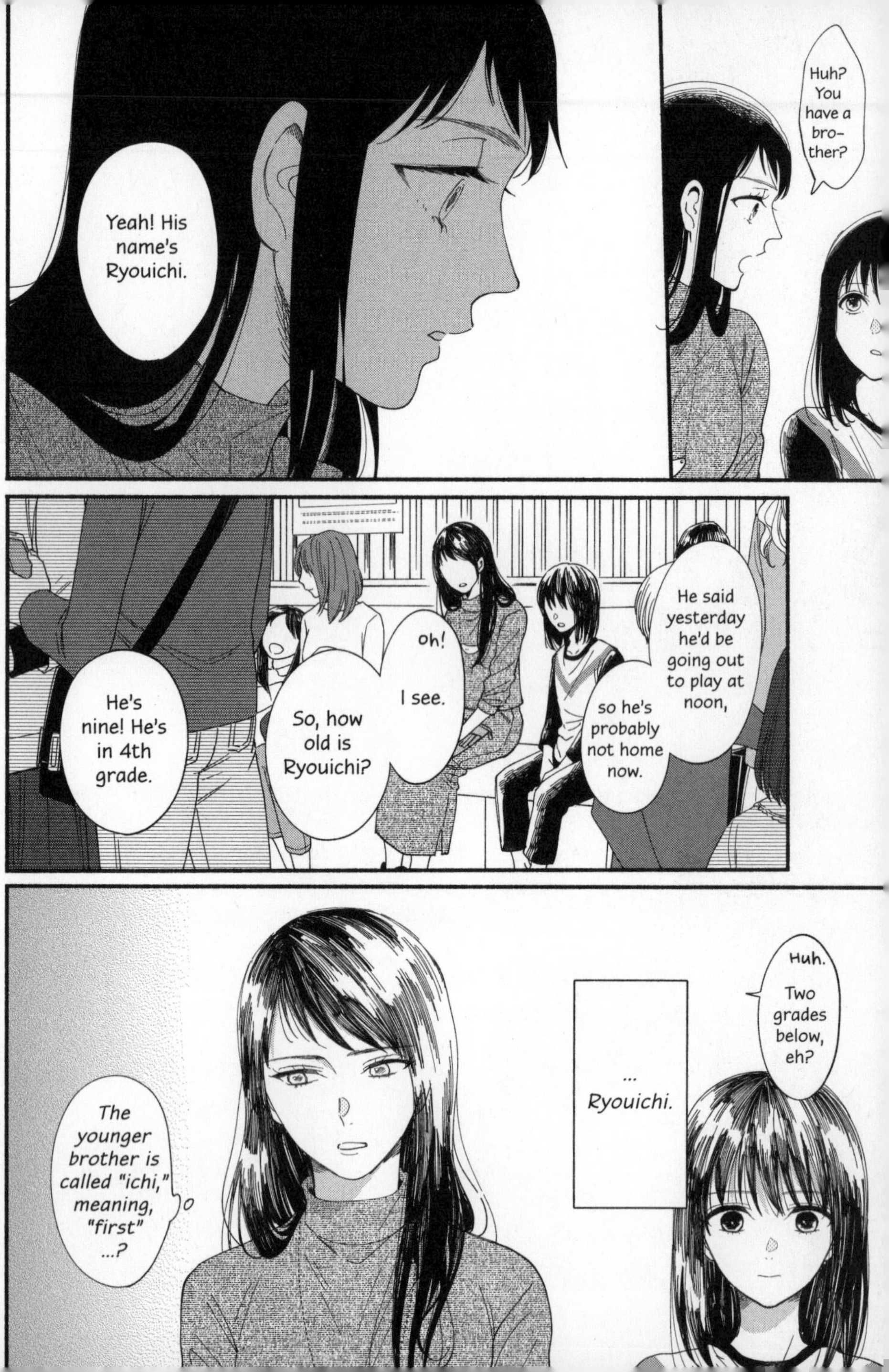
Huh? You have a brother?
Yeah! His name's Ryouichi.
He said yesterday he'd be going out to play at noon,
so he's probably not home now.
Oh! I see.
So, how old is Ryouichi?
He's nine! He's in 4th grade.
Huh. Two grades below, eh?
... Ryouichi.
The younger brother is called "ichi," meaning, "first" ...?

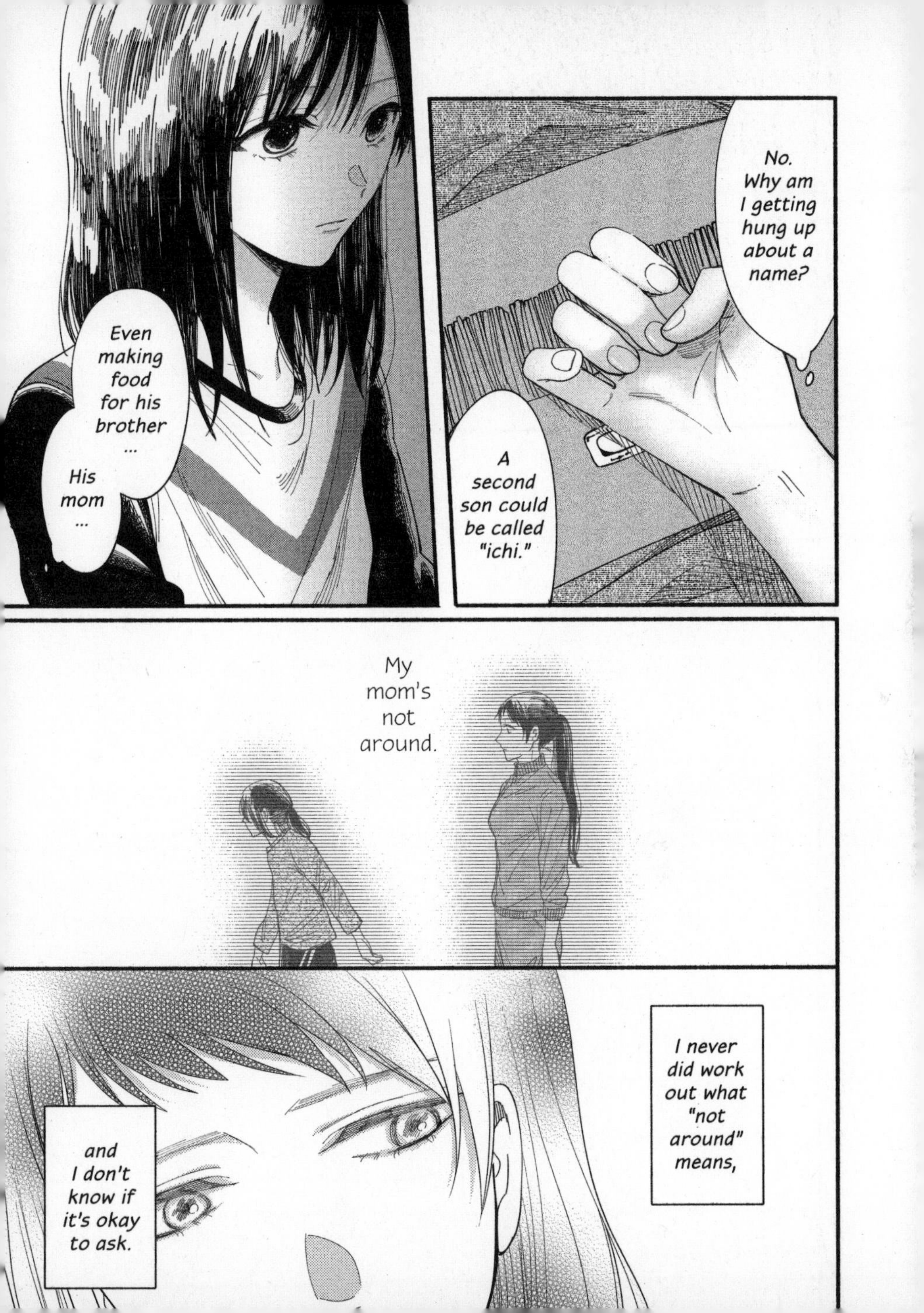
No. Why am I getting hung up about a name?
A second son could be called "ichi."
Even making food for his brother ...
His mom ...
My mom's not around.
I never did work out what "not around" means,
and I don't know if it's okay to ask.

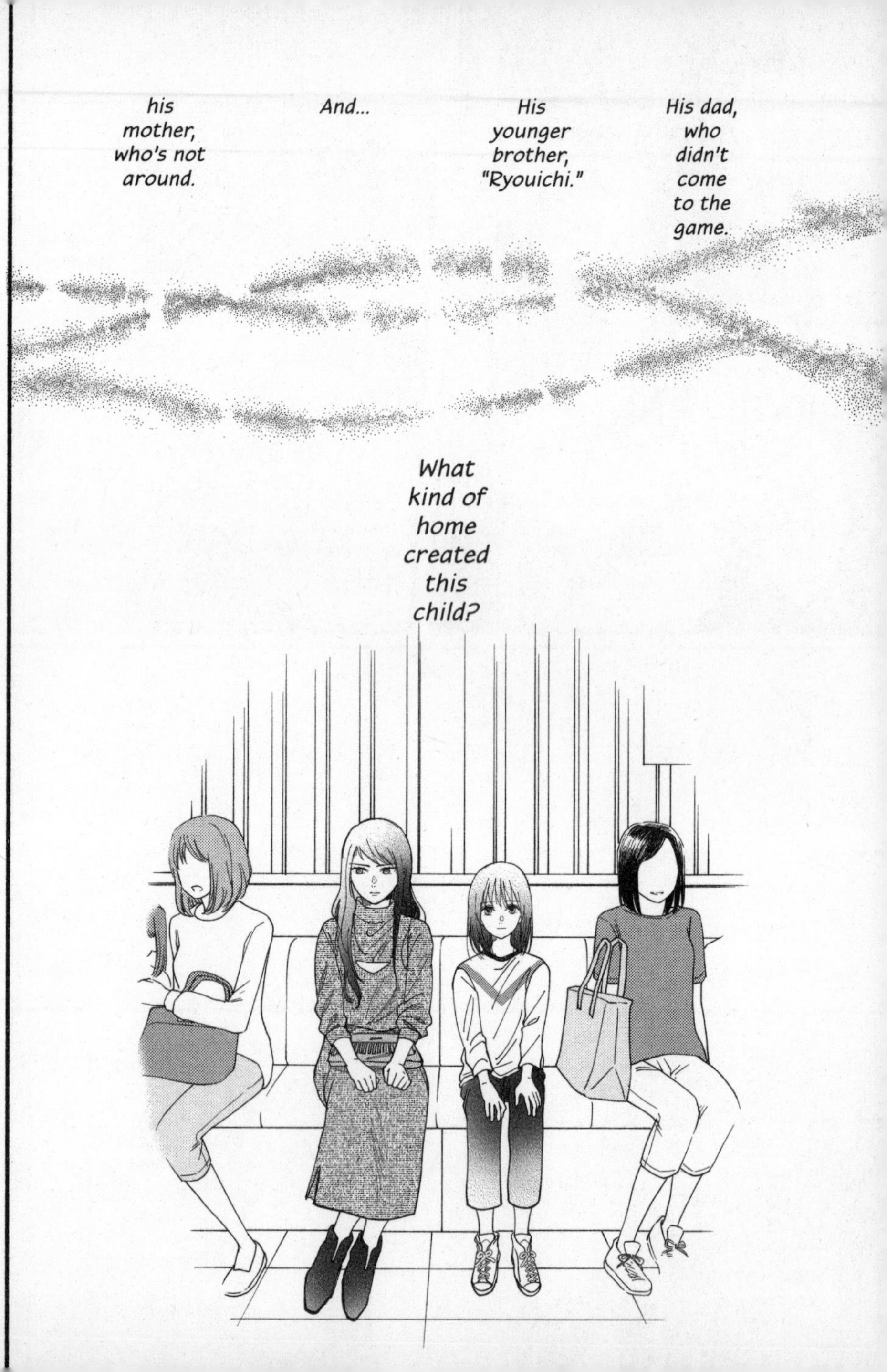
His dad, who didn't come to the game.
His younger brother, "Ryouichi."
And...
his mother, who's not around.
What kind of home created this child?

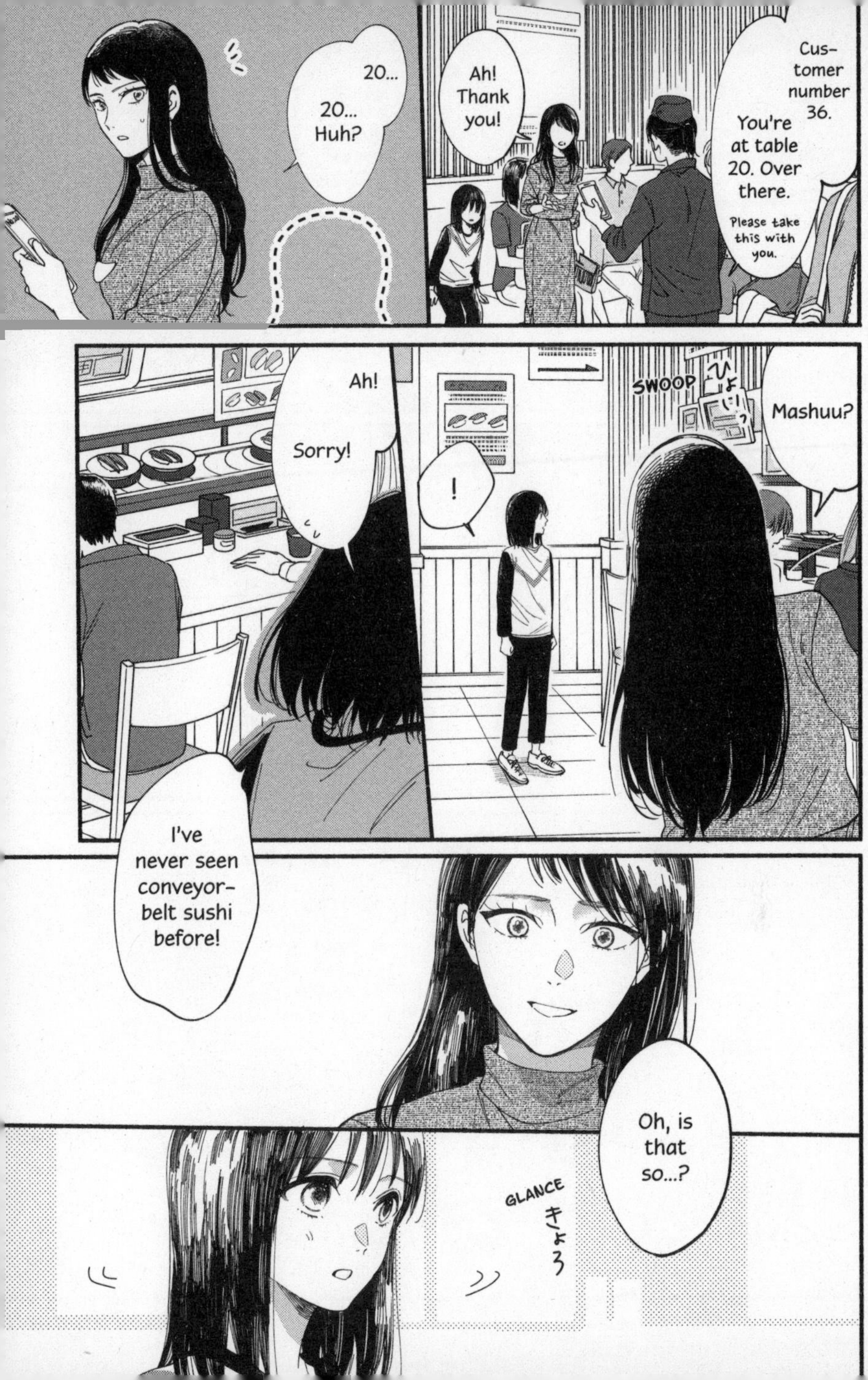
Cus-tomer number 36.
You're at table 20. Over there.
Please take this with you.
Ah! Thank you!
20...
20... Huh?
Mashuu?
SWOOP
ひょい?
!
Ah!
Sorry!
I've never seen conveyor-belt sushi before!
Oh, is that so...?
GLANCE
きょろ

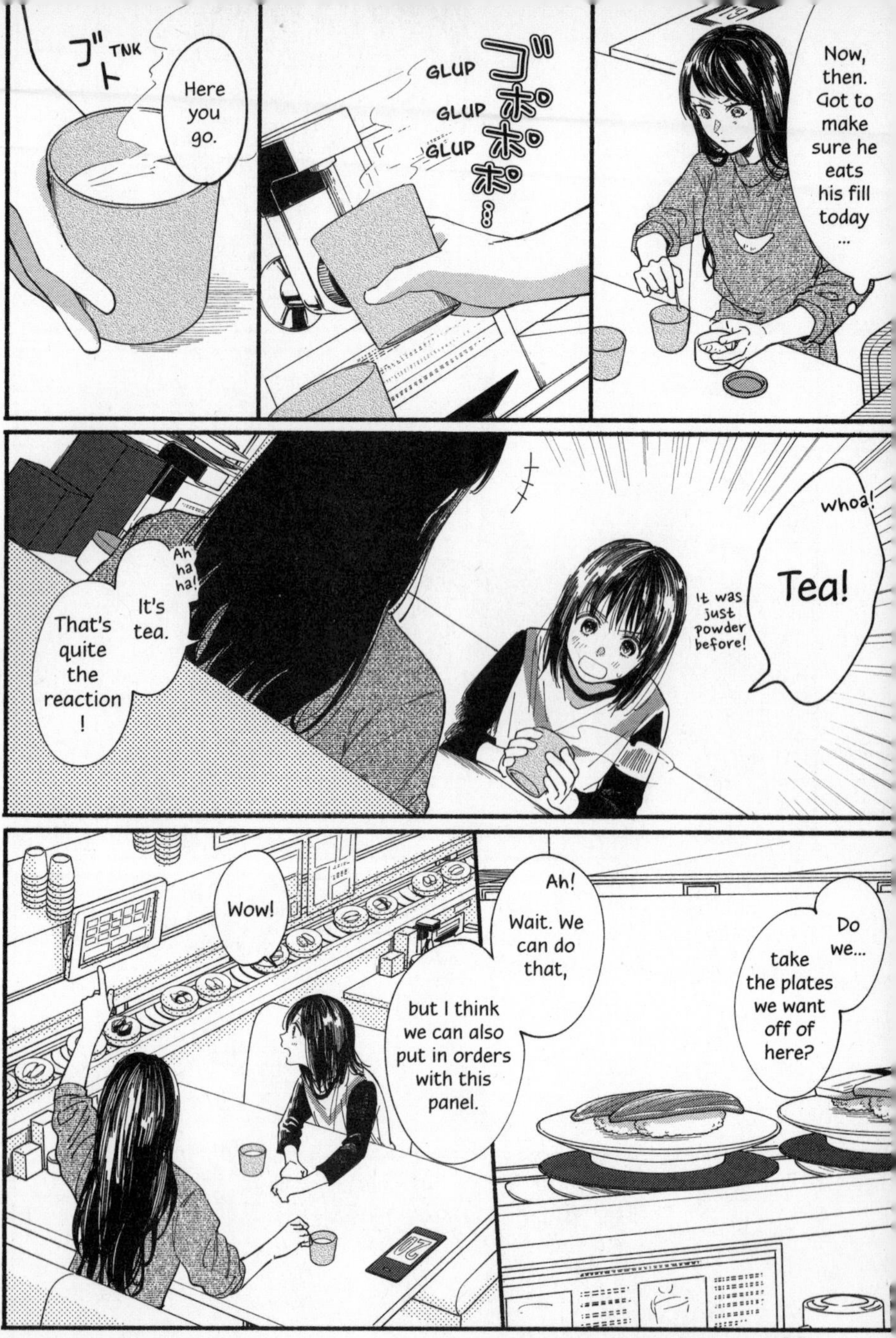
Now, then. Got to make sure he eats his fill today ...
ゴポポポ…
GLUP GLUP GLUP
ゴト
TNK
Here you go.
Tea!
whoa!
It was just powder before!
Ah ha ha!
It's tea.
That's quite the reaction!
Do we... take the plates we want off of here?
Ah!
Wait. We can do that,
but I think we can also put in orders with this panel.
Wow!

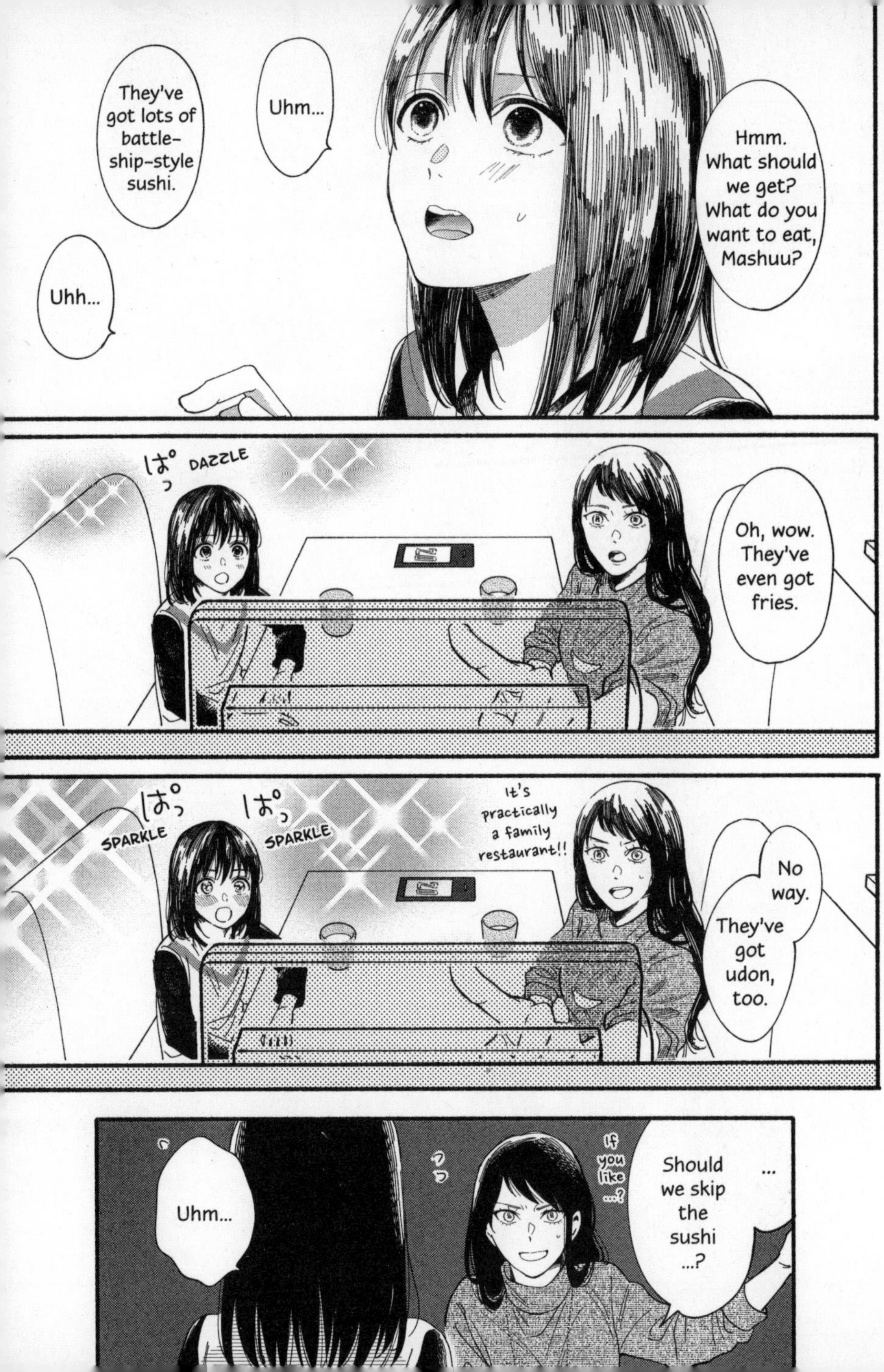
Hmm. What should we get? What do you want to eat, Mashuu?
Uhm...
They've got lots of battle-ship-style sushi.
Uhh...
Oh, wow. They've even got fries.
ぱっ DAZZLE
No way. They've got udon, too.
It's practically a family restaurant!!
ぱっ SPARKLE
ぱっ SPARKLE
...
Should we skip the sushi ...?
If you like ...?
Uhm...

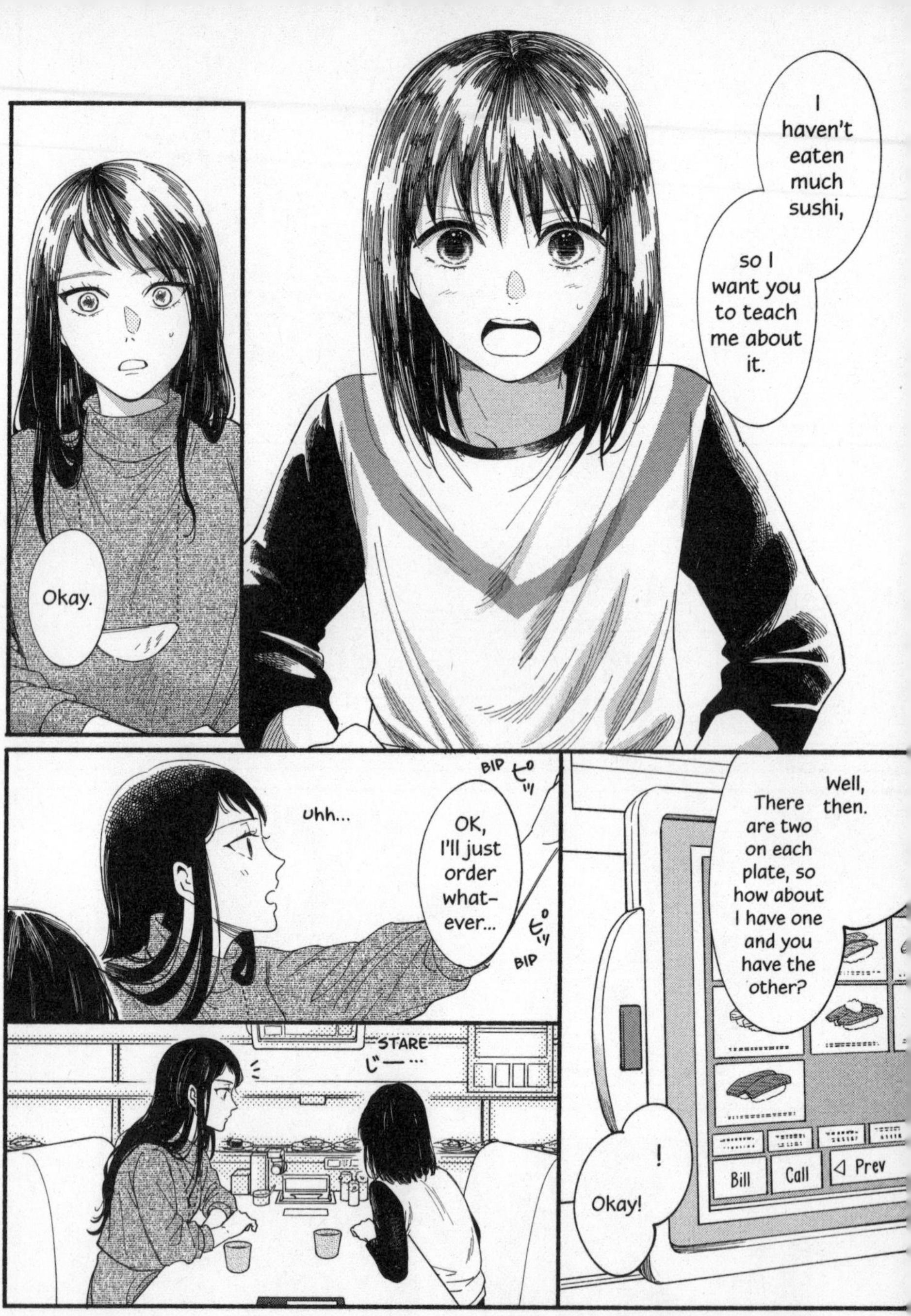
I haven't eaten much sushi,
so I want you to teach me about it.
Okay.
Well, then.
There are two on each plate, so how about I have one and you have the other?
Bill
Call
◁ Prev
!
Okay!
BIP ピッ
OK, I'll just order whatever...
uhh...
ピッ BIP
STARE じー…

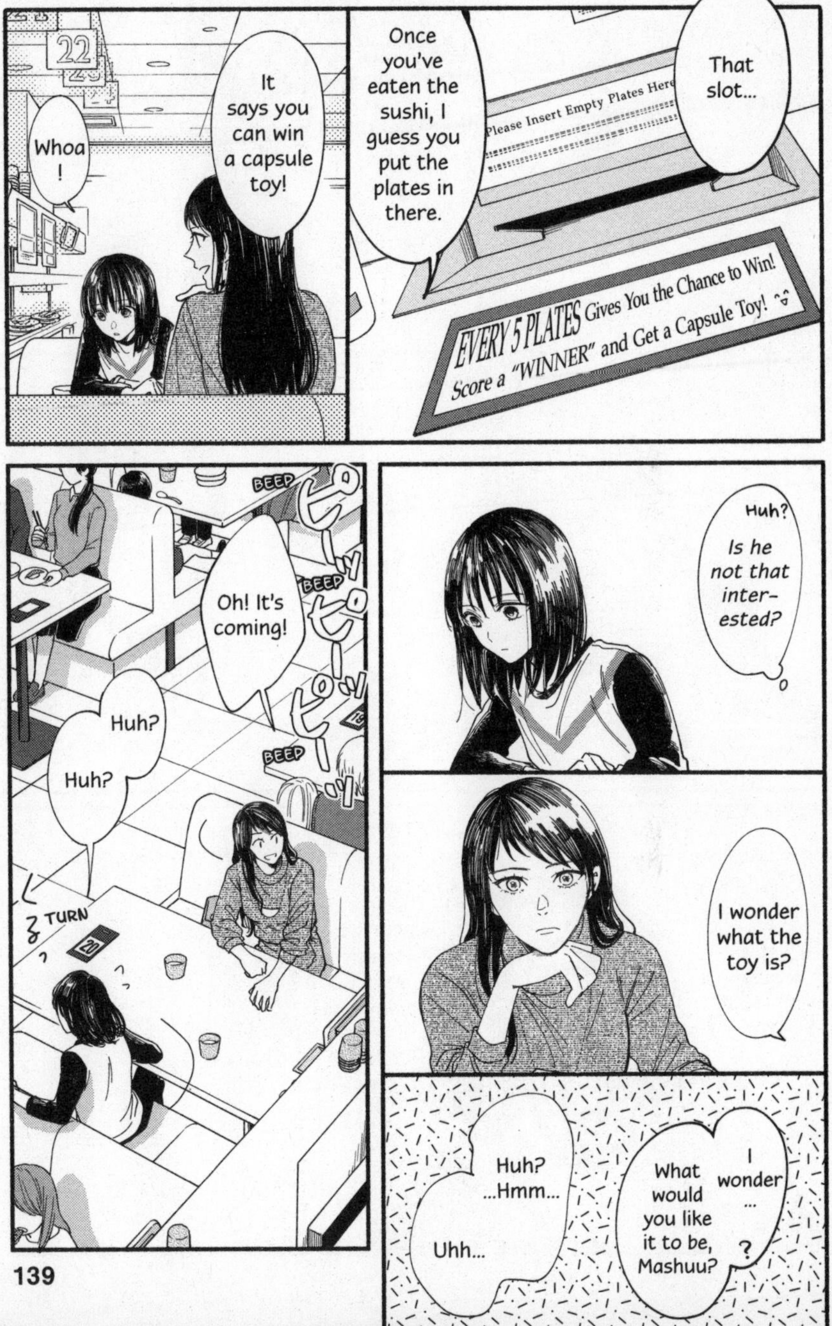
That slot...
Once you've eaten the sushi, I guess you put the plates in there.
Please Insert Empty Plates Here
EVERY 5 PLATES Gives You the Chance to Win!
Score a "WINNER" and Get a Capsule Toy!
It says you can win a capsule toy!
Whoa!
Huh? Is he not that inter-ested?
I wonder what the toy is?
I wonder...?
What would you like it to be, Mashuu?
Huh? ...Hmm...
Uhh...
BEEP
BEEP
Oh! It's coming!
BEEP
Huh?
Huh?
TURN

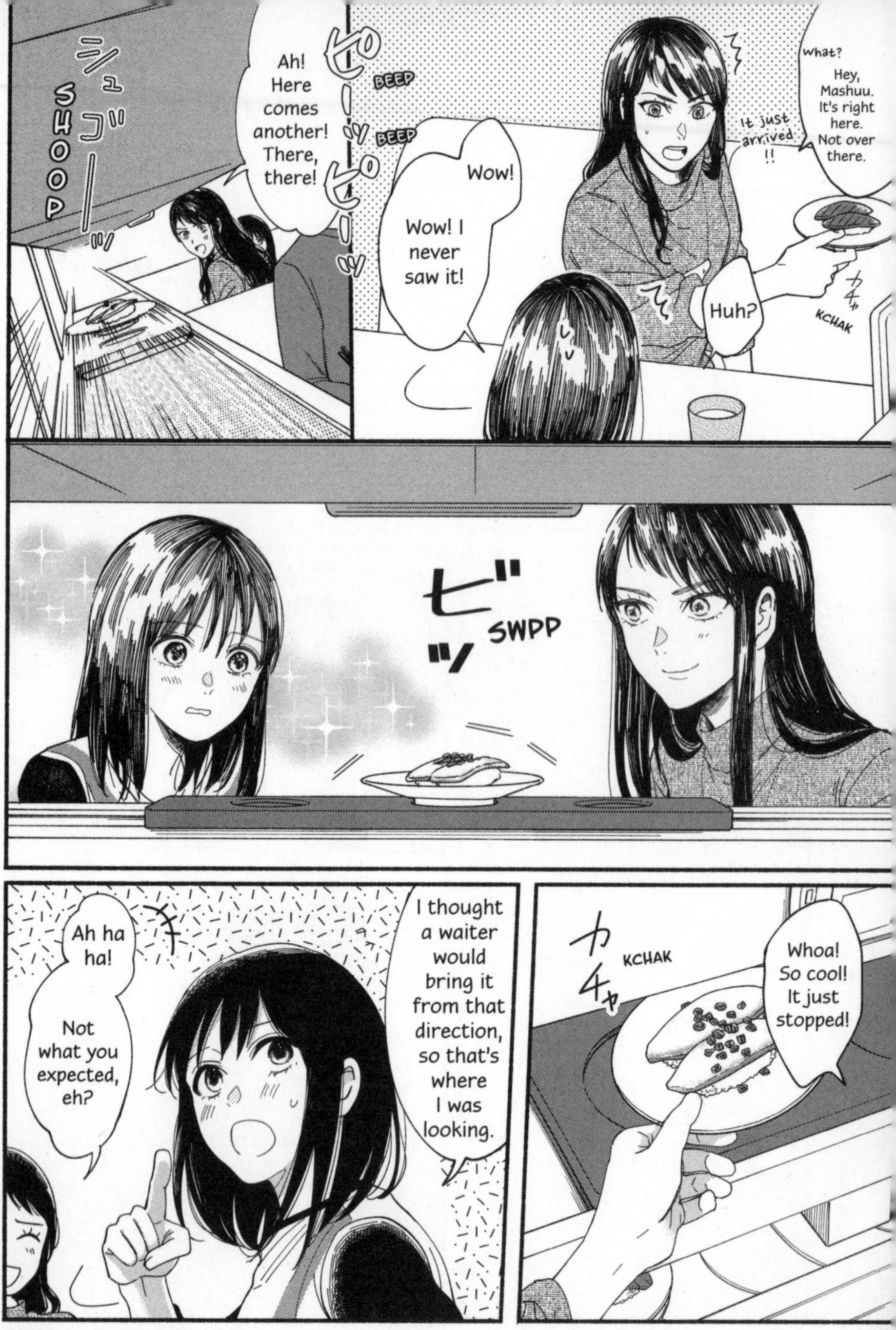
what?
Hey, Mashuu. It's right here. Not over there.
It just arrived !!
Huh?
KCHAK
Wow!
Wow! I never saw it!
BEEP
BEEP
Ah! Here comes another! There, there!
SHOOP
SWPP
KCHAK
Whoa! So cool! It just stopped!
I thought a waiter would bring it from that direction, so that's where I was looking.
Ah ha ha!
Not what you expected, eh?

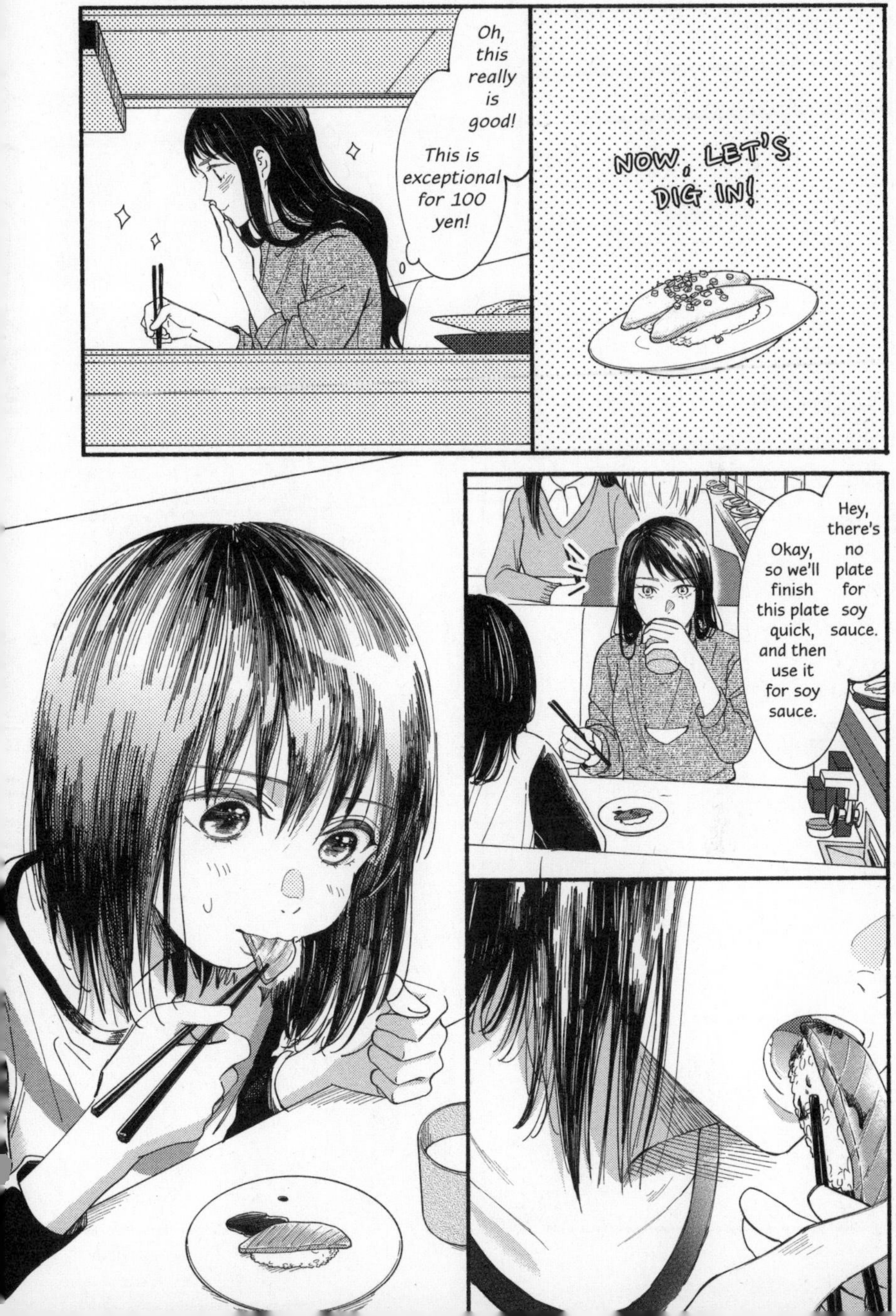
NOW, LET'S DIG IN!
Oh, this really is good!
This is exceptional for 100 yen!
Hey, there's no plate for soy sauce.
Okay, so we'll finish this plate quick, and then use it for soy sauce.

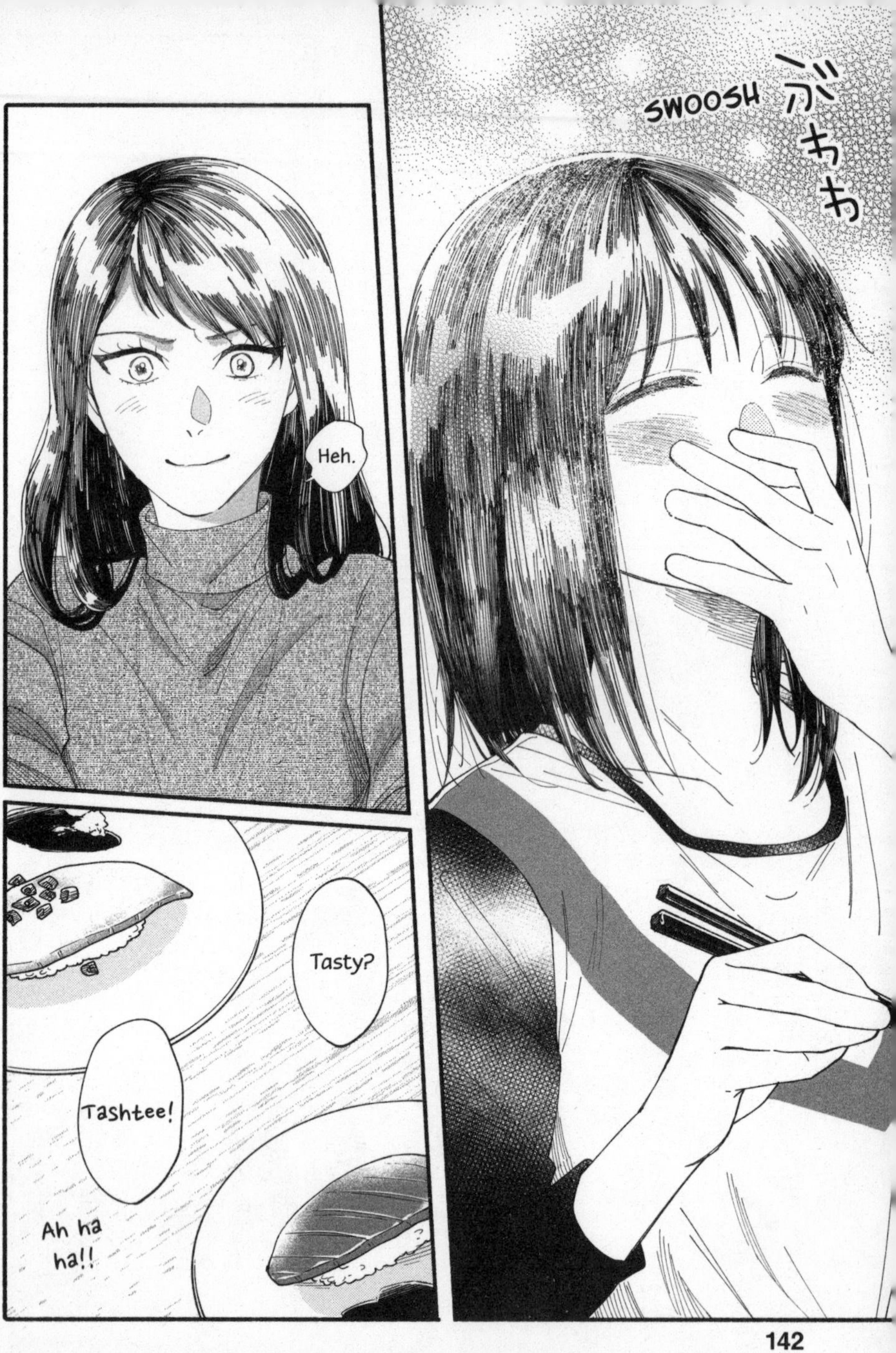
SWOOSH
Heh.
Tasty?
Tashtee!
Ah ha ha!!

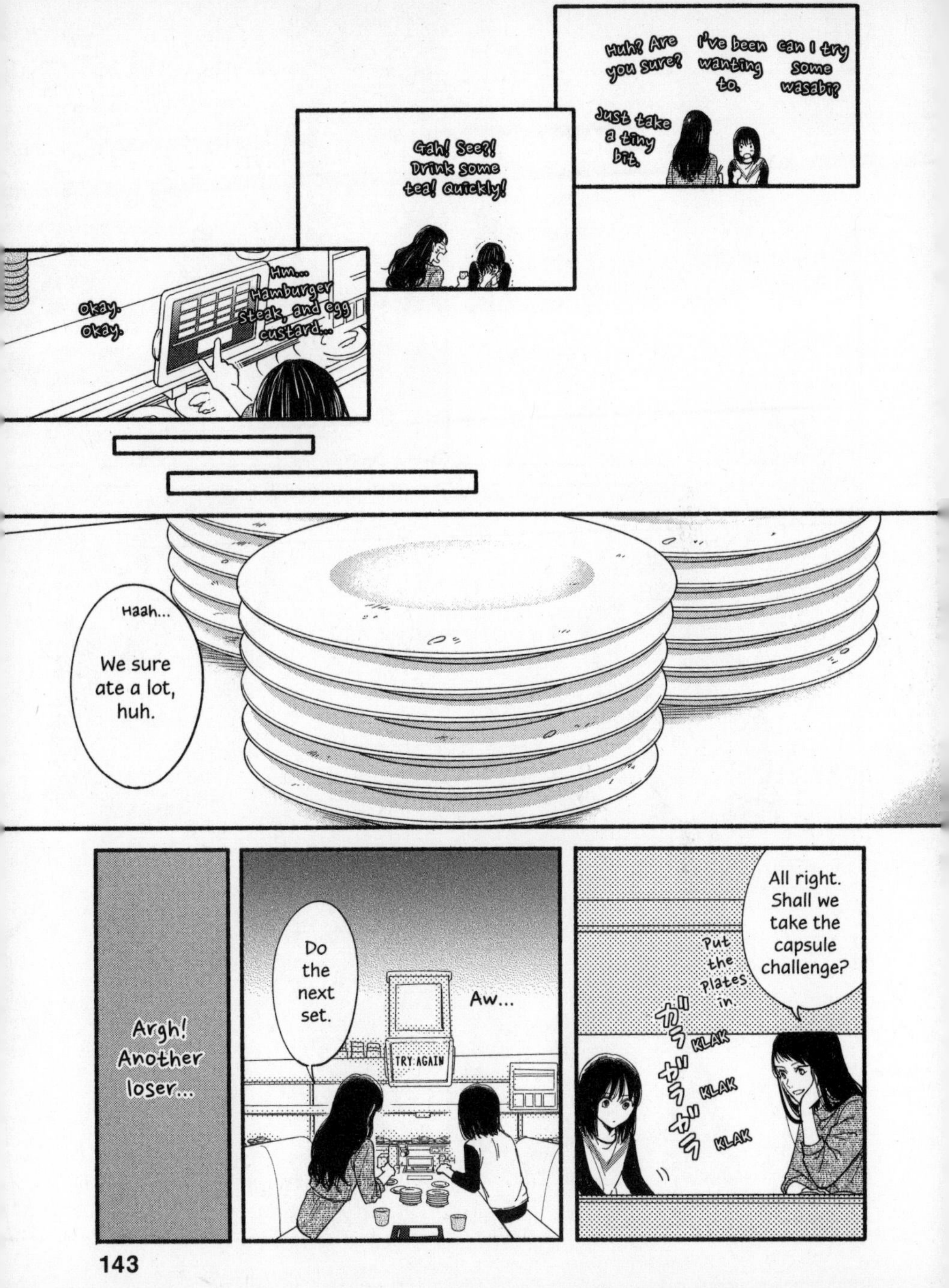
Can I try some wasabi?
I've been wanting to.
Huh? Are you sure?
Just take a tiny bit.
Gah! See?! Drink some tea! Quickly!
Hm... Hamburger steak, and egg custard...
Okay. Okay.
Haaah...
We sure ate a lot, huh.
All right. Shall we take the capsule challenge?
Put the plates in.
ガラ KLAK
ガラ KLAK
ガラ KLAK
Aw...
Do the next set.
TRY AGAIN
Argh! Another loser...

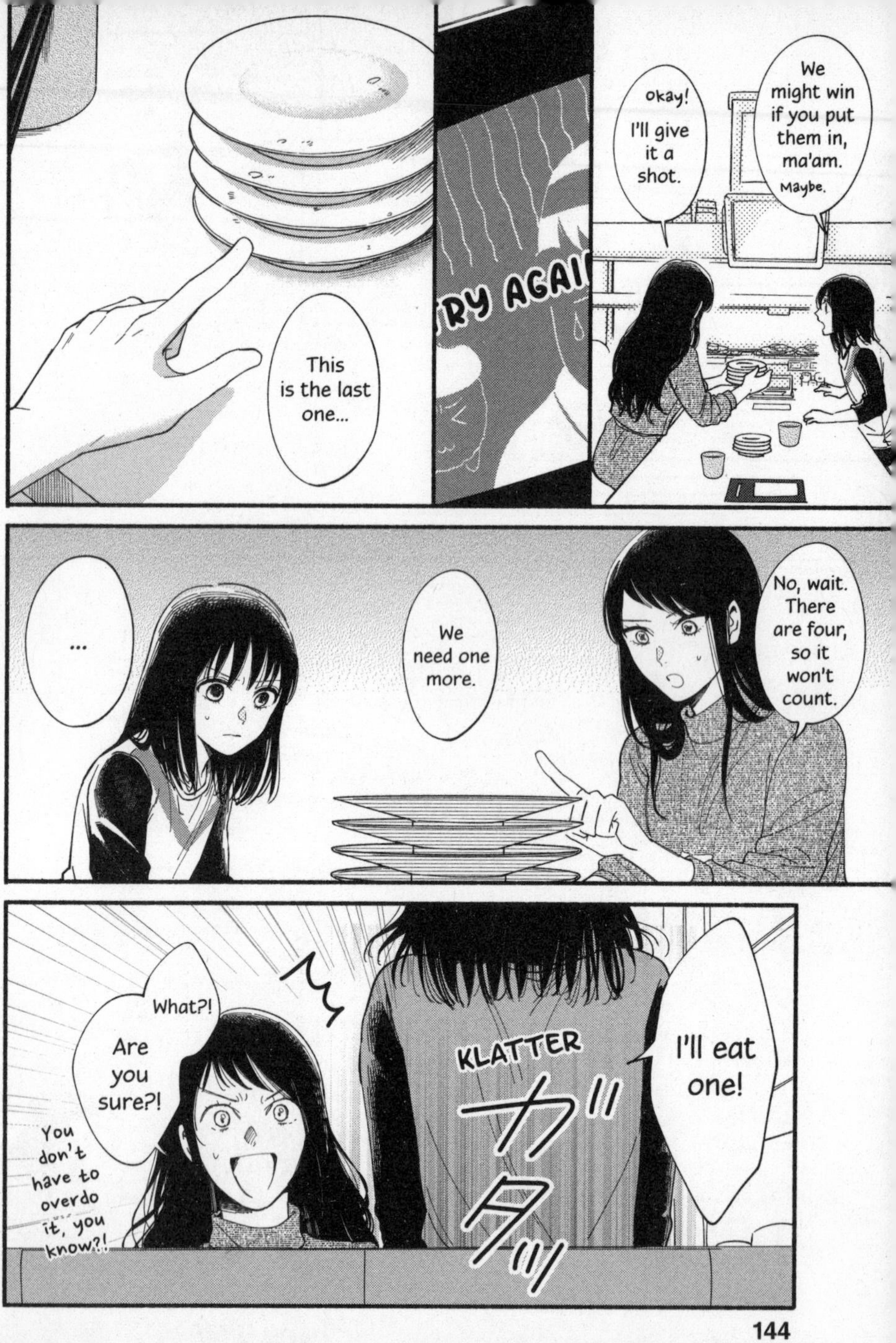

We might win if you put them in, ma'am. Maybe.
Okay! I'll give it a shot.
TRY AGAI
This is the last one...
No, wait. There are four, so it won't count.
We need one more.
...
I'll eat one!
KLATTER
ガタッ
What?! Are you sure?!
You don't have to overdo it, you know?!

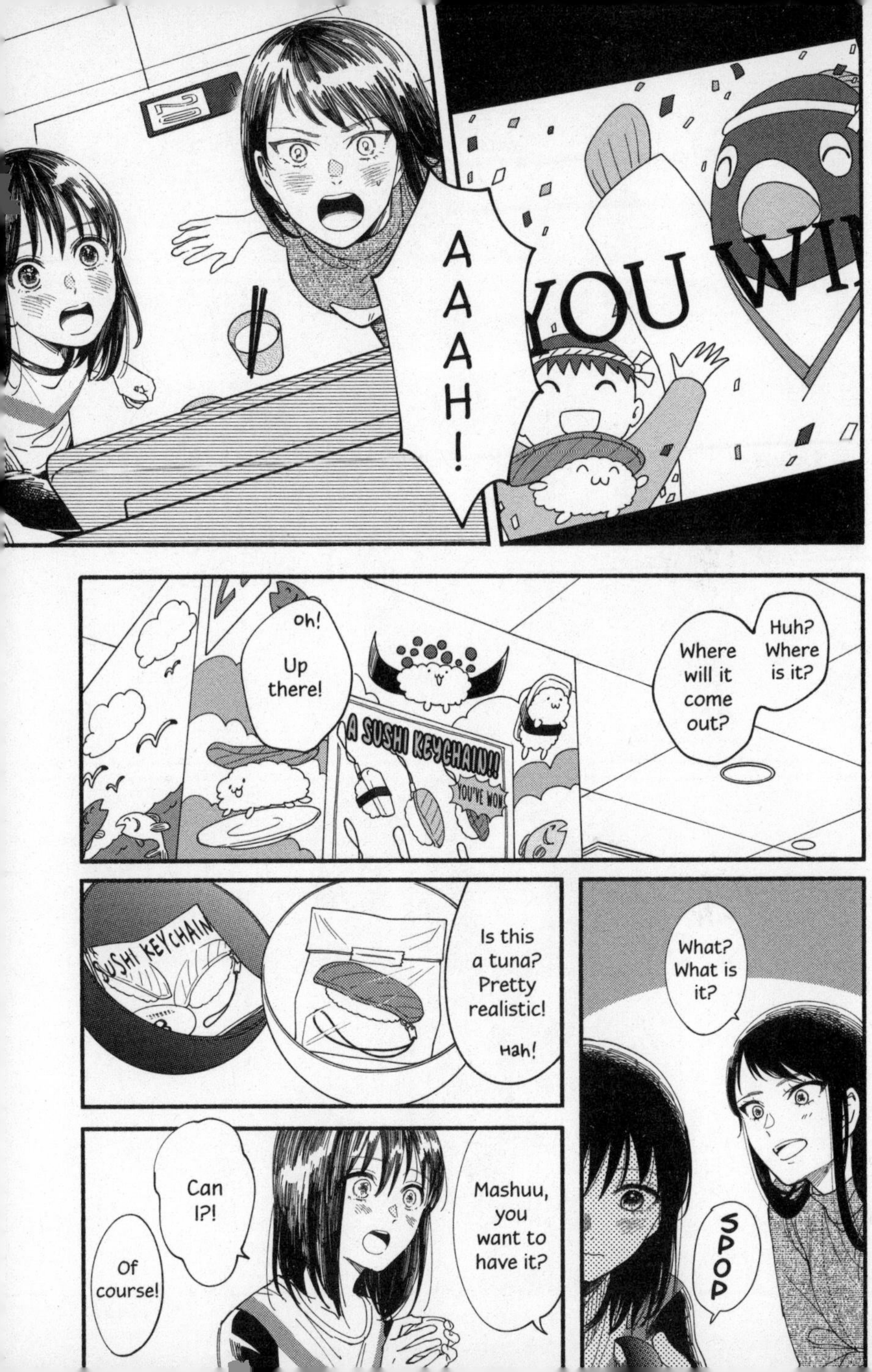
YOU WI
AAAH!
Huh? Where is it?
Where will it come out?
A SUSHI KEYCHAIN!!
YOU'VE WON
oh!
Up there!
What? What is it?
SPOP
SUSHI KEYCHAIN
Is this a tuna? Pretty realistic!
Hah!
Mashuu, you want to have it?
Can I?!
Of course!

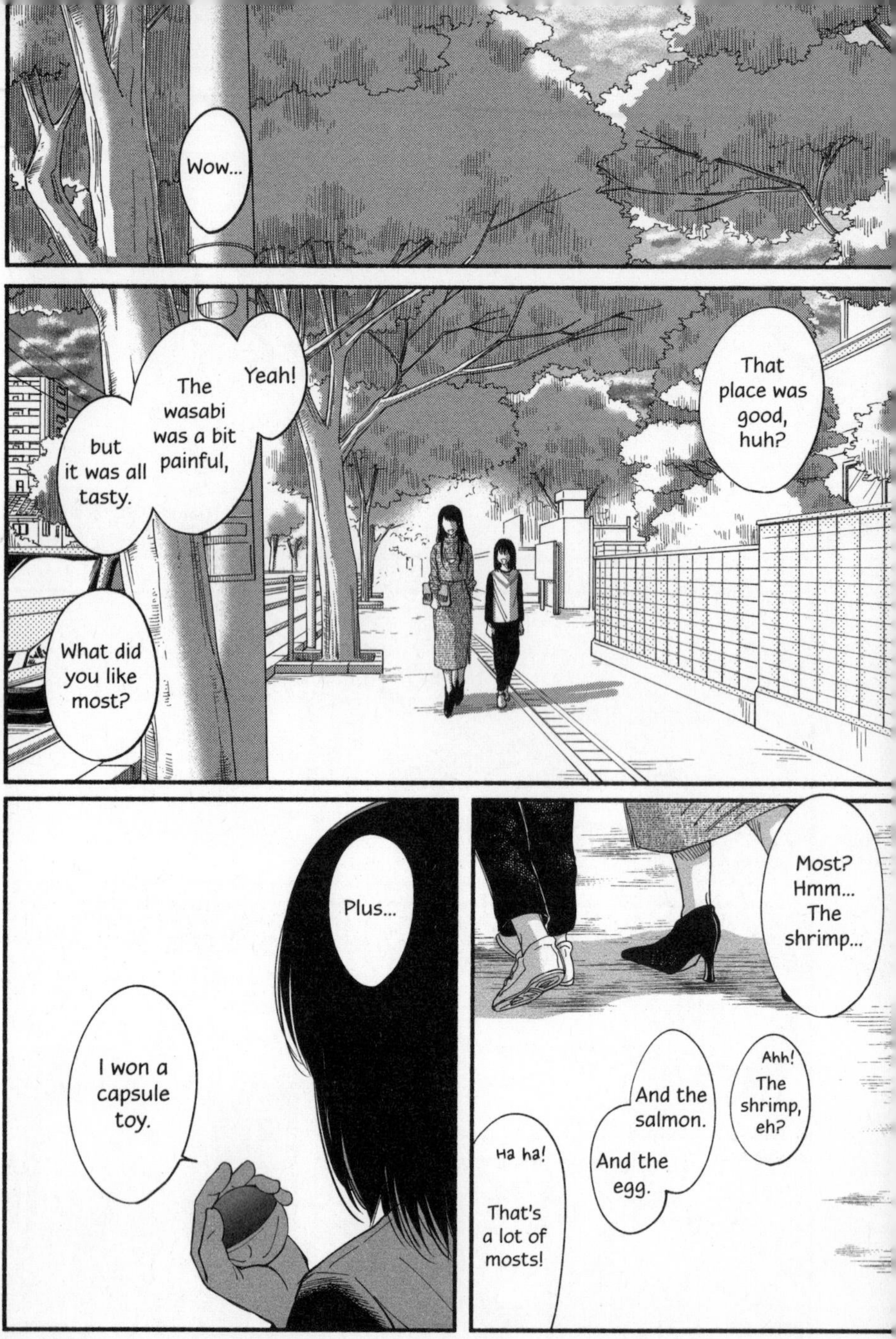
Wow...
That place was good, huh?
Yeah!
The wasabi was a bit painful,
but it was all tasty.
What did you like most?
Most? Hmm... The shrimp...
Ahh! The shrimp, eh?
And the salmon.
And the egg.
Ha ha!
That's a lot of mosts!
Plus...
I won a capsule toy.

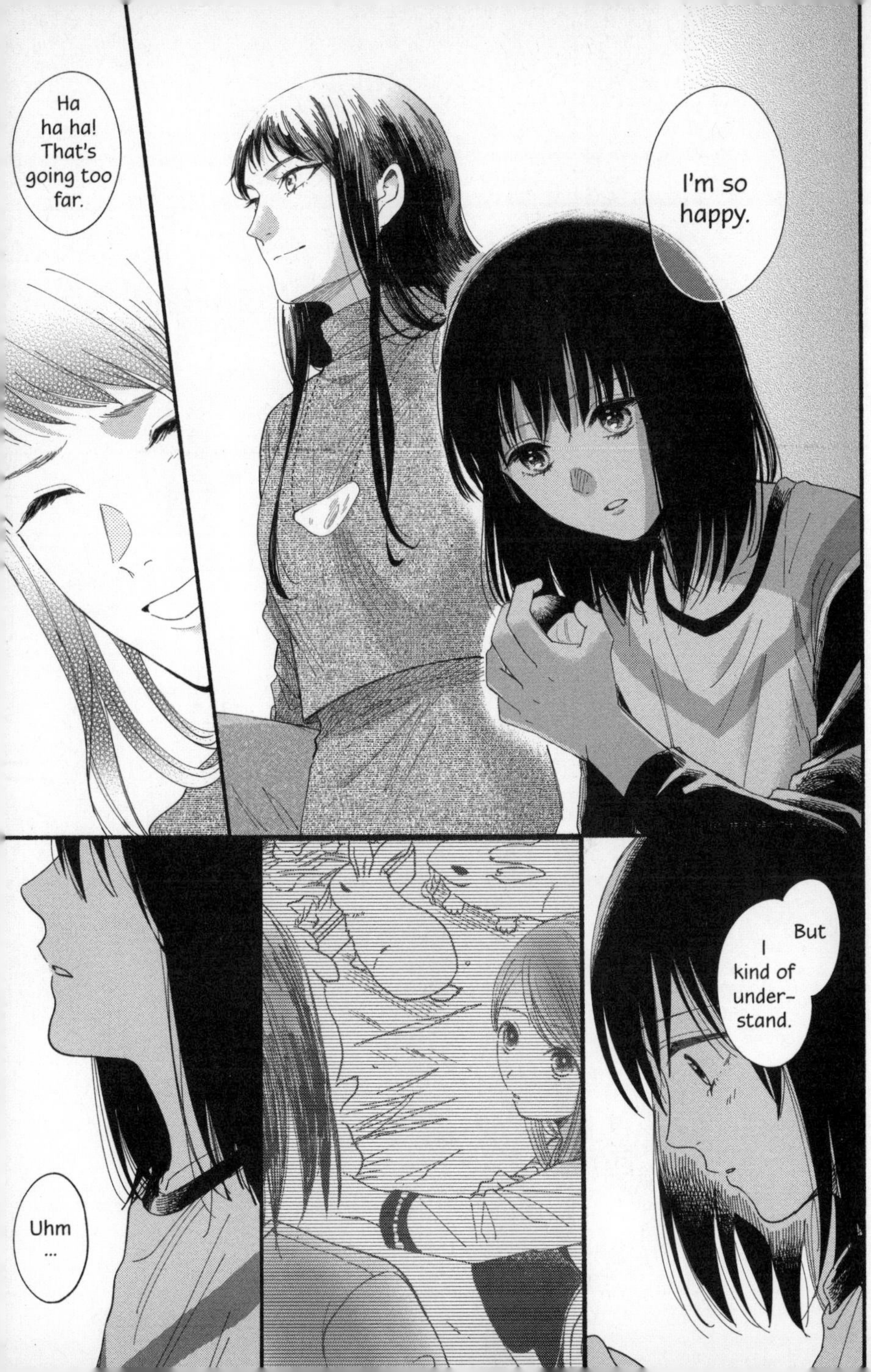
I'm so happy.
Ha ha ha! That's going too far.
But I kind of under-stand.
Uhm ...

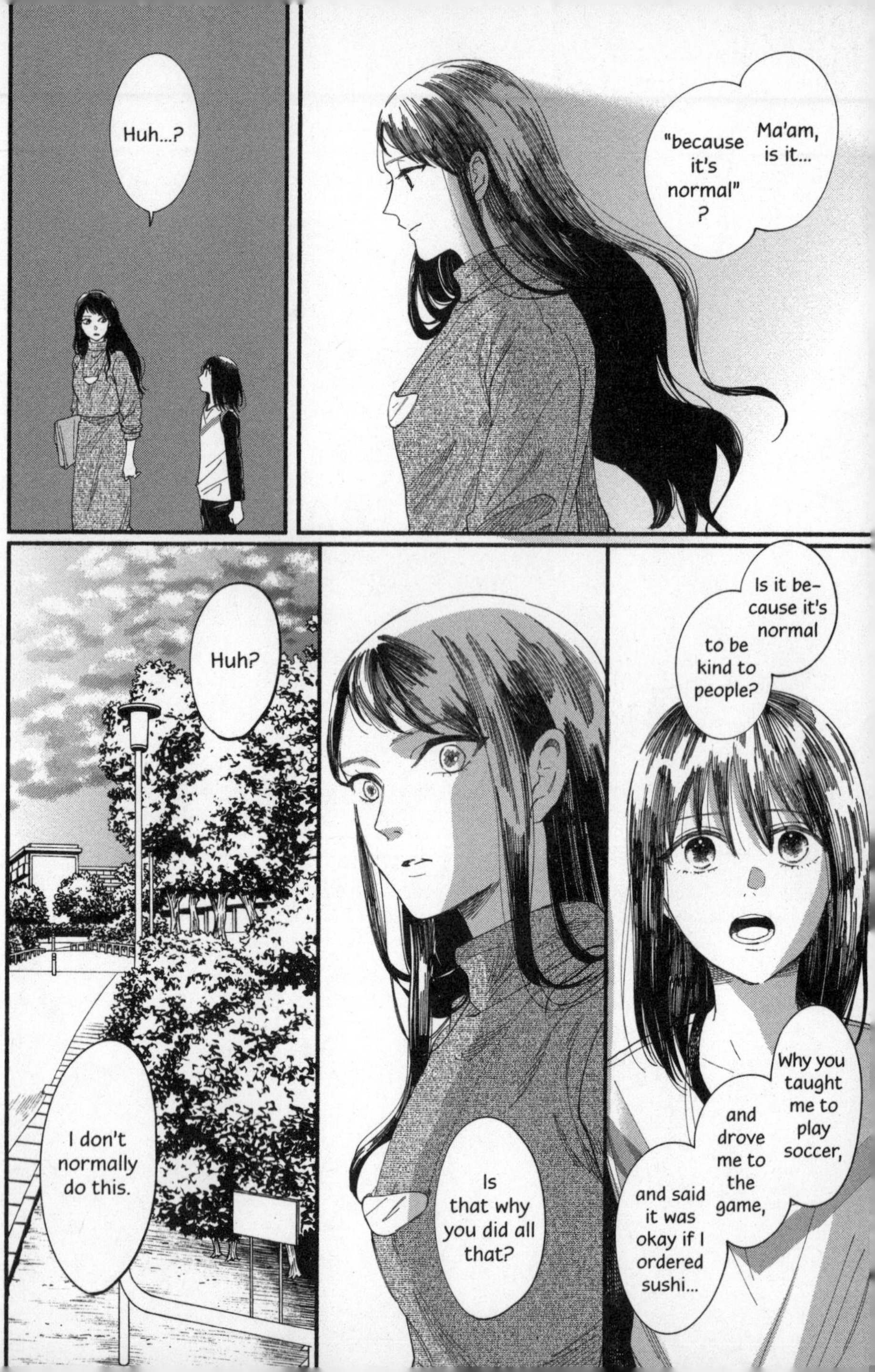
Ma'am, is it...
"because it's normal" ?
Huh...?
Is it be-cause it's normal to be kind to people?
Why you taught me to play soccer,
and drove me to the game,
and said it was okay if I ordered sushi...
Is that why you did all that?
Huh?
I don't normally do this.

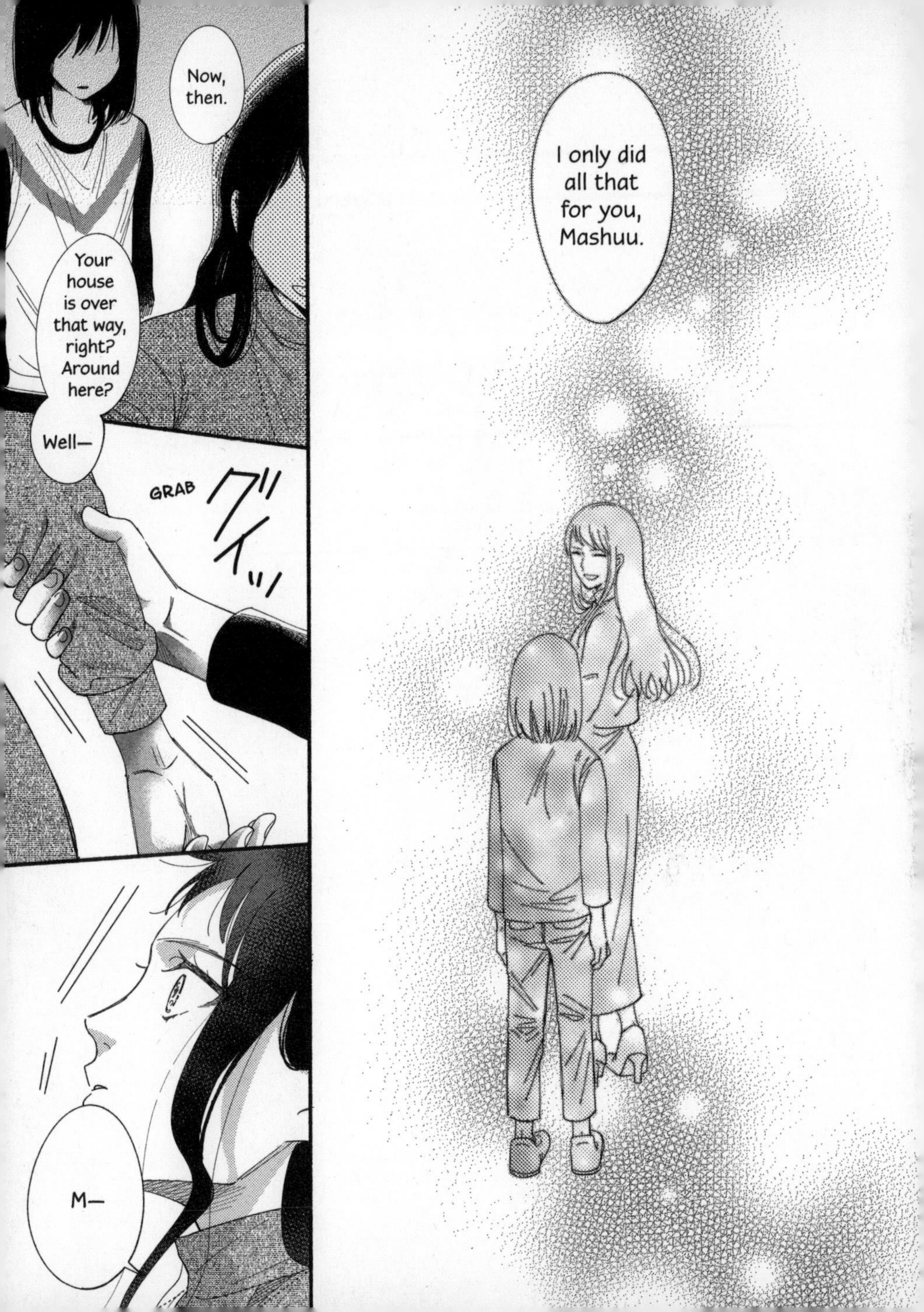
I only did all that for you, Mashuu.
Now, then.
Your house is over that way, right? Around here?
Well—
GRAB
グイッ
M—

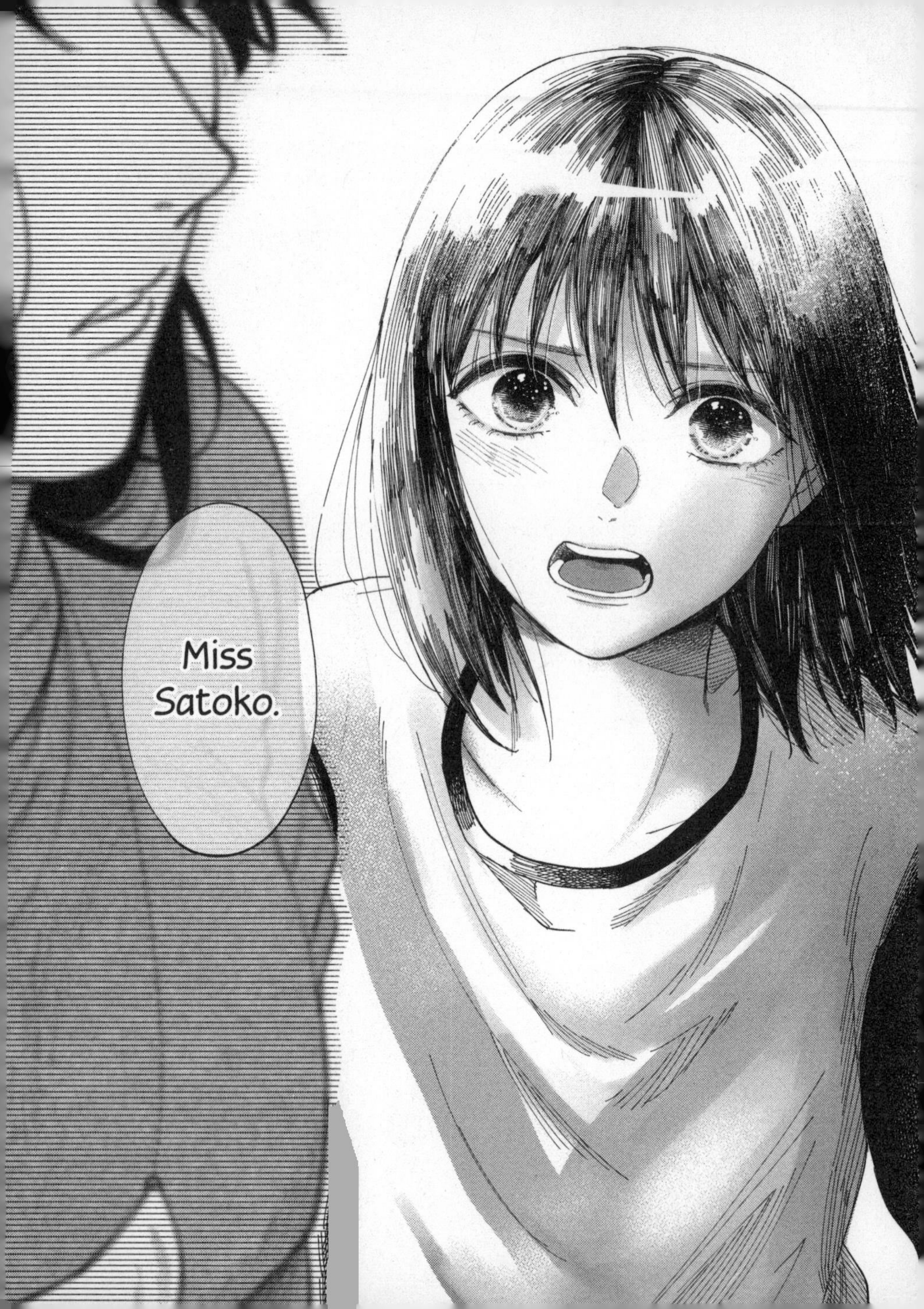
Miss Satoko.

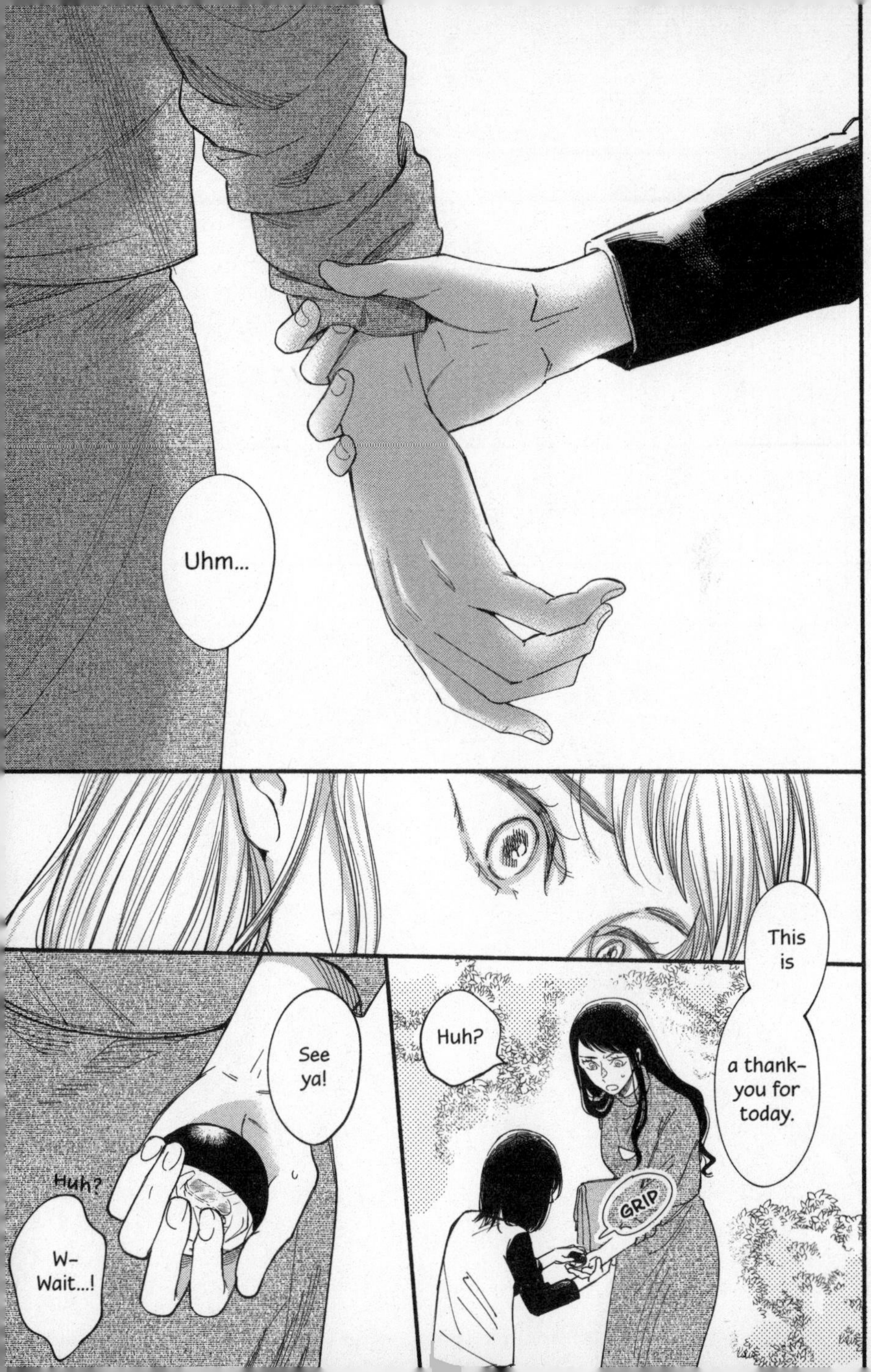
Uhm...
This is a thank-you for today.
GRIP
Huh?
See ya!
Huh?
W- Wait...!

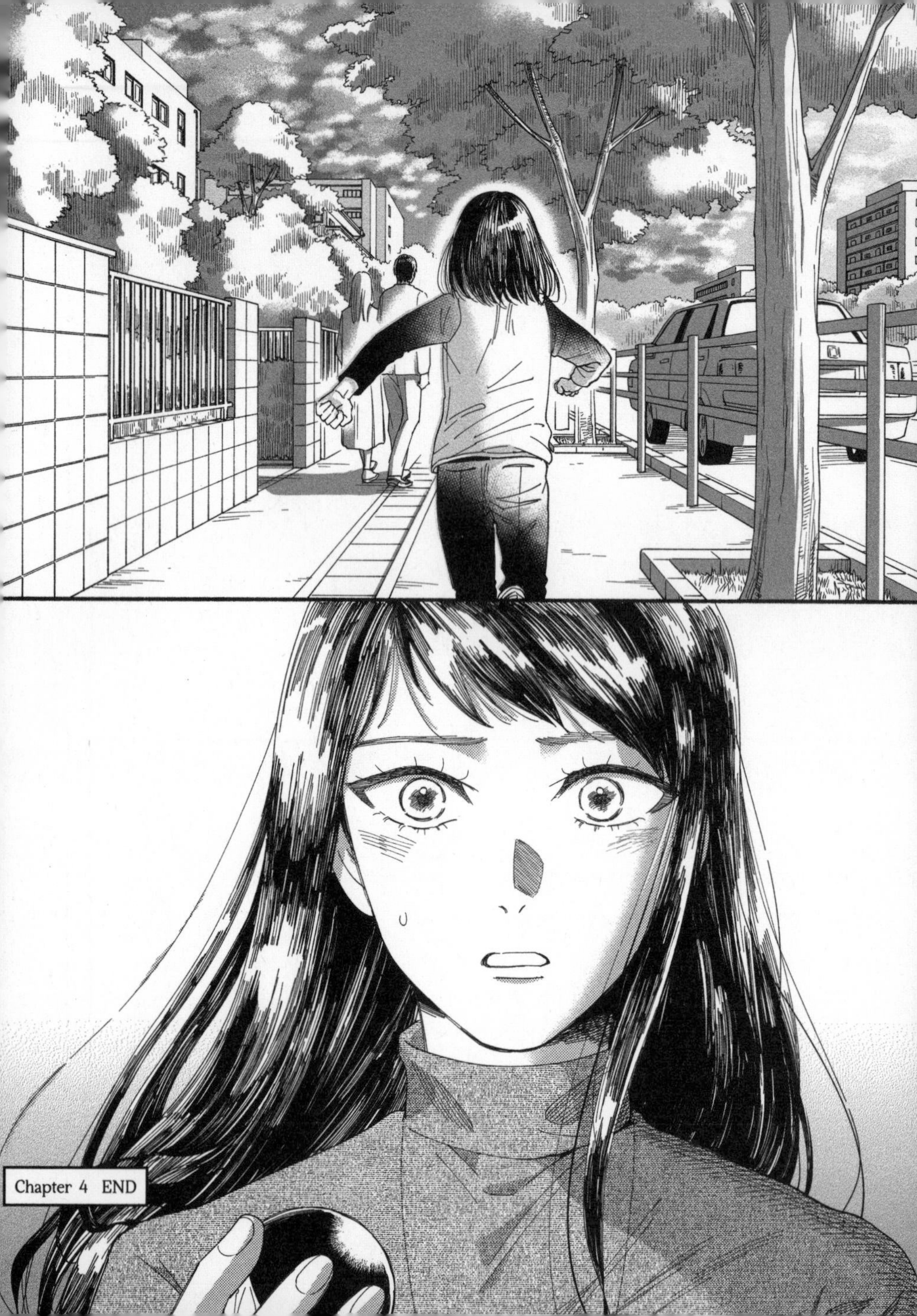
Chapter 4 END

TO BE CONTINUED IN VOLUME 2

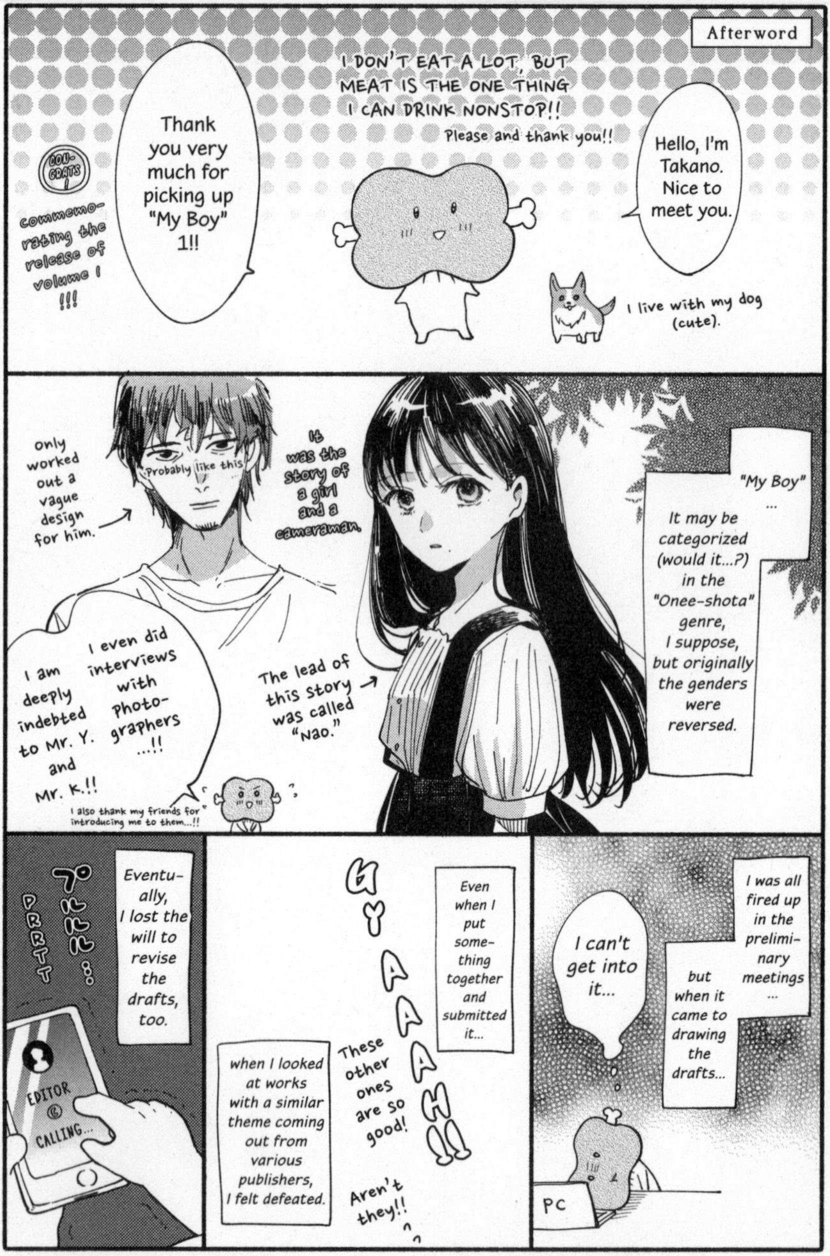
Afterword
Hello, I'm Takano. Nice to meet you.
I DON'T EAT A LOT, BUT MEAT IS THE ONE THING I CAN DRINK NONSTOP!!
Please and thank you!!
I live with my dog (cute).
Thank you very much for picking up "My Boy" 1!!
CON-GRATS!
commemorating the release of volume 1 !!!
"My Boy"... It may be categorized (would it...?) in the "Onee-shota" genre, I suppose, but originally the genders were reversed.
It was the story of a girl and a cameraman.
The lead of this story was called "Nao."
only worked out a vague design for him.
Probably like this
I even did interviews with Photographers ...!!
I am deeply indebted to Mr. Y. and Mr. K.!!
I also thank my friends for introducing me to them...!!
I was all fired up in the preliminary meetings...
but when it came to drawing the drafts...
I can't get into it...
PC
Even when I put something together and submitted it...
GYAAAAH!!
These other ones are so good!
when I looked at works with a similar theme coming out from various publishers, I felt defeated.
Aren't they!!
Eventually, I lost the will to revise the drafts, too.
プルルル…
PRRTT
EDITOR CALLING...

*Onee-shota = coupling of Onee-san (young woman) + shota (boy).

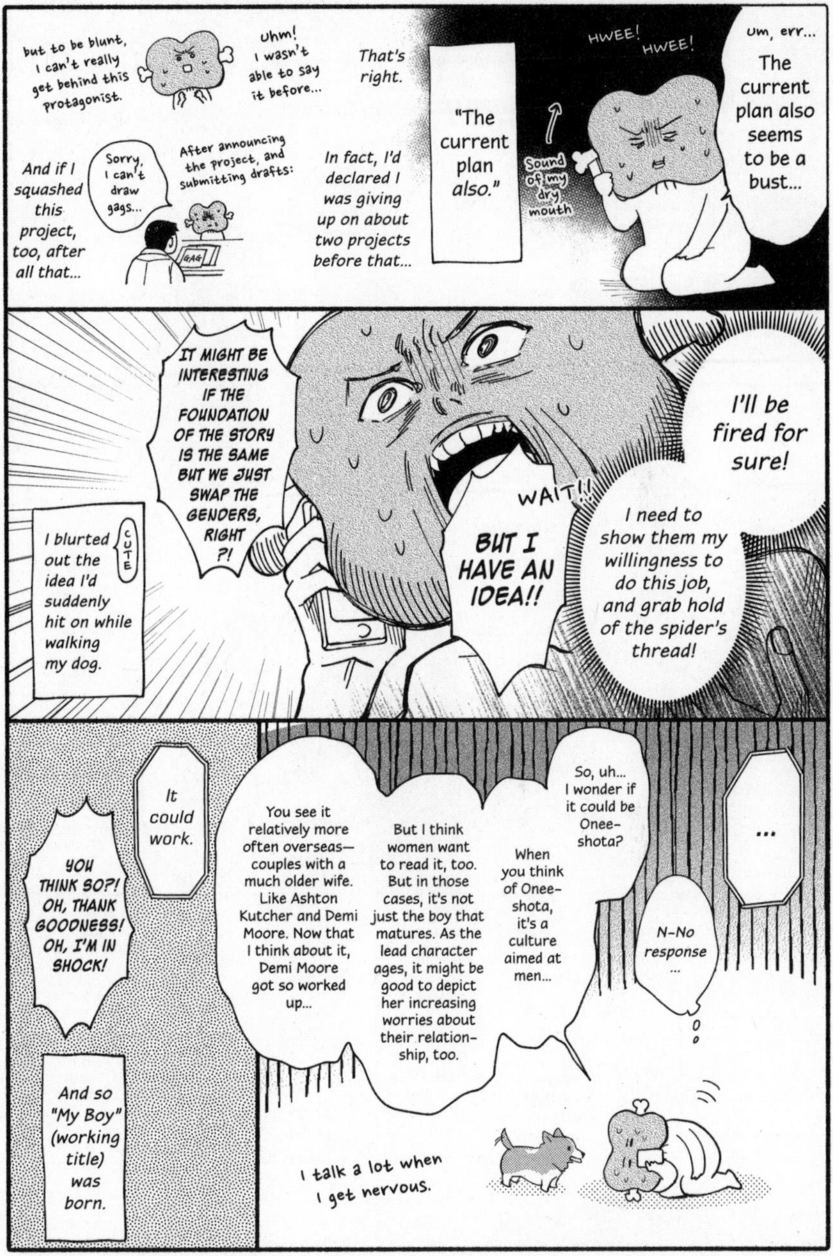
Um, err...
The current plan also seems to be a bust...
HWEE! HWEE!
Sound of my dry mouth
"The current plan also."
That's right.
Uhm! I wasn't able to say it before...
but to be blunt, I can't really get behind this protagonist.
In fact, I'd declared I was giving up on about two projects before that...
After announcing the project, and submitting drafts:
Sorry, I can't draw gags...
GAG
And if I squashed this project, too, after all that...
I'll be fired for sure!
I need to show them my willingness to do this job, and grab hold of the spider's thread!
WAIT!!
BUT I HAVE AN IDEA!!
IT MIGHT BE INTERESTING IF THE FOUNDATION OF THE STORY IS THE SAME BUT WE JUST SWAP THE GENDERS, RIGHT?!
CUTE
I blurted out the idea I'd suddenly hit on while walking my dog.
...
So, uh... I wonder if it could be Onee-shota?
N-No response...
When you think of Onee-shota, it's a culture aimed at men...
But I think women want to read it, too. But in those cases, it's not just the boy that matures. As the lead character ages, it might be good to depict her increasing worries about their relationship, too.
You see it relatively more often overseas—couples with a much older wife. Like Ashton Kutcher and Demi Moore. Now that I think about it, Demi Moore got so worked up...
I talk a lot when I get nervous.
It could work.
YOU THINK SO?! OH, THANK GOODNESS! OH, I'M IN SHOCK!
And so "My Boy" (working title) was born.

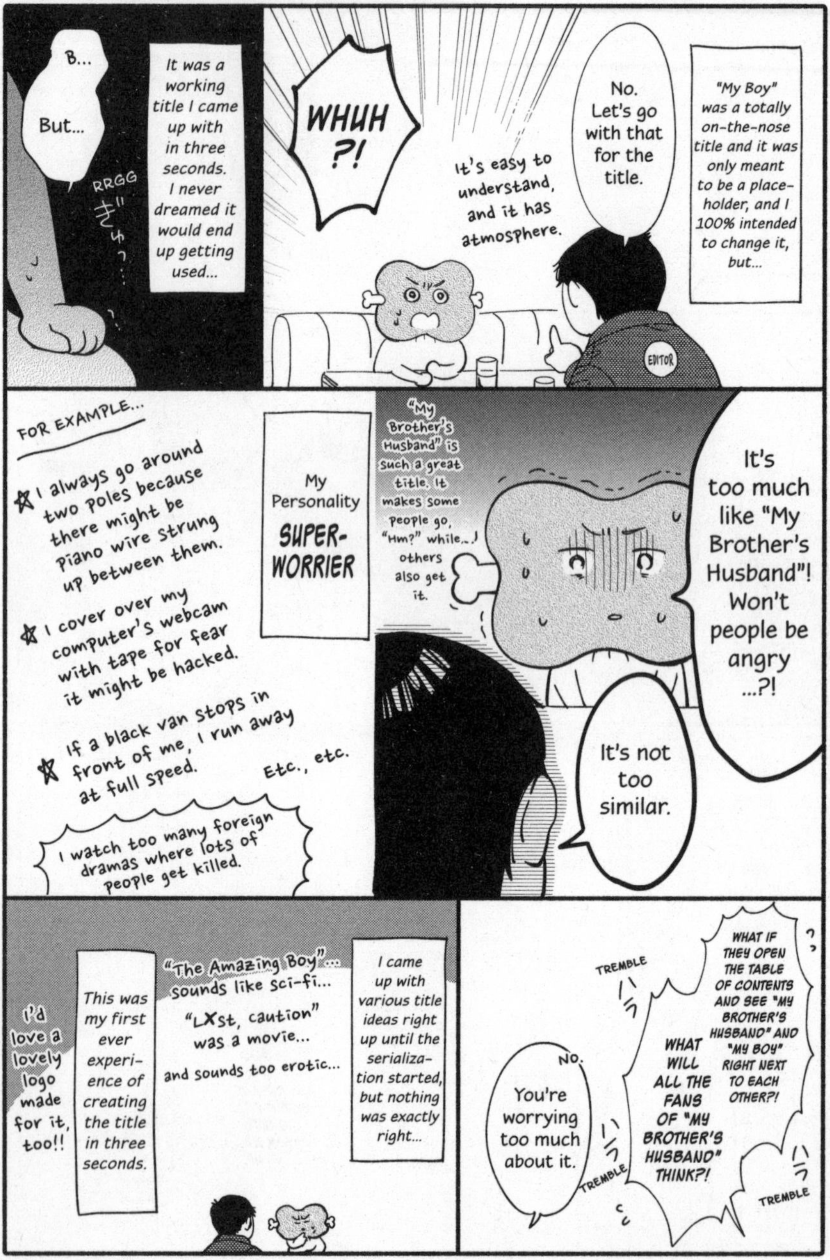
"My Boy" was a totally on-the-nose title and it was only meant to be a place-holder, and I 100% intended to change it, but...
No. Let's go with that for the title.
It's easy to understand, and it has atmosphere.
EDITOR
WHUH ?!
It was a working title I came up with in three seconds. I never dreamed it would end up getting used...
B... But...
RRGG
It's too much like "My Brother's Husband"! Won't people be angry ...?!
"My Brother's Husband" is such a great title. It makes some people go, "Hm?" while others also get it.
It's not too similar.
My Personality SUPER-WORRIER
FOR EXAMPLE...
I always go around two poles because there might be piano wire strung up between them.
I cover over my computer's webcam with tape for fear it might be hacked.
If a black van stops in front of me, I run away at full speed.
Etc., etc.
I watch too many foreign dramas where lots of people get killed.
WHAT IF THEY OPEN THE TABLE OF CONTENTS AND SEE "MY BROTHER'S HUSBAND" AND "MY BOY" RIGHT NEXT TO EACH OTHER?!
WHAT WILL ALL THE FANS OF "MY BROTHER'S HUSBAND" THINK?!
TREMBLE
TREMBLE
TREMBLE
No.
You're worrying too much about it.
I came up with various title ideas right up until the serialization started, but nothing was exactly right...
"The Amazing Boy"... sounds like sci-fi...
"LXst, caution" was a movie...
and sounds too erotic...
This was my first ever experience of creating the title in three seconds.
I'd love a lovely logo made for it, too!!

⚠ "My Brother's Husband" ("Ototo no Otto") by Gengoroh Tagame was a super popular serial that ran in Futabasha's "Weekly Action," and "My Boy" actually runs in the same magazine.

About the "Shota" ("Boy")

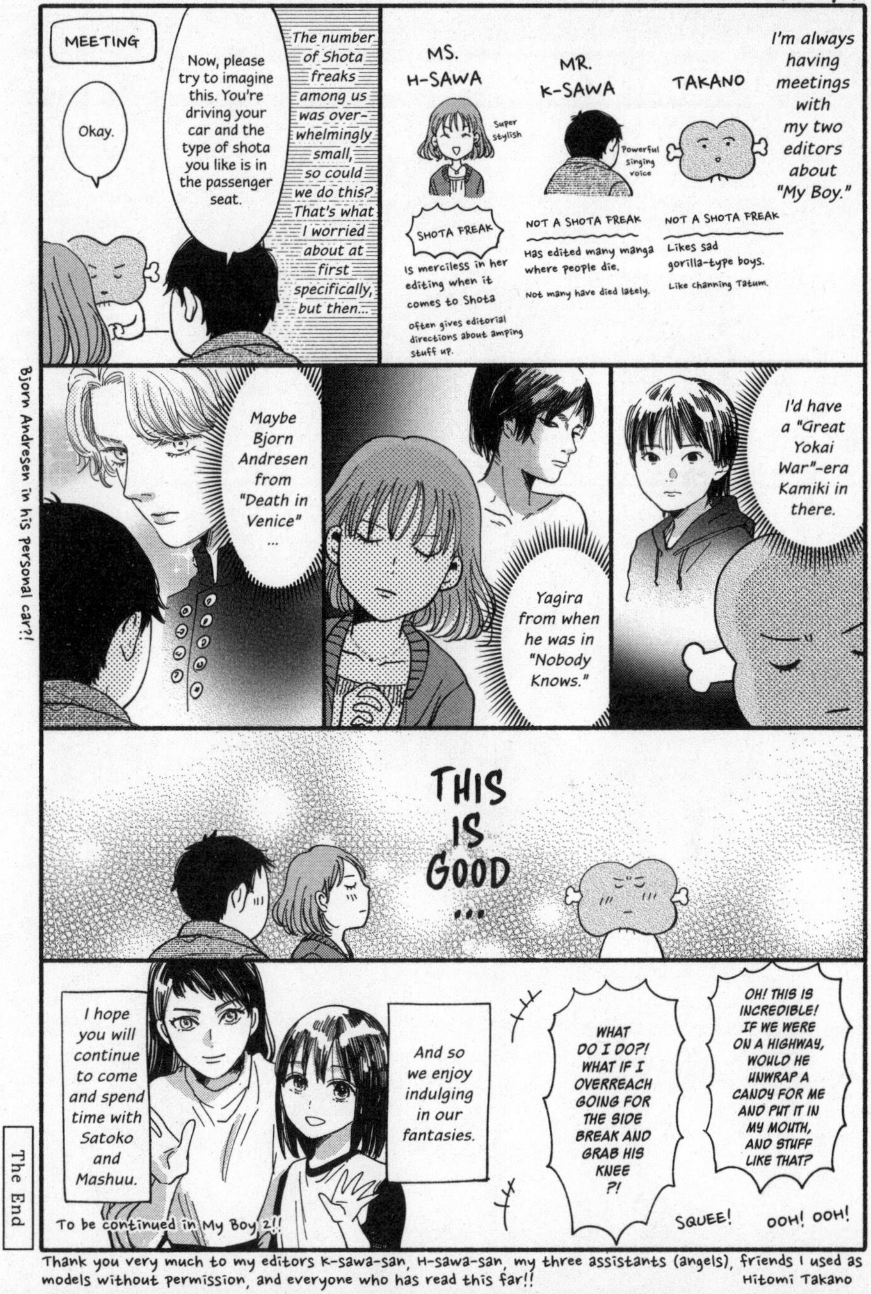
I'm always having meetings with my two editors about "My Boy."
TAKANO
NOT A SHOTA FREAK
Likes sad gorilla-type boys.
Like Channing Tatum.
MR. K-SAWA
Powerful singing voice
NOT A SHOTA FREAK
Has edited many manga where people die.
Not many have died lately.
MS. H-SAWA
Super stylish
SHOTA FREAK
Is merciless in her editing when it comes to Shota
Often gives editorial directions about amping stuff up.
The number of Shota freaks among us was over-whelmingly small, so could we do this? That's what I worried about at first specifically, but then...
MEETING
Now, please try to imagine this. You're driving your car and the type of shota you like is in the passenger seat.
Okay.
I'd have a "Great Yokai War"-era Kamiki in there.
Yagira from when he was in "Nobody Knows."
Maybe Bjorn Andresen from "Death in Venice" ...
Bjorn Andresen in his personal car?!
THIS IS GOOD ...
OH! THIS IS INCREDIBLE! IF WE WERE ON A HIGHWAY, WOULD HE UNWRAP A CANDY FOR ME AND PUT IT IN MY MOUTH, AND STUFF LIKE THAT?
OOH! OOH!
WHAT DO I DO?! WHAT IF I OVERREACH GOING FOR THE SIDE BREAK AND GRAB HIS KNEE ?!
SQUEE!
And so we enjoy indulging in our fantasies.
I hope you will continue to come and spend time with Satoko and Mashuu.
To be continued in My Boy 2!!
The End

Thank you very much to my editors K-sawa-san, H-sawa-san, my three assistants (angels), friends I used as models without permission, and everyone who has read this far!!

Hitomi Takano

Next Volume

A 30-year-old office worker for whom time has stopped.

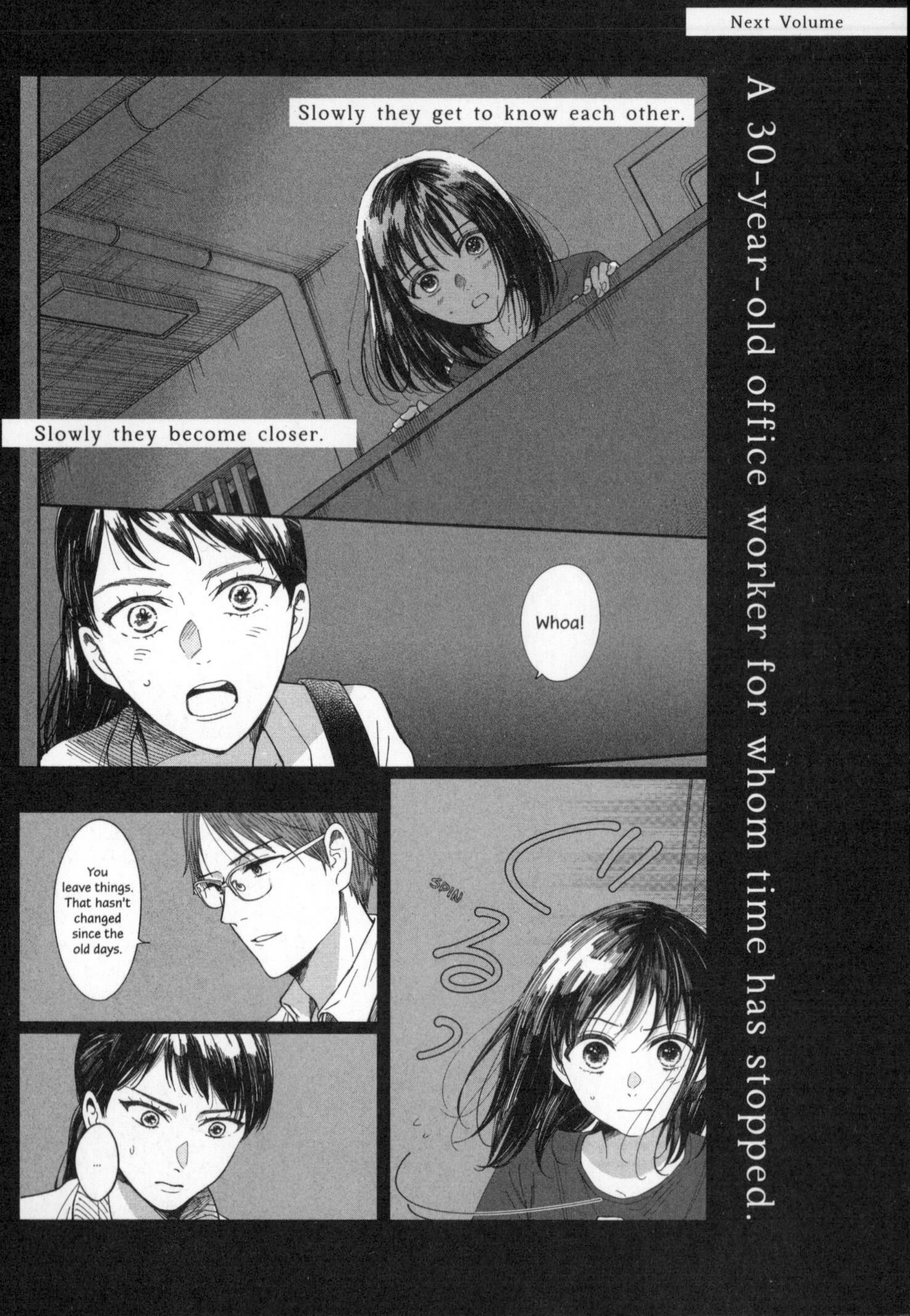

Slowly they get to know each other.
Slowly they become closer.
Whoa!
SPIN
You leave things. That hasn't changed since the old days.
...

His smile connects both of their
pasts to the present.

MY BOY

Volume 2 on sale Summer 2018

MY BOY 1

Translation: Kumar Sivasubramanian
Production: Risa Cho
            Rina Mapa

WATASHI NO SHONEN
© HITOMI TAKANO 2016
All rights reserved.

First published in Japan in 2016 by Futabasha Publishers Ltd., Tokyo.
English language version produced by Vertical, Inc.
Under license from Futabasha Publishers Ltd.

Translation provided by Vertical, Inc., 2018
Published by Vertical Comics, an imprint of Vertical, Inc., New York

Originally published in Japanese as *Watashi no Shounen 1* by Futabasha Publishers Ltd., 2016
Watashi no Shounen first serialized in *Gekkan Akushon*, Futabasha Publishers Ltd., 2016 -

ISBN: 978-1-945054-87-7

Manufactured in the United States of America

First Edition

Vertical, Inc.
451 Park Avenue South
7th Floor
New York, NY 10016
www.vertical-comics.com

Vertical books are distributed through Pengiun-Random House Publisher Services.